CULTURES IN CONFLICT:
THE FOUR FACES OF INDIAN BUREAUCRACY

CULTURES
IN CONFLICT

*The
Four Faces
of Indian
Bureaucracy*

STANLEY J. HEGINBOTHAM

NEW YORK & LONDON   1975
COLUMBIA UNIVERSITY PRESS

This study was prepared under the auspices of the Southern
Asian Institute, Columbia University, New York. The
Southern Asian Institute seeks a deeper knowledge of that
vast and tumultuous area stretching from Pakistan in the
West to Indonesia and the Philippines in the East. To
understand the problems facing its leaders and diverse
peoples requires sustained study and research. Our
publications are intended to contribute to that better
understanding.

The Andrew W. Mellon Foundation, through a special
grant, has assisted the Press in publishing this volume.

LIBRARY OF CONGRESS CATALOGING IN PUBLICATION DATA

Heginbotham, Stanley J
    Cultures in conflict.

    Bibliography: p.
    Includes index.
    1. Bureaucracy.   2. Local officials and employees—Tamil
Nadu.   3. Community development—Tamil Nadu.   4. Tamil Nadu—
Social conditions.   I. Title.
JS7025.T33A43   354'.54'8201   74-31206
ISBN 0-231-03888-7

To the Memory of
Wayne Ayres Wilcox

1932–1974

Preface

This book discusses bureaucracy and bureaucratic behavior in a setting characterized by conflicting and changing cultural patterns. Indian bureaucrats, many of whom were raised in traditional Hindu environments, are studied as they carry out their duties in formal bureaucratic structures that are strongly reminiscent of the pre-Independence British administration. Rules, regulations, procedures, control mechanisms, and basic management practices have remained essentially unchanged over the past twenty-five years. Other features of bureaucratic life, however, have been substantially modified by two reform movements. One, led by Mahatma Gandhi, is indigenous to India. The other, espoused by numerous western development specialists with experience in Indian rural development, is foreign. Both the Gandhian ideology and the ideology of "community development" have had substantial impact on the bureaucracy's goals, its training programs, the creation and organizational structure of new agencies, and the patterns of relationships bureaucrats maintain with citizens and politicians.

The past three decades have produced a wide range of fruitful insights on bureaucratic behavior patterns and their consequences for both institutions and individuals in culturally homogeneous settings. This book builds on these insights by examining behavior patterns in a situation where conflicting cultural attitudes, values, and institutional traditions are added to the now-classic patterns of conflict that have been studied in western bureaucracy.

I shall explore five matters of practical and theoretical importance in the course of my analysis: The characteristics of four cultural traditions that have a bearing on contemporary patterns of bureaucratic behavior in India; the points of conflict between these various traditions; the consequences of these conflicts for the nature of administrative processes and efficiency; the effect of these conflicts on the individuals who are members of the bureaucracy; and the nature of the causal relationship between cultural patterns, attitudes and values, bureaucratic structure, and individual behavior within that structure.

This study of bureaucratic behavior began as an examination of the role of politics and administration in India's program for economic development. It was conceived of as a case study focusing on a program that became in 1967—and remains to this day—the key to the Indian strategy for agricultural development: the program for the popularization of newly developed high-yielding varieties of food grains. In geographic scope, the study is limited to the state of Tamil Nadu (formerly Madras), and within the state, it examines developments within North Arcot District.

Acknowledgments

The field research for this study was conducted in 1967 and 1968, supported by a generous grant from the Foreign Area Fellowship Program of the Joint Committee of the American Council of Learned Societies and the Social Science Research Council. Subsequent financial support for the writing of this manuscript, as well as the dissertation on which it is based, was provided by the Southern Asian Institute at Columbia University. The Institute's director, Howard Wriggins, has been a source of support, encouragement, and sound advice throughout the lengthy process of transforming raw field materials into this volume.

I am deeply indebted to the countless public servants in India—and especially in Tamil Nadu—who talked with me, answered my questions, and shared broad aspects of their working lives with me. That they almost always did so with patience and candor is a tribute to the traditions of Indian public administration. Similarly, the people of Marusoor and of numerous other villages in North Arcot District were generous in their cooperation with my inquiries and observations. I was fortunate to have the skilled research assistance of Mr. K. Sivakumar during much of my stay.

Many other individuals have contributed to the development of this project at different stages in its evolution. Myron Weiner, Lucian Pye, and Frederick Frey provided diverse, but complementary and enormously beneficial, forms of support and direction during the preparation of my dissertation. Among those who read later drafts and offered useful criticism and suggestions were Howard Wriggins, Ainslie Embree, Wayne Wilcox, John Briscoe, Geraldine Alpert, and John Boyle. Leslie Bialler served as a skilled, patient, and understanding editor, and Andrée Mounier was sensitive to intellectual concerns in her design work. Estelle

Cooper and Carole Graszler typed various versions of the manuscript with commendable efficiency and forebearance.

My wife, Connie, not only shared with me the inevitable turmoil inherent in the fieldwork for a project of this nature, but also made extensive and invaluable suggestions for the final revision of the manuscript.

Contents

CULTURES IN CONFLICT:
THE FOUR FACES OF INDIAN BUREAUCRACY

 PART ONE

Culture and Bureaucracy

CHAPTER ONE

Introduction

Any reasonably intelligent and sensitive observer who has dealt extensively with public bureaucracies in different societies can attest to the
dissimilarities in patterns of bureaucratic behavior and operations among
various nations. One may simply recognize that there are different
"feels" to similar agencies in different countries, or may have anecdotes
that illustrate those differences and their consequences. The same observer, however, is also likely to be quite aware of striking similarities
in bureaucratic pathologies that transcend national boundaries.

The goal of comparative public administration is to develop a single
conceptual model within which both the patterned similarities and the
local distinctiveness of bureaucracies in different cultural and historical
settings can be described and analyzed. The fields of public administration and organization theory have made great strides in the development
of our understanding of behavioral dynamics in public bureaucracies.
The empirical base on which this body of theory has been developed is
largely confined, however, to American—and some other Anglo-
Saxon—organizations. Nevertheless, the growing body of research on
organizational behavior in other parts of the world is generally supportive of those findings.

It is important that we continue to explore and document the degree
to which our generalizations on organizational dynamics are applicable
in nonwestern cultural settings. The very notion of a field of *comparative*
public administration, however, assumes that there are important differences across systems and that these can be conceptualized and related
to each other. For the most part research done on the public bureaucracies of Asia, Africa, and Latin America has not been directed toward
that end, but has consisted of analyses of institutional structures and
their relevance for the needs and goals of the specific society. This re-

3

search has often emphasized the historical evolution of bureaucratic roles and the problems of bureaucracies in adjusting to the new requirements of greater involvement in developmental processes and greater responsiveness to democratic political processes.

Striking though the differences are between the ways in which Indian and British civil servants operate within similar structures, the culturally determined characteristics of these bureaucracies have received very little academic attention. In the late 1950s and early 1960s the attempts within the discipline of political science to develop more general conceptual models of political cultures floundered because of a number of formidable obstacles. Some tentative efforts to define the elements of a comparative study of organizational culture were made during this period, but the same set of obstacles appears to have discouraged further exploration and development in this area.

Because the obstacles to the development of a comparative study of political cultures appear to have discouraged research into the comparative analysis of organizational cultures, it is worth reviewing the more important of those obstacles. It is an extraordinarily complex task to relate, in any systematic way, the general cultural orientation of a society to its political structure and patterns of political behavior.

First, the problems of establishing categories that permit the comparison of similar aspects of two different cultures are deceivingly complex. The categories we customarily use may differ greatly in their salience from culture to culture. It is possible to compare the highly elaborated social structure of India with the much more diffuse social structure of Cambodia, but it is much more difficult to deal with the fact that this dimension of the cultural environment is a far more important determinant of political processes in India than in Cambodia. With no clear or generally applicable guidelines for determining the relative importance of different components of cultures for the explanation of political processes, one becomes dependent upon the impressions of the individual analyst. Thus, Richard Solomon sees the dynamics of Chinese politics stemming from the aggression and hostility produced by traditional Chinese child-rearing patterns.[1] Jean Grossholtz, on the other

---

[1] *Mao's Revolution and the Chinese Political Culture* (Berkeley: University of California Press, 1971).

hand, sees Philippine politics as being shaped by a traditional pattern of exchange relationships.[2] These two studies give us little to compare between China and the Philippines. We learn little about patterns of exchange relationships in China from Solomon and little about the evolution of hostility and aggression in the Philippines from Grossholtz. We remain uncertain as to whether this difference in emphasis is truly a product of dramatically different political dynamics, a product of the radically different types of source material available to the authors, or a product of their radically different perceptual processes and predispositions.

One solution to this problem is to focus on the explicitly political dimensions of culturally determined attitudes and values. Thus, Almond and Verba, in their classic study of civic culture, ask a series of identical questions of citizens from five nations that specify differences in their subjective orientations to the political process.[3] The problem with this process is that it is very difficult to extract from the resulting analysis any sense of the internal coherence and dynamics of these very different cultures.

Second, almost any analyst of a political culture sooner or later becomes aware that he is grossly distorting reality in an attempt to fit diverse views, personalities, and experiences into a model of a single political culture. The skilled and sophisticated researcher can isolate attitudinal dimensions along which the distribution of a population is relatively narrow. In the process, however, he may ignore other dimensions, which are important in the political dynamics of the society but are hidden by great differences in attitudes across subcultures.

The third and perhaps most serious obstacle is our inability to understand and explain the dynamics of political processes within any single cultural environment. The emergence of a bewildering variety of new nations in the post-World War II era forced the discipline to reexamine political change at the societal level. We have only begun to make sense out of extraordinarily complex processes of change on the basis of data drawn from radically different cultural environments in which the evolution of political institutions and processes is differentially advanced,

---

[2] *Politics in the Philippines, A Country Study* (Boston: Little, Brown, 1964).
[3] Gabriel A. Almond and Sidney Verba, *The Civic Culture: Political Attitudes and Democracy in Five Nations* (Princeton, New Jersey: Princeton University Press, 1963).

following different patterns, and progressing—or regressing—at different rates. Where there has been so little basic understanding of, or agreement on, the underlying dynamics of the process, the presence of important cultural differences only serves to complicate the analysis and obscure comparable dynamics.

One approach to this problem has been to use culture as a primary explanatory variable in an attempt to get at the political development process. Thus, for example, Lucian Pye noted that the attitudes and values of Burmese civil servants and politicians were impediments to the development of a mature political processes in that nation.[4] Numerous other analysts saw the ambivalence of Frenchmen toward authority as a key source of the apparent inability of that nation's political processes to establish stable governmental operations. As the critics of these pioneering and often extremely insightful authors have never failed to point out, however, the focus on cultural patterns has resulted in serious inattention to social, economic, and structural phenomena that offer alternative explanations of the same phenomena or at least raise doubts as to the significance that should be attached to the cultural dynamics.

Another way to attack this problem is to develop a conceptual model that essentially ignores cultural variations. Though such an approach does not necessarily deny that culture has an impact on political systems, it tends to understate the significance of those political dimensions heavily influenced by cultural phenomena and to treat cultural phenomena as residual categories that might account for patterns that cannot be explained by the more "objective" economic, social, technological, and structural factors.

The comparative study of formal organizations has undoubtedly been influenced in its development by the failure of political scientists to effectively resolve the problems of integrating cultural variations into a reasonably rigorous comparative framework. The 1950s and 1960s did see some tentative explorations into the cultural determinants of bureaucratic behavior but, creative and imaginative though some of these attempts were, they were not followed up by a substantial number of empirical studies.

One of the earliest and most ambitious of such attempts was Fred

[4] Lucian W. Pye, *Politics, Personality and Nation Building: Burma's Search for Identity* (New Haven: Yale University Press, 1962).

Riggs's effort to develop idealtypic models of organizations in industrial and traditional (or, in Riggs's terms, agrarian) societies. In his subsequent elaboration of this work, Riggs develops a third model; that of the transitional or "prismatic" society. Though the Riggs models do not apply to any specific society, they do attempt to relate patterns of organizational behavior to what Riggs sees as some of the cultural concomitants of different levels of social and economic complexity.[5]

Two less ambitious, but more successful, efforts to relate cultural patterns to organizational behavior dealt with case studies in specific countries. Michel Crozier describes and explains patterns of bureaucratic behavior in two French organizations within the context of organization theory developed out of research done in the United States and Great Britain.[6] Crozier then goes on to show how specific elements of the behavioral patterns in the bureaucracies he studied are related to French cultural patterns that have previously been described by other authors. He uses cultural phenomena as residual variables, but does show how they can be employed to lend greater explanatory power to a body of empirical theory.

In what is perhaps the most successful attempt to employ cultural concepts in the analysis of organizational behavior, James Abegglen suggests that patterns of authority and compliance in Japanese factories differ very substantially from those in the United States and that these differences stem from Japanese perceptions of the role of authority figures in traditional Japanese family institutions.[7]

The later 1960s and early 1970s have seen a few additional excursions into cultural patterns of organizational behavior, but this field continues to be stigmatized—erroneously—by the low esteem in which general political culture studies are now held by political scientists.

Cultural variables can be incorporated into political analysis much more successfully within a specific field whose basic dynamics are understood than they can be in the amorphous and ill-defined area of societal political development. Where, for example, one can begin to specify the

[5] Fred W. Riggs, *Administration in Developing Countries: The Theory of Prismatic Society* (Boston: Houghton Mifflin, 1964).
[6] Michel Crozier, *The Bureaucratic Phenomenon* (Chicago: University of Chicago Press, Phoenix Books, 1964).
[7] James C. Abegglen, *The Japanese Factory: Aspects of its Social Organization* (Glencoe, Illinois: Free Press, 1958).

relationship between certain types of supervision and the inclination of subordinates to take initiative, it may be fruitful to explore patterns of supervision among authorities in traditional social institutions. Or, where behavioral patterns in line and staff roles in one country differ markedly from patterns found in similar roles in other countries it may be useful to explore how roles associated with line and staff functions are performed in the traditional institutions of the two societies.

Though there are a number of issues within the area of organizational behavior that remain unsettled, the field does work with reasonably well-developed conceptual tools and a relatively sophisticated understanding of behavioral dynamics. We understand something of the behavioral consequences of formal structures and are further aware of the great importance of informal patterns of communication and friendship in organizations. We are aware of the implications of compliance systems for morale, performance, and the exercise of initiative.

Given this set of conceptual tools, the problems of introducing cultural variables are considerably less severe than they are at the level of the analysis of whole political systems. What is needed is a further set of conceptual tools that provides a linkage between cultural patterns and bureaucratic behavior. It does not do great violence to the present state of organizational theory to separate out four components of analysis which are generally dealt with as independent variables.

1. *Formal Structure.* This includes such elements as the nature and shape of the line hierarchy: the number of hierarchical levels and the span of control (or number of subordinates) assigned to each level; the location and elaboration of staff functions within the hierarchy; and the basis and extent of functional specialization and accompanying coordinating or areally defined roles.

2. *The nature of the compliance system* through which the leadership of the organization attempts to influence the behavior of its subordinate employees. In any system this involves achieving a balance between a highly elaborated set of control mechanisms that are expensive to maintain and tend to thwart the exercise of any initiative and a more casual compliance system that can exercise only minimal influence on the behavioral patterns of subordinates.

3. *Working norms* and the patterned distribution of functions within

the organization. What forms of behavior, in short, is the compliance system attempting to maintain?

4. *The relationship between the organization and its clientele.* What channels of access do the clients have to influence the operation of the bureaucracy? What spheres of organizational activity are considered legitimate areas of client concern? How are clients perceived and to what extent is it felt that client satisfaction is an important goal of the organization?

In some cases researchers do provide us with some insights as to how the structure, compliance system, working norms, and client orientation of a bureaucracy has developed. Etzioni, for example, suggests that the nature of the compliance system of a bureaucracy is closely related to its tasks.[8] Brian Smith, in a comparative analysis of field organizations, indicates that the historical evolution of governmental functions has shaped the degree to which public bureaucracies are organized along functional or areal lines.[9] Robert C. Wood, on the other hand, suggests that in the case of the United States the evolution of heavily functionally oriented bureaucracies was in large part a product of a federal political structure.[10] As a further example, Philip Selznick, in his study of the Tennessee Valley Authority, shows how a particular ideological orientation of one bureaucracy led to a specific and unusual pattern of relationships with clients.[11]

These impressionistic insights notwithstanding, most of the rigorous analytical work in organizational behavior has treated these variables as givens and has been concerned with exploring their consequences. This strategy has yielded a number of very valuable insights into the dynamics of bureaucracy, but has left us with an underdetermined explanatory model. Even though we have a reasonably sophisticated understanding of the consequences of using certain types of compliance systems in conjunction with specific organizational structures, we are often at a loss to understand why it is that an agricultural bureaucracy in

---

[8] Amitai Etzioni, *A Comparative Analysis of Complex Organizations: On Power, Involvement and their Correlates* (New York: Free Press, 1961).
[9] Brian C. Smith, *Field Administration: An Aspect of Decentralisation* (London: Routledge and Kegan Paul, 1967).
[10] Robert C. Wood, in *Area and Power; A Theory of Local Government,* ed. Arthur Maass (Glencoe Illinois: Free Press, 1959).
[11] Philip Selznick, *TVA and the Grass Roots* (Berkeley: University of California Press, 1949).

India uses a system of very close supervision whereas one in the United States accords the field officer a great deal more autonomy and exerts much less intrusive supervision. Nor are we able to explain on the basis of existing theory why it is that within Indian agricultural administration a structure that was designed to sustain organizational patterns of very flexible supervision, an advisory staff role, and great responsiveness to expressed clients' needs should in fact have rapidly turned into an organization characterized by very close and elaborate supervision, extensive staff roles in program planning and personnel evaluation, and rather specific prescriptions as to what clients ought to want and the circumstances under which they should get services from the bureaucracy.

In order to begin to understand dynamics such as these, it is essential that we see structure, compliance systems, working norms, and client relationships not as independent variables but rather as intervening variables that are the products of cognitive models of organization that shape the structural designs, procedural rules, operating behaviors, and management strategies in the bureaucracies of any society. These models may be carefully developed and highly elaborated views of the workings of an institution or they may be relatively crude and ill-defined notions of what an organization ought to look like. In either case, there is usually a constellation of views as to three interrelated sets of cognitive orientations. First, perceptions as to the broad goals and critical dynamics of an organization. Second, perceptions of the motivations, loyalty, and responsiveness to various incentives and disincentives among different classes of a population, who man—or are expected to man—different levels within the organization. Third, a similar set of perceptions relating to clients which the bureaucracy is expected to serve, protect, or regulate.

There would appear to be three major sources of cognitive models of organizations. First, the broad nexus of attitudes, values, and social institutions that define a cultural tradition which has, at some point in its history, sustained an independent and autonomous pattern of existence is likely to have produced at least some elements of a cognitive model of organizations. This study, for example, will argue that within the cultural tradition of southern India, there exists an implicit conceptual model of organization that is highly sophisticated and elaborated.

Historical experience with formal organizations constitutes the second major source for cognitive models of organizations. European colonial powers, for example, extended their bureaucratic structures into much of the nonwestern world, and new administrative patterns evolved that were the products of separate cultural traditions and thus of separate cognitive models of organization. The resulting historical experience produced new cognitive models of organizations, which shaped recruitment and socialization patterns within those organizations and also influenced the way in which subsequent organizations were designed.

Explicit ideological movements that seek to modify existing cultural dynamics or to synthesize elements of different cultural traditions are a third major source of cognitive models of organization. Such movements may be as sophisticated and detailed in their organizational imperatives as Marxism-Leninism or as rudimentary and suggestive as the community development movement that evolved in many of the new nations of Africa and Asia in the years following the post-World War II achievements of independence.

The construct of a cognitive model of organization permits a more sophisticated introjection of cultural dynamics into the analysis of organizational dynamics than has heretofore been attempted. It suggests that one should consider cultural orientations, historical experiences, and ideological movements as alternative sources of different cognitive models of organizations, which might simultaneously develop within a single setting and shape the structure and character of a specific organization. This approach discourages the simplistic view that the analysis of a single cultural tradition is a useful construct for understanding organizational behavior.

This study explores the organizational structure of and behavioral patterns in the development administration of the Indian state of Tamil Nadu. The specific empirical focus is on that part of the bureaucracy which was responsible for the implementation of a program to popularize the use of high-yielding varieties of rice in 1967 and 1968. It argues that four different cognitive models of organization were, in differing degrees, significant in the evolution of both the organizational structure and the patterns of organizational behavior of that bureaucracy. The first model is a product of a highly sophisticated and well elaborated cultural tradition of south India. It contains broad ramifications for compliance systems, motivational patterns, staff and line relationships, and working norms that apply to almost all organizations in south India. The second model derives from the historical experience of British colonial bureaucracies in India and rivals the first model in importance as a force shaping bureaucratic dynamics. The third model is a product of the community development movement which was articulated by a number of theorists and practitioners of social change in Asia and Africa during the late 1940s and early 1950s. These men were themselves from the West or were Indians who had been heavily influenced by western ideas. This model had a major impact on the structure of the bureaucracies with which this study is concerned and on the attitudes, values, and working norms of many of the individuals in its lower levels. The fourth model is a product of the Gandhian movement in India. Of less significance for our purposes than the other three, it has nevertheless had important effects on the working norms of many participants within the Tamil agricultural bureaucracy.

These models are not unrelated to each other. Though the traditional south Indian culture greatly predates British notions of colonial bureaucracy, both developed in preindustrial settings, and therefore are in some sense "traditional." Clearly, however, they reflect roots in radically different cultural traditions, one Indian, the other western.

In one sense, then, the Gandhian and community development traditions can be seen as allied efforts to modernize their respective precursors in the Indian and western traditions. In another sense, however, the dharmic and Gandhian traditions can be seen as reinforcing aspects of Indian culture that stand in opposition to specifically western qualities of the British colonial and community development traditions. Conceiving of change along the two dimensions of modernization and westernization, then, the four traditions can be seen as cases which fall into the four cells of a two-by-two table:

Modernization

	TRADITIONAL	MODERN
INDIAN	dharmic	Gandhian
WESTERN	British colonial	community development

Westernization

Clearly this categorization does some violence to reality. The complexity and specialization of British colonial bureaucracy certainly suggest a much greater degree of modernization than does the pattern of relationships that characterizes Tamil village life. Community development ideology represents, in many respects, a rejection of the larger scale, highly differentiated—and thus modern—character of western bureaucracy in its search for patterns appropriate to the fostering of development in village communities. Gandhi, in his reformulation of some features of Indian norms, also rejects much that one would think of as modern in revisionist Hindu thought.

The value of the typology is not, however, in its categorization of the four traditions, but in its suggestions as to the nature of the changes in attitudes, values, and expectations that are experienced with movement from one tradition to another. The incongruities and conflicts between dharmic and colonial bureaucratic thought primarily reflect differences in Indian and western approaches to organization. The Gandhian revisions of dharmic views, though partial and representing a particular strain of thought, involve modernization of a traditional ethic. The movement from a dharmic view to a community development view of organization, this categorization suggests, involves processes both of modernization and westernization. One begins to disentangle the two processes by observing them in the context of the British colonial and Gandhian traditions. Where dharmic and community development ideologies conflict on a specific issue, reinforcement of the dharmic view by the Gandhian tradition suggests that an issue of westernization is involved. Conversely, where British colonial notions are supportive of a dharmic view in opposition to Gandhian and community development approaches, an aspect of modernization would seem to be at issue.

One can see contemporary Tamil bureaucracy, then, as simultaneously experiencing and trying to come to terms with the conceptually distinct processes of modernization and westernization. It is in the examination of the conflicting and reinforcing character of the cognitive models of organization that derive from these cultural, historical, and ideological roots that one begins to better understand the differences and relationship between the two processes.

In the following chapter, each of these cognitive models of organization will be presented in the context of the cultural tradition, historical experience, or ideological movement that produced it. Chapter 3 shows how those cognitive models shaped the evolution of development bureaucracy structure in Tamil Nadu. This sets the stage for the three descriptive chapters of Part II which contain a narrative presentation of specific examples of bureaucratic behavior in the context of a particular geographic and program setting. The cognitive models, structure, and empirical context are then tied together in a series of three chapters which explore, and attempt to explain, the nature of the bureaucratic compliance system, the nature and function of work norms in the bureaucracy, and patterns of relationships between bureaucrats and their farmer clients.

In substantive terms, this study analyzes how and why a small but diverse group of Indian bureaucrats carried out an agricultural development program in 1967 and 1968. The program was a substantial success, but it is less important to understand why that was so than it is to understand the effect of institutional and cultural forces that caused individuals to behave the way they did. In five years the agricultural programs, problems, and prospects of North Arcot District have changed substantially. The bureaucratic apparatus which is charged with planning and bringing about rapid social and economic change in India remains, however, the product and the prisoner of the same structural and cultural constraints which shaped its patterns of behavior five years ago.

To argue, however, that the quality and character of the administrative process observed in the development bureaucracy of North Arcot and the agricultural bureaucracy of Tamil Nadu is representative of the bureaucratic process throughout India would be patently false. The *mix* of cultural traditions, bureaucratic structures, agricultural conditions, and administrative personnel found in this setting was unique. The education, technical training, and integrity of Tamil bureaucrats are probably considerably better than would be found in many Indian states. The efficiency, responsiveness, and competence of the Agricultural Department staff are probably greater than in other departments within the same state. And finally, the administrative skills and the enthusiasm for agricultural programs of the district Collector, combined with the suitability of North Arcot for the innovations being sponsored by the Agriculture Department, undoubtedly contributed to the relatively smooth operation of this program during this year in this district.

The importance of this study for understanding Indian developmental bureaucracy lies in the fact that these same four cognitive models of organization have contributed significantly to administrative structure and practice throughout the subcontinent. The nature of the mix of traditions, as well as the levels of competence and integrity of bureaucrats, varies from state to state, but many general patterns found in this setting will be recognized by those who observe bureaucracies elsewhere in India. Indeed, insofar as certain of the conflicts between cognitive models that shape behavior in Tamil bureaucracy are manifestations of greater traditionality or modernity in approaches to organizations, they are likely to generate common patterns throughout much of postcolonial bureaucracy. Thus, the emphasis in this study is less on how a specific bureaucracy performed in implementing a specific program than it is on identifying patterns of behavior and seeking to discover the roots of those patterns.

The Evidence

A wide variety of sources provided information about the nature of the working experience, behavior, and attitudes of the bureaucrats and farmers whose lives were, in some substantial measure, involved in the High Yielding Varieties Program (HYVP) in 1967 and 1968.

1. *Observation* of actual behavior patterns among bureaucrats and farmers provided a sense of much that was going on in the implementation of a program. Visits to fields made by extension agents; staff meetings in a variety of field offices; the processing of files, reports, and correspondence; the selling of agricultural supplies to farmers; the inspection of subordinates and their work—these activities and many others, when observed and listened to with care, revealed much about the individual bureaucrat's behavior and gave clues as to his attitudes, perceptions, and values.

2. *Interviews*—especially when carried out in the context of a specific work situation—supplemented information about behavioral patterns that came from observations, and revealed much about the background, attitudes, perceptions, and values of individuals at various points within the bureaucracy.

3. The examination of the bureaucracies' *written records* provided evidence about patterns and content of communications within the system. Minutes of meetings that I had attended showed not only what was felt to be important, but also what was felt to be best left unsaid. Required

reports that are filed periodically by extension agents, and then forwarded to and consolidated by successive layers in the bureaucracy, indicated the nature and quality of much of the program information that
moved from the field to program planners and evaluators. Responses to
such reports, as well as evaluative documents in planning and programming offices, indicated the way such reports were used. Discrepancies between what extension personnel did and what they entered in
their monthly reports reflect their sense of how they would like to appear
to their superiors.

4. *Time-use surveys* provided a detailed sense of how individuals of
specific job descriptions spent their working days. Since it was especially
difficult to get a coherent view of the work of extension agents, who
were frequently traveling to and from villages and were engaged in a
wide variety of tasks, they were systematically surveyed with respect to
their activities during individual working days. They were asked to fill
out a one-page form on the day it was received in the mail, indicating the
one type of activity that took the largest amount of their time during
each half-hour period during the working day.

5. *Stories* told by respondents in answer to the question "What story
would you tell to your younger brother in order to give him a good example of proper performance of duty?" indicated some of the media of
cultural communication through which ideas, attitudes, and norms about
bureaucracies were transmitted. This question was asked as part of a
written survey administered to 401 local extension personnel in North
Arcot District.

In India, as in many traditional societies, the story is one of the
most important of the styles used in the transmission of cultural norms.
Folk tales and stories of the great tradition of Hinduism both proclaim
standards of behavior and reflect implicit assumptions about the nature
of human intercourse. Indeed, the process of drawing analogs out of
stories—as well as other sources—forms a dominant means of reasoning
in Indian society.

Moreover, it is widely held in India that giving advice is the most
effective method for changing attitudes. Since giving advice is an appropriate thing for a status superior to do, and since the elder-brother–
younger-brother dyad is a relationship that was familiar to many respondents, this formulation of a question, combining the giving of advice

with the medium of the story, appears to have struck a responsive chord in many respondents. Of the 401 respondents to the questionnaire, 247 wrote coherent stories, many of which were rich sources of information and insight.

6. *Anthropological data* on the nature and meaning of duty in south Indian village settings helped to clarify the attitudes and values that young villagers brought with them as they entered the development bureaucracy. Unfortunately for these purposes, anthropologists have largely ignored traditional indigenous analyses of the village order, but have deduced, on the basis of their own observations, the nature of village social organization. Though we have, as a result, learned much about ritual, transactional, and power relationships in villages, our knowledge of connotations surrounding such concepts as duty in village settings has been fragmentary.

In the past several years, however, Indian anthropologists have begun to explore village level interpetations of the nature of the village community. K. Ishwaran, in his study of Shivapur in Dharwar District of Mysore State, describes village perceptions of inter-caste relationships and numerous aspects of individual duty within this system.[12] K. S. Mathur, in his writings on the Malwa village of Potlod in Indore District of Madhya Pradesh, also devotes considerable attention to "the Hindu values of life"—including the value of duty—as seen in the village.[13]

These descriptions of village perceptions, in addition to the considerable anthropological literature on patterns of village organization in India,[14] provide important clues necessary to understand the sense of

[12] K. Ishwaran, *Tradition and Economy in Village India* (London: Routledge and Kegan Paul, Ltd., 1966).

[13] K. S. Mathur, *Caste and Ritual in a Malwa Village* (Bombay: Asia Publishing House, 1964). Both Ishwaran and Mathur have difficulty integrating and reconciling professed attitudes and values with actual patterns of behavior. Moreover, both present a coherent view of the community that is their own synthesis of multiple views, making it difficult to determine how much of the synthesis derives from their own broader knowledge of Hinduism, how much is present in the views of individual members of the community, and how broadly within each village these perceptions of the village community are held. Mathur is forthright in his admission that his own upper-caste status placed considerable restrictions on his ability to explore questions in detail with members of the lower caste (p. 11).

[14] See, among others, Louis Dumont, *Homo Hierarchicus: An Essay on the Caste System* (Chicago: The University of Chicago Press, 1970); Bernard S. Cohn, "Anthropological Notes on Disputes and Law in India," *American Anthropologist* 67, no. 6, part 2 (December, 1965)

duty that the new bureaucrat brings with him from his village environment and the sets of values that he can use to justify the behavior patterns and attitudes he adopts in the bureaucratic environment.

7. *The literature of the great tradition of Hinduism* has been used to
suggest patterns of thought in Indian tradition that may have played a
role in shaping contemporary values, attitudes, perceptions, and behavior. It is, of course, much too simple to suggest that because a given
value is present in the literary tradition of a culture, that value must also
be current among the members of that culture. Even if the presence of
that value were empirically demonstrated, there is still no guarantee that
the value was instilled by the literary tradition.

The literary products of Hinduism's great tradition therefore enter
this study for the most part through the conduit of respondents who
spontaneously chose great tradition stories as the ones they would use as
examples of proper performance of duty or who made allusions to such
stories in other contexts. Nevertheless, a familiarity with the tradition is
valuable both because it facilitates identification of themes and patterns
in the stories, and because the writings of the great tradition suggest the
significance of and explanations for behavior, perceptions, and values
that might otherwise go unobserved or be misunderstood.[15]

Each of the types of evidence employed in this study contributed to
an understanding of how the Tamil bureaucrat behaved in the environment of an agricultural development program and what factors led to
those behavioral patterns. The primary focus of the study, however, is
on attitudes, perceptions, values, and behavior—not on method or ap-

---

pp. 82–122; William H. Wiser, *The Hindu Jajmani System* (Lucknow: Lucknow Publishing
House, 1936); Walter C. Neale, "Reciprocity and Redistribution in the Indian Village:
Sequel to Some Notable Discussions," *Trade and Markets in the Early Empires*, eds. Karl
Polanyi et al. (Glencoe, Ill.: The Free Press, 1957).

[15] Dumont argues strongly for the use of Indian literary heritage in the attempt to understand an Indian social structure. "In sociological studies the universal can only be attained
through the particular characteristics, different in each case, of each type of society. Why
should we travel to India if not to try to discover how and in what respects Indian society
or civilization, by its very particularity, represents a form of the universal? In the last analysis, it is by humbly inspecting the most minute particulars that the route to the universal
is kept open. If one is prepared to devote all the time necessary to studying all aspects of
Indian culture, one has a chance, under certain conditions, of in the end transcending it,
and of one day finding in it some truth for one's own use." *Homo Hierarchicus*, pp. 3–4.

proach. Consequently, the organization of material is built around substantive themes rather than bodies of data, and the various sources of
data are drawn on as they reveal something about the themes and issues
under consideration.

 CHAPTER TWO

Four Cognitive Models
of Organization

The Dharmic Model

The dharmic approach to the nature of bureaucracy stems from the ethos of social, economic, and political life in Indian villages, rather than from the experience of large, formal organizations. The patterns of thought, calculation, and behavior that characterize village life are generalized into a set of norms and values that influence the nature of the individual's behavior in an alien and unfamiliar structure such as a bureaucracy.

Some norms and values, of course, are village specific; many detailed rules of behavior are relaxed when a villager leaves for a distant town or city. Others are so fully internalized that an individual continues to apply them even when confronted by a new environment. The concept of duty, for example, is central to most Indians in their handling of work situations, whether in their native village or a massive state bureaucracy. Some of the precise connotations differ from setting to setting, but many of the general orientations remain constant.

To understand the orientations toward behavior in a bureaucracy that derive from a village ethic, we should begin by reviewing some of the central features of Indian village organization as they pertain to the closely related spheres of production, distribution, influence, and status. From these features—and the way in which they are perceived by villagers—we may draw inferences about some of the central orientations toward motivation, authority, work habits, and structure that influence behavior of civil servants brought up in the ethos of village norms.

Anthropological evidence suggests that most Indian villages have long been reasonably coherent, integrated, and largely self-contained communities. Individuals living within a definite "village" area have been found to interact with each other in economic, social, ritual or dispute-

20

resolution matters. A wide range of needs in each of these spheres is met within the village. This does not mean, however, that the village is either fully integrated or fully self-sufficient. The role of one group may be limited to the performance of certain economic functions. Factionalism may prevent certain forms of interaction from bridging two hostile segments of the village. And an increasing variety of goods is likely to be imported from outside the village. Nonetheless, a complex pattern of interaction generally does tie the village together into a coherent and meaningful whole.[1]

The centrality of caste in the composition of Indian villages is also well recognized. Occupational, ritual, and hierarchical features of caste generally structure the nature of social and ritual relationships and determine many of the contours of economic interchange within villages. The evidence from numerous village studies of recent years indicates that many villages contain a broad distribution of numerous castes. As Bernard Cohn points out, however, this may be more a reflection of the anthropologist's desire to study multicaste villages than reliable evidence of the dominant pattern of caste composition in Indian villages.[2] Many villages, especially in the south of India, appear to have smaller numbers of castes, and not infrequently, one caste dominates to the near exclusion of all others.

One feature of caste is its close association with occupation. Numerous smaller castes have quite specific occupations with which they are associated. It is clear, however, that there is not a one-to-one correlation between specific castes and specific occupations. It seems, rather, that certain occupations are the preserves of specific castes, whereas other occupations are open to any with the resources and skills to pursue them. Occupations that can be conducted largely independently—farm-

---

[1] Recent writings have also provided a corrective for the view, widely held some years ago, that the village community is a fully self-sufficient entity. Parents generally go outside of their own village to find marriage partners for their children; certain types of disputes are resolved with the help of mediation from outside the village, and a variety of ritual, economic, and entertainment services are frequently obtained from outside the village community. That the village is dependent on outside institutions for a variety of important functions should not, however, be allowed to obscure the fact that most villages have traditionally provided the bulk of their own needs from within.

[2] Bernard S. Cohn, "Anthropological Notes on Disputes and Law in India," *American Anthropologist* 67, no. 6, part 2 (December 1965): 86.

ing and animal husbandry—are generally open, and those involving patterned relationships with other groups—service and ritual occupations—are reserved for specific castes.[3] Thus, members of a smithing caste have exclusive *rights* to service the smithing needs of a village; at the same time, they have the full and inalienable *responsibility* for doing so as well. Within this limitation, however, members of the caste retain the option to pursue certain other occupations, as long as they are not the exclusive preserve of another local caste.

In the recent past, land has been the dominant and controlling factor in the production of goods in the village economy. Those owning land produced and controlled the distribution of food. Labor involved in the production of food and in the providing of a multitude of services has been conventionally paid in kind, from the product of the land.

As a result of this economic reality, a pattern of vertical economic relationships has generally supplemented the horizontal ties of caste. Each major land owner has maintained regular exchange relationships with specific individuals or families from most or all of the various service and laboring castes represented in the village. Thus, agricultural laborer families of one caste might be divided by their economic loyalties to two or more landowners.

The generic term that has come to be applied to this common pattern of economic exchange is the *jajmani* system. Throughout much of northern India, the term *jajman* refers to the landowner who exchanges products of the land for the services of a specific group of clients, or *kamin*, with whose families he has traditionally maintained relationships.[4] The term *baluta* is also used in describing these relationships, but it appears that this refers to village servants in general, rather than the specific kamin of specific jajmans. In the area of Mysore studied by Ishwaran, the broad pattern of exchanges is termed the *aya* system.[5]

Irrespective of regional names, the patterns of exchange share cer-

[3] K. S. Mathur, *Caste and Ritual in a Malwa Village* (Bombay: Asia Publishing House, 1964), pp. 153, 160.

[4] Descriptions of this system enter into ethnographic accounts of most northern Indian villages. See also, T. O. Beidelman, *A Comparative Analysis of the Jajmani System* (Locust Valley, N.Y.: Association for Asian Studies, 1958); William H. Wiser, *The Hindu Jajmani System* (Lucknow: Lucknow Publishing House, 1936).

[5] K. Ishwaran, *Tradition and Economy in Village India* (London: Routledge and Kegan Paul, Ltd., 1966), pp. 36–49.

tain characteristics. At harvest times, landowners turn over to the individuals who have served them during the year or the previous season a certain share of their crops, depending on the nature of the service. The specific shares are traditionally established and simple to measure, though an external analyst trying to calculate the share of the total produce that went to various members of the community found that analysis of the total system was unmanageably complex.[6] In addition to annual payments of grain, other traditional forms of in-kind payments are made on more frequent bases. Service castes may exchange services with each other and appear to provide certain services to laborers in return for little or no direct payment.

The dynamics of the system are extremely complex and take in a wide range of activities. The specifically jajman-kamin relationship is supplemented by other types of exchanges. Extensive debtor-creditor relationships exist in which it is commonly agreed that no short-range attempt will be made to pay off the principal. The creditor is, however, clearly in the position of authority in the relationship and has the dominant leverage in the case of any disagreement. As numerous analysts have pointed out, the landowner is generally in a comparable position in relationship to those who provide services to him. He does need their services and it is to his advantage to maintain correct relations with them, and indeed, to foster loyalty and indebtedness by going beyond his customary obligations. In the case of serious conflict, however, the landowner has the power over the primary resource—land—and doing battle with him is risky indeed. Only when there are independent sources of income—when the servant has his own land or members of his family are employed outside the village—is the balance of power not firmly in the hands of those who own land.[7]

As a participant conceptualizes these relations, however, he places them in the broader context of order and authority represented in the

[6] Walter C. Neale, "Reciprocity and Redistribution in the Indian Village: Sequel to Some Notable Discussions," in *Trade and Markets in the Early Empires*, eds. Karl Polyani, et al. (Glencoe, Ill.: The Free Press, 1957).

[7] Edward B. Harper has argued cogently that the *jajmani* type of village exchange depends on a subsistence type of economy independent of a money economy. He points to the existence of a very different pattern of relationships in a Malnad community where the subsistence conditions are not met. See his "Two Systems of Economic Exchange in Village India," *American Anthropologist* 61, no. 5, part 1 (October 1959).

concept of dharma. The literature dealing with dharma is vast and the subtleties of content and meaning that have been imputed to the term are complex and varied. At its most general level, dharma is seen as the governing principle of the universe. It is the source and nature of order and balance among all aspects of the universe. At the level of political theory and philosophy, dharma is the principle that regulates the activities of various components of the Hindu nation or kingdom. The king is seen as the upholder and enforcer of dharma.

The village is also seen in the context of the operation of dharma. The patterns of interaction among individuals within the village are thought to be based on the cosmic ordering, insofar as it can be understood and replicated by mortals. For the individual, dharma represents those specific activities which are his responsibility to perform. The compelling beauty and coherence of the philosophical system is that it so effectively relates the individual to his society. When each individual fulfills the duties traditionally accepted as his dharma he at once furthers his own religious development and makes an essential contribution to the stability, order, balance, and continuity of the social units of which he is a part.

The relationship between the philosophical system of the great tradition of Hinduism and the conceptual framework that structures social and religious phenomena in the daily lives of Indian villagers is complex and only partially understood. In both the village of Potlod studied by Mathur and K. Ishwaran's Mysore village, however, dharma is reported to be a concept that is central to the villagers' understanding and explanation of the nature of their village community. In the villages of Tamil Nadu the term dharma is not commonly used in its traditional Sanskrit meaning, but the Tamil word *kademai* is remarkably equivalent. It appears that an important concept in the philosophical aspects of Hinduism is also significant in the lives and social perceptions of individual inhabitants of villages. Their sophistication and understanding of the concept, however, may well be quite limited, and we are dependent in large part on the writings of Mathur and Ishwaran for evidence on the nature of village perceptions. Though this is clearly an area of study that needs further field research, the material now available is sufficient to indicate the general directions of these perceptions.

A Village View of Community

Duty is the primary principle on which this village view of community is based. Each individual has complex sets of actions he must perform. The whole range of these actions, taken together, constitutes his dharma. These duties lay out, in highly specific terms, approved patterns of relations within the family, the caste, and the village. They cover one's religious, hygienic, economic, and social interactions. Mathur notes:

> Religious traditions lay down with meticulous care how a person should behave and live in order to lead a proper life. The traditions one is most concerned with for guidance in one's life and behavior are the traditions of one's caste or *jati* (i.e., his *jati-dharma*). These prescribe for the caste rules for proper (*dharmic*) living in everyday life, and prohibit what is traditionally considered to be improper for the caste.[8]

The duties of individual members of the village are intimately connected with the social order of the community. As Mathur points out,

> In the social sense, *dharma*—or *dharam* as it is popularly known to the people of Potlod village—is composed of all those elements, moral rules and ethical codes, beliefs, concepts and theories, rights and observances, that are designed to hold together the social system. The social function of *dharma* is to hold together, maintain, and perpetuate a given social order. . . . According to the Hindu view of life, it is only righteous action—righteous in a given context—that can serve this purpose—of perpetuating a social order. And thus *dharma* comes to be equated with and mean all 'righteous belief and action,' that is, a proper way of living and behaving in society.
> *Dharma* is the Hindu scheme of values. The Hindu belief is that *dharma* is the law of the universe, and society the manifestation of the divine law. Most village Hindus believe that if the tenets of *dharma* are not properly adhered to, the prescribed rites not performed in the right way, and the taboos or ritual avoidances not observed, in short, if the *dharma* is allowed to decay, there is bound to be chaos and disorder, and society will come to an end.[9]

It is the complex set of economic, ritual, and service interactions that, by indirectly linking each member of the community to every other member, unites personal dharma (duties) with social dharma (order). The jajmani (or aya) system constitutes one aspect of these interactions.

[8] Mathur, *Caste and Ritual*, p. 5.   [9] *Ibid.*, pp. 94–95.

Though it is clear to the western analyst that such an economic institution fosters gross inequalities in economic power, Ishwaran suggests that villagers see it in a somewhat different light:

> An important point to note about these transactions is that they present a variety of relationships. They are believed to be of mutual benefit, and both parties are governed by such a belief. They involve economic and social relations of give and take. . . . The central principle here is the *Dharma* or "duty." All the parties are equalized as persons with duties. These duties should be performed without any grumbling. The client/tenant notion is completely foreign to the spirit of the *Aya* system. Who gives and who takes is a matter of shifting perspectives and contexts.[10]

The complexities of exchange relationships in the village community have already been noted. Mathur suggests that villagers see not only the economic exchanges, but the entire village system, to be beyond their understanding.

> The nature of *dharma*, the people say, is extremely complex, more so for ignorant, unread, and untutored minds. The principles of *dharma* are unfathomably deep, and so, for all practical purposes, the average common man should generally follow the path trodden by his ancestors and predecessors, in accordance with the best available traditions of the class or caste to which he happens to belong.[11]

Thus, one does not perform duties in accordance with one's understanding of what the ramifications will be for the entire community. Rather, the system depends on the empirical realization that traditionally sanctioned duties, when aggregated into a village system, have normally produced a stable, coherent, and relatively equitable system. As Ishwaran notes,

> Such a complicated machinery cannot work without some all-pervasive belief or spirit. This belief that animates the system as a whole is the belief that the system is good because it has been proved to be good. Otherwise, how did their ancestors accept it and hand it on to them? This belief is also

---

[10] K. Ishwaran, *Tradition and Economy*, pp. 37–39. Clearly, exposure to nontraditional theories of microeconomics is changing these perspectives rapidly. The concern of this portion of the study, however, is with the village of fifteen to twenty years ago. The perspectives which Ishwaran and Mathur describe, though now being rapidly eroded, were undoubtedly much more widespread when our respondents were village children.

[11] Mathur, *Caste and Ritual*, p. 86.

pragmatically supported by the fact that the system leads to mutual benefit and hence must be good.[12]

"Tradition," Mathur's villagers feel, "is thus the best and most important source of *dharma*, one which takes precedence over all the other sources, literary or mythical." [13]

For most people in the village, then, the goal of "living a proper life" does not involve calculating the consequences of action, or acting in order to achieve certain consequences, but rather simply fulfilling the expectations of their roles. Mathur, in relating a popular village story, makes this point:

> Being born in a particular caste . . . is not in a man's hands. . . . But having been born into a particular caste and station of life, it is incumbent upon a person to live righteously in accordance with the traditions of his caste for that and that alone is his *dharma*. To abandon the duties related to one's caste and profession is considered to be both shameful and sinful.[14]

Indeed, it is considered a virtue in village life to be able to persevere in the performance of duty even though the obvious manifest consequences of doing so appear to be entirely negative.

MOTIVATION

In the Tamil village conception, motivation, as understood in the west, is irrelevant. The will, desires, and needs of the individual are not the roots of analysis; rather, the needs of the social order, the role of the individual in meeting those needs, and the religious advancement achieved as a result of the disciplined meeting of those needs are the important components of the individual's work environment. Thus, the individual has a set of duties and rights clearly defined for him by the social context. Personal options are not defined and the development of individual preferences is not encouraged. Rather the individual learns that the socially approved posture is one of allegiance to one's duty simply because it is one's duty.

It is clear in this conception, however, that the individual's duty involves limiting his need for and expectations of personal benefits in order to maintain the balance and harmony of the social community. It is

[12] Ishwaran, *Tradition and Economy*, pp. 48–49.   [13] Mathur, *Caste and Ritual*, p. 86.
[14] *Ibid.*, p. 87.

equally clear that, all attempts at socialization notwithstanding, many individuals will be tempted to stray from the path of duty. This is recognized explicitly in the distinction made between dharma and danda. The necessary complement to the definition of the cosmic ordering—dharma—is the existence of an authority—danda—to enforce the pattern of rights and duties that sustain the ordering.

In this definition of the problem, then, the use of incentives to induce individuals to comply with expectations is foreign and incongruous. Self-deprivation is inherent in duty; duty is by nature in conflict with short-term material self-interest.

AUTHORITY AND CONTROL

In the village, the most important authority is that of tradition. The authority of individuals consequently plays a lesser role than in many societies, and that role is closely related to the basic ordering principle of the village.

Where tradition defines so much of human intercourse, the role of personal authority is twofold: first, to resolve cases of doubt or dispute as to what precisely are the rights and duties of individuals or families in a given setting; second, to reestablish the proper pattern of rights and duties when they have been violated. In most villages the first function is the major preoccupation of leaders. Though the cosmic ordering of a social community cannot be fully comprehended by any individual, in times of conflict one turns to village or caste elders who have demonstrated a capacity for the mediation and resolution of disputes. Bernard Cohn has cited numerous studies suggesting that precisely this capacity to mediate disputes is considered the most important attribute of a village leader.[15]

The dispute is likely to be taken to a council of elders whose goal is not to assign guilt for a specific action, but rather to resolve the dispute without destroying the village relationships. One is, in short, trying to reestablish the social order, the pattern of dharma. In another article, Cohn has pointed out that the dispute resolution process examines the entire nexus of relationships among parties to the dispute.[16] The history

[15] "Anthropological Notes on Disputes and Law in India," pp. 85–98.
[16] In "Some Notes on Law and Change in North India," *Economic Development and Cultural Change* 8, no. 1 (October 1959): 79–93.

of perceived slights is of importance because every action must be evaluated in light of the exchange relationships of which it is a part. Every individual is given an opportunity to present his view and the elders begin to sense the lines along which a compromise solution can be drawn. The criterion for a proper resolution of the conflict is not a legalistic right or wrong, but rather its acceptability to the concerned parties. If a solution is seen as creating an equitable ordering of relationships, it is likely to be a close approximation to the dharmic ordering. Susanne Rudolph describes this consensual tradition in the following terms:

> When the council of five, the panchayat, speaks as one, it is said to be the voice of God; it gives expression to the consensus of the traditional moral order. The apotheosized village republic, representative, deliberative, and harmonious, rests on the moral basis of *dharma* and *karma* of sanctified custom, in which rank and distance, privilege and obligation, rights and duties, are acquired at birth and legitimized by religion. . . .
>
> . . . The consensus context, unlike the adversary, assumes that some traditionally recruited body . . . will reach a decision after all who should be have been heard and discussion has revealed what most, if not all, agree is the proper disposition of the problem. . . . Support is determined not by a show of hands, but by weighing the participants' sense of the moral fitness of things. Village consensus grows out of the belief that there is one right answer to a problem, that testimony and deliberation are important in finding it, and that the applied moral sense of the group's members partakes of their common traditional cultures.[17]

Enforcement is normally a less important function of authority figures in the village setting. In part this is because the norms and expectations relating to doing one's duties are clear and the demands on any one individual are rarely felt to be unduly burdensome. Perhaps more important is the everpresent threat of social ostracism which is an enormously powerful deterrent to nonperformance of duty. Compliance with the traditional demands of duty, however, is seen as very important to the stability of the village system. The relative infrequency of punishment reflects the effectiveness of the deterrence system, rather than the weakness of enforcement powers.

Because of the high degree of perceived interdependence, any fail-

---

[17] In "Consensus and Conflict in Indian Politics," *World Politics* 13, no. 3 (April 1961): 386–87.

ure in the performance of duty is seen as having a complex and far-reaching set of possible ramifications. This helps to make clear the heavy emphasis Joan Mencher found on punishment for mistakes in child-rearing practices in Kerala. She relates that "many old men and women speak of the canings they received for having made mistakes. . . . When I asked what was so wrong about making a mistake, older people were usually speechless." [18] The concept in Malayalam that Mencher translates as "a mistake" appears to be the equivalent of *adharmic* behavior as it is understood in Potlod and Shivapur. A mistake is viewed with such concern because it is seen as threatening the stability and order of the social system.

Though enforcement of duty does not frequently arise in village settings, dharma cannot be maintained, the writings of the great tradition suggest, without danda, the coercive function to enforce the pattern of duties. As with the meaning of many Sanskrit terms, the precise definition of danda has evolved considerably over the centuries. At each point, however, danda has referred to the enforcement and implementation of dharma. The scope of activities subsumed in the role of implementation has changed, but it has generally focused on the necessity of inducing individuals, through coercion, to follow their dharma.

As Drekmeier points out, dharma was not seen as a condition that could be achieved and maintained without constant surveillance. Without external constraints placed on him, each individual would be tempted to act in his immediate self-interest, violating the cooperative and self-restraining injunctions of dharma:

> The constant reiteration of the need for coercion (*danda*) in the preservation of the *dharmic* order suggests a cynical view of human nature. In addition to the *Mahabharata*, the *Kautaliya* and the *Kamandakiya*, the *Manusmriti* and the *Shukranitisara* all attest to the natural depravity of man. The suspicion of human nature that dominates Hindu thought can be summed up in the words of Manu: "a guiltless man is hard to find. A society without constraints is no society at all: men feed on one another as do the beasts of the jungle and the fish in the sea." [19]

[18] "Growing Up in South Malabar," *Human Organization* 22, no. 1 (Spring 1963): 57.
[19] Charles Drekmeier, *Kingship and Community in Early India* (Stanford: Stanford University Press, 1962), p. 249.

V. R. Ramachandra Dikshitar, in his study of *Hindu Administrative Institutions,* quotes a number of early texts on the nature of danda: [20]

> Repression of crime is known as *danda.* Owing to the possession of this virtue, the king himself is known as *danda.* The administration of the king is called *danda niti.* (*Kamandaka*)
>
> It is through fear of *danda* that the whole earth is made fit for enjoyment. (*Manu*)
>
> It is *danda* that rules the subjects, it is *danda* that protects all. It is *danda* that keeps awake and guards people when they are asleep and hence the learned style *danda* itself as *dharma.* (*Manu*)
>
> The power of *danda*, and especially the dread of it, is such that even the Devas, Asuras, Gandharvas, Rakshasas, Pathagas, and Uragas, do their duty loyally. (*Mahabharata*)

The point to be noted here is that dharma and danda are seen as clearly separate concepts that are intimately related in the processes of governing. Indeed, the administrative process would seem to involve the determination of dharma, followed by the application of danda. Although precedent exists in the Hindu tradition for a coercive and punitive dandic authority, it rarely operates openly in the village setting. Rather it is the threat of sanctions imposed by a social order that tends to keep the individual on the path of duty.

PERCEPTIONS OF WORK

In the traditionally slowly changing environment of the village it is almost always possible for an individual to complete the range of duties custom has assigned to him. As conditions do change, the nature of exchange relationships is slowly redefined by resolving disputes on a case-by-case basis. When personal emergencies arise, the individual looks to his family or to his caste for temporary relief. Thus, situations in which it is impossible for an individual to do his duty rarely arise.

There follow from this fact four self-evident behavioral prescriptions, which profoundly influence attitudes toward work. These prescriptions are not made explicit in the village ethic because the conditions they address do not arise in a slowly changing social and economic envi-

[20] (Madras: University of Madras, 1929), pp. 6, 10.

ronment. They become of special interest, however, under conditions of more rapid change.

First, the question of the relative importance of duties does not arise. Since a failure in the performance of any task is seen as threatening the balance and order of the social system, all tasks are clearly important. Since the performance of one almost never conflicts with the performance of any other, the need to establish criteria for determining their relative importance does not arise. Dharma is very clear: one does all of one's duties.

Second, for the same reason the problem of determining which of one's duties should be accomplished and which should be neglected does not arise. It is essential and possible to fulfill all of them.

Third, one does not calculate what resources are available before determining what one's duties are. Rather the duties come first and determine how one's resources are to be used.

Fourth, in most circumstances there are no meaningful and acceptable explanations for failures to carry out one's assigned duties. Failure is viewed very seriously and is seen simply as a straying from the path of dharma. One makes up excuses, but with the expectation that they will be treated as such. Mencher writes, "If one were 'caught in a mistake' one would try to find a good rationale for it since admitting a mistake was an affront to a good Nayar's dignity and never failed to arouse hostile feelings which could not be expressed directly toward the 'accuser.' " [21]

In addition to prescribing that it is feasible and important to do all of one's assigned duties, the dharmic tradition also clearly indicates appropriate attitudes toward doing those duties. Of primary importance is the basic precept that one does not calculate the consequences of what one does. Since the cosmic ordering, even within a village, is so complex as to defy the comprehension of any one individual, it is foolhardy to try to anticipate the results of one's actions. Theory is combined with pragmatism in the view that the traditionally derived pattern of rights and duties has maintained both order and balance in the village. It must, therefore, be a close approximation to the dharmic order. Therefore, the very clear directive of the dharmic view of bureaucracy is that one follow

[21] Mencher, "Growing Up," p. 57.

the precise behavioral pattern that is defined as one's duty. One does not question its purpose or concern oneself with its consequences. One does not work to achieve results. Rather one carries out assigned tasks. Perhaps Vinoba Bhave expressed the concept most clearly in a recent statement he made in reply to a question about whether or not the work he was then engaged in would succeed: "Fire merely burns. It does not care whether anyone puts a pot on it, fills it with water and puts rice in it to make a meal. To burn is the limit of its duty."

Initiative, creativity, and originality are characteristics that are highly valued in growth- and change-oriented cultures. However, where stability and order are primary values and are achieved in the context of a static technology and economy, such characteristics are not appreciated. Thus, in the dharmic view, one values the individual who can stick to traditionally sanctioned behavior patterns. New ideas and new ways of doing things disrupt an established balance, change the distribution of goods, and thus threaten to create conflict. The product of a dharmic cultural setting is not, as a result, likely to search out new ways of doing things in a bureaucratic setting. Nor is he likely to expect or value such behavior among his subordinates.

Even within a setting where innovation is not expected, one can make judgments as to the quality of an individual's performance. In the dharmic view, however, quality is seen within the context of the goal of maintaining the social balance and order. As a result, acts are seen as being of two types; what one does either promotes or disrupts the stability and balance of the community. Ishwaran reports this perception as follows:

> If one gets inside the mental workings of the people, one notes that none in Shivapur thinks overtly in terms of caste or status. The categories that prevail are normal/abnormal. To behave in accordance with *Dharma* is normal, and to violate *Dharma* is abnormal. If one behaved abnormally one would be legitimately putting one's self beyond the pale of village society, and indeed, out of all social existence.[22]

Mathur states the principle very clearly and succinctly: "All that is *dharma* is good and right, and conversely, all that is not *dharma* (or a-*dharma*) is bad, wicked and wrong." [23] To try to fit behavior into a qualitative

[22] Ishwaran, *Tradition and Economy*, p. 73.   [23] Mathur, *Caste and Ritual*, p. 83.

continuum of worst-bad-fair-good-better-best is, then, inappropriate because the quality of behavior is essentially dichotomous.

Thus, the dharmic tradition provides its adherents with a set of norms relating to work that differ in many important ways from the norms of a growth- and change-oriented society. It does not prepare an individual for situations of work overload. The concept of setting priorities is a foreign one, as is the notion of calculating costs and benefits in order to determine optimal work strategies. One does not strive to achieve results, nor does one feel concern if the performance of one's duty produces what appear to be undesired consequences. One keeps to established procedures and standards—neither seeking innovations nor quality of work that exceeds the traditional system-maintaining norms.

The British Colonial Model

The character of the British imperial tradition of administration was shaped by its central problem: to provide order and collect taxes over a vast area with a very small number of representatives of the raj. The system was dependent in its day-to-day operations on Indian subordinates, but the trust accorded to those subordinates was minimal.

The lack of trust became a ritual and unquestioned part of the tradition of the British elite during the latter decades of the imperial administration. A part of the myth perpetuated by many of the British officials was the view that Indian subordinates had no moral scruples, were inveterate liars, and schemed incessantly among themselves. Two great novels of the imperial era, Forster's *A Passage to India* and George Orwell's *Burmese Days*, are scathing indictments of the blind prejudice and racism that had become institutionalized features in many quarters of the British Indian establishment.

The bases of that pattern, however, were firmly rooted in the early experience of the British administration in India. During the early nineteenth century, while the British were groping to establish and extend their authority, the Indians who served their imperial needs had little understanding of, appreciation for, or loyalty to the principles, personnel, or traditions of the British raj. Their loyalties were to their own social and religious institutions.

The British were soon forced to recognize these facts. The most comprehensive and revealing account of the British coming to grips with a highly organized Indian effort to subvert the imperial design of the raj to the benefit of caste and family factions is presented in Frykenburg's classic study of Guntur District.[24] Frykenburg documents the rise of a family of Marathi-speaking Brahmans who, during the 1830s and 1840s, dominated the higher levels of the district bureaucracy and managed to subvert completely the revenue operations of the British administration. One highly organized faction, the Nyapati, was deeply entrenched in key positions; and during a period of weak and transient British collectors, it systematically falsified records on a massive scale, extorting millions of rupees from the villagers and diverting them from the British coffers into their own pockets.

British civil servants, dependent on Indian staffs, developed personal allegiances to competent members of the Brahman elite who, in turn, used their influence with British officials as weapons in their struggles to destroy competing factions. The leader of the Nyapati faction, for example, was enormously successful in gaining the trust of the British establishment. When a new collector of Guntur, John Goldingham, discovered the nature and extent of the Nyapatis' bureaucractic sabotage, he attempted to appoint as *Huzar Sheristadar*—the principal native revenue officer—the leader of a competing faction who had exposed the Nyapati wrongdoings. Such was Nyapati influence with the British Board of Revenue, however, that the appointment was rejected and the collector virtually forced to accept the leader of the Nyapati in his place.[25]

The repeated efforts of Goldingham and his successor to press charges against and remove key officeholders of the Nyapati faction were consistently reversed, and the faction remained in almost total control of the district administration from 1837 until 1845, when an independent commission spent six months gathering detailed evidence, extracted from recalcitrant and hostile officials, that clearly revealed the scope of Nyapati corruption.[26]

Though Guntur was an extreme case, similar interests and intrigues pervaded virtually every south Indian district. In Coimbatore District a shrewd civil servant, Casee Chetty, built a powerful financial empire by

[24] Robert Frykenburg, *Guntur District, 1788–1844: A History of Local Influence and Central Authority in Southern India* (Oxford: Clarendon Press, 1965).
[25] *Ibid.*, pp. 100–110, 122–35.   [26] *Ibid.*, pp. 192–229.

manipulating grain markets and public works funds over which he had gained control.[27] The Montgomery Report of 1844 revealed that the collector of Rajamundry (like Guntur, a district in the delta of the Godavari River of the Telegu country) "had all but abandoned the administration of his district to the tender mercies of the Desasthas [Maharata Brahmans] in the Huzur Cutcherry [district headquarters]."[28] Frykenburg concludes that "the tendency of Desastha Brahmans in charge of a Huzur Cutcherry to combine in a subversive manner was not confined to Guntur, but was general throughout south India."[29] He quotes a British Commissioner of the period, Henry Ricketts, as follows: "In every district, in a greater or less degree, the whole body of public servants form a combination bound together by strong ties of interests (not only out of fear of injury) and often of family or caste connection, to maintain abuses."[30]

Recognizing the alien pattern of caste and family loyalties that were of preeminent importance to the native administrative establishment, British officialdom tried not so much to establish a competing focus for loyalties, as to establish and enforce increasingly elaborate rules, which reduced the opportunities for corrupt practices, improved the capacity of the bureaucracy to punish offenders, and increased the legitimate financial and status rewards available within the bureaucracy.[31]

As a result of this serious threat to British authority, record-keeping procedures were tightened, control over financial transactions was made more elaborate, the size and complexity of the surveillance establishment were increased, and numerous rules designed to prevent the rise of family empires within the bureaucracy were introduced.

Over the years the procedures for checking and double-checking on the behavior of each individual in the administrative establishment became increasingly sophisticated, eliminating ever more elaborate attempts to defraud the British raj. Although this procedure gave the British masters more effective control over the behavior of their Indian subordinates, it had little effect on their perceptions of the base nature of Indian motivations.

Corruption and fraud were by no means limited to the ranks of In-

[27] Mariadas Ruthnaswamy, *Some Influences That Made the British Administrative System in India* (privately printed, University of Madras, 1939), pp. 303–306.
[28] Quoted in Frykenburg, *Guntur District*, p. 193.   [29] *Ibid.*, p. 235.   [30] *Ibid.*
[31] *Ibid.*, pp. 215–16.

dian subordinates. The senior civil service grew out of the corps of British officials of the East India Company, who knew many ways to accumulate personal wealth while in the Company's service. As the British began to assume revenue collection functions, increasing restraints were put on the British officials, and in 1793 the category of "covenanted" servants was established. In return for generous salaries, these senior officials agreed not to carry out personal financial manipulations.[32]

By such means were attempts made to increase the loyalty and legitimate gains of the British so as to assure their compliance with the interests of the bureaucracy. Men of "good" family with a common ethic and loyalty were chosen for positions. Their college training in Britain emphasized an elitist moral code of loyalty and honesty. The esprit de corps was strengthened in training programs and in probationary service in the field.[33]

Whereas Indians had held senior posts in the Moghul revenue administration, they were excluded from "covenanted" ranks in the Company. In 1833 it became illegal to exclude candidates on grounds of religion, birth, descent, or color; but it remained clear that the tastes, intellectual traditions, and moral ethics of aristocratic Christian England remained the *sine qua non* of admission to the senior ranks of the Company and, after the establishment of the Indian Civil Service (ICS) under the British Government, to that august club as well.[34]

Thus, the imperial administrative tradition developed two clearly defined tiers. Historians have documented in painful detail the efforts of qualified Indians to gain access to the upper tier and the barriers that were placed in their paths.[35] Of much greater significance for the development of traditions within the bureaucracy itself, however, were the divergent patterns of control, motivation, and work habits that developed in the two tiers.

The small and elite ICS was a self-regulating corps. Its members

[32] Richard Symonds, *The British and Their Successors: A Study in the Development of the Government Services in the New States* (London: Faber and Faber, 1966), p. 26. However, the practice of making handsome profits from nonsanctioned enterprises continued well into the nineteenth century.

[33] B. B. Misra, *The Administrative History of India, 1834–1947: General Administration* (London: Oxford University Press, 1970), pp. 177–81.

[34] Symonds, *The British and Their Successors*, pp. 29 ff. and Misra, *The Administrative History of India*, pp. 171–77.

[35] See, for example, Misra, *The Administrative History of India*, pp. 186–248.

were taught that the mark of their superiority was their capacity to comply with the needs of the system without supervision. The ICS officer operated within the parameters of a system of rules, but the assumption of honesty and judgment that pervaded his position made judicious breaking or circumventing of the rules reasonably common.

The training of the ICS officer did not so much prepare him for the specifics of district office as it fostered the self-confidence and analytical skills needed to take charge and act with assurance and initiative in unfamiliar circumstances. At a time when well-placed Indian subordinates were extorting vast sums, not only from the Company but from villages as well, the "covenanted" officer and later the ICS officer came to symbolize the trustworthy and selfless man of justice who could be looked to by the common villager for protection from the depredations of the revenue bureaucracy.[36]

The lower tier developed in an entirely different context. Assumptions of dishonesty, the elaboration of supervisory and control mechanisms, and the limitation of independent authority shaped its traditions. After preliminary collection of data and establishment of land revenue procedures and tax levels, the bureaucratic enterprise settled into the routine of keeping a complex operation in motion. The lower tier consisted of a massive clerical staff involved in performing routine chores, policing itself through the regular adherence to carefully prescribed procedures and the preparation of documents in the form of "files," which were placed before a member of the upper tier for a substantive decision. Offices were organized to maximize the efficient operation and decision-making of a single individual.

A central tenet of British imperial organization was the rotation of upper-tier officers between district field assignments and departmental posts in the state capital. With fairly rapid turnover of decision-making personnel, it was perceived as imperative that the permanent establishment be prepared to provide background and orientation on each issue coming before the decision-makers.[37]

In practice, when a letter requiring a decision was received, the of-

---

[36] For an interesting view of the British self-image, see Allen J. Greenberger, *The British Image of India, a Study in the Literature of Imperialism, 1880–1960* (London: Oxford University Press, 1969) pp. 58–61.

[37] For a candid statement of "tenure" policy, see *Report of the Government of India Secretariat*

fice would first establish it as a file and attach to it any relevant prior correspondence or documents. In order to save the officer's time, clerks would summarize contents of the file, write "notes" designed to conceptualize the central issues involved, and, in most cases, draft the officer's reply. Often, however, the possibility that other departments or offices might be concerned with the case had to be considered. This would result in a "referral" to one or more offices, where the case again would be noted, considered by the officer, and returned to the originating office. The officer might then ask for further information, issue drafting instructions, or simply return the draft presented to him for "fair copying." When a reply was prepared to the officer's satisfaction it was typed, signed, and mailed. And finally, because officer turnover was so frequent, filing was seen as being of great importance.

A number of pathologies developed out of this system over time. First, since "noting" was one of the few ways in which men of the lower tier could show their mettle, it developed into an elaborate and highly stylized art form. In 1899, Lord Curzon described the noting process as "a dismal ordeal of irresponsible loquacity"; 21 years later Llwellyn Smith found conditions little better, and 25 years after Smith wrote Sir Richard Tottenham still found "excessive noting" to be a major problem in office procedures. The various remedies attempted had only marginal and temporary effect.[38]

Second, referral procedures were often used as delaying techniques. When a clerk or deputy secretary was uncertain about how to handle a problematic case, his actions could often be delayed for several weeks by a well devised referral. Other subterfuges were often employed to avoid making decisions on painful or puzzling cases.[39]

Both the excessive noting and various forms of delaying tactics, however, were little more than symptoms of a more fundamental problem with the administration. Whereas training for the upper tier was

---

Procedure Committee (The Llwellyn Smith Report), Delhi, 1920. Reprinted in 1963 by National Institute of Public Administration, Karachi, Pakistan, p. 41.

[38] Misra, The Administrative History of India, pp. 133–36; The Llwellyn Smith Report, p. 80; and Reports on the Reorganization of the Central Government, 1945–46 (The Tottenham Reports). Reprinted in 1963 by the National Institute of Public Administration, Karachi, Pakistan, p. 51.

[39] Misra, The Administrative History of India, pp. 136–39; Llwellyn Smith Report, pp. 79–80.

reasonably successful in producing creative, capable, and thoughtful men, the educational system feeding the lower tier did little more than grind out young men who were able to memorize massive amounts of material irrespective of their ability to understand it. At the turn of the century, Lord Curzon described the Indian system of higher education as "a huge system of active but often misdirected effort, over which, like some evil phantom, seemed to hover the monstrous and malefficient spirit of CRAM." [40]

The clerical staffs, then, had neither the training nor the experience to gain practical understanding of field problems. They lacked the perspective of the upper tier officers and were deprived of opportunities to develop skills and learn how to take initiative or exercise independent judgment. Their training and job descriptions produced functionaries capable of performing highly routinized clerical activities. Delays and ritualized forms were an inevitable product of the very characteristics that gave the system its stability and continuity.

The British techniques for handling their Indian subordinates relied heavily on the firmness—indeed harshness—of a remote and powerful authority. The common perception was that subordinates would respond only out of fear. Thus, a constant sense of threat was seen as important to the maintenance of proper discipline and order.

As Allen Greenberger has pointed out, the primary analogy used in the British analysis of British-Indian relations was that of the parent-child situation. The conclusion to be drawn was that a firm hand was in order:

> For the British to do their duty as parents it is naturally most important that they recognize both their superior position and the fact that the Indians, because of their "racial character," must be treated as dependents. Half of the British mistakes in India are blamed on the "false" British notion of kindness in treating Indians as the British themselves would like to be treated. . . . Particularly in the stories of the Mutiny there is a constant theme that much of the trouble was due to the British failure to realize their own power and to use it. Marqueray's statement that the reason why his troops remained loyal, unlike those of the other English commanders, was because he relied on fear rather than kindness to control his men is one expression of this idea. [41]

[40] Symonds, *The British and Their Successors*, pp. 44–55 (quote of Curzon, p. 51).
[41] Greenberger, *The British Image of India*, pp. 58 and 59.

Greenberger quotes from Percival Christopher Wren's novel of the 1940s, *The Dark Woman,* to indicate the continuation well into the twentieth century of the tradition of treating Indians as children who need a firm hand:

> Stacy Burlestone was by nature essentially and fundamentally a kindly man; but long residence in the East and a wide experience of Orientals had led him to the conclusion, right or wrong, that, to the Eastern mind, kindness and weakness are synonymous terms. . . . He knew that the Indian's mental attitude towards the kindly and easy European is inevitably tinged with contempt; and that his translation of "kind" is a word indistinguishable from "soft." [42]

The harshness of the compliance system, though perpetuated by the parent-child analogy, was reinforced by three additional factors. First, the clear differentiation between the self-discipline of the upper tier and the need for close supervision in the lower tier was an important factor in sustaining the pride and the esprit de corps of the upper tier. Perpetuation of the tradition that members of the subordinate service couldn't be trusted to work independently and without supervision lent an air of superiority and clear separateness to the ICS. Even with the evolution of a middle tier, the Provincial Civil Services, the gap between the ICS and the other tiers remained unbridgeable.

Second, the ICS–non-ICS gap was reinforced by a cultural and social gap. The British sense of cultural, religious, and moral superiority was heightened and perpetuated by the exclusion of Indians from the social life of British communities. The loyalties of Indian subordinates were directed toward caste, family, and village networks which remained quite separate and distinct from their overt associations with the British administration. And the British superiors, vaguely aware and uncomprehending of this other world of their subordinates, saw it as mysterious, treacherous, and to be avoided. Thus, whereas British social life was extensively integrated with the business of the raj, Indian social patterns were, for the most part, clearly separated. The trust, friendship, association, and common interest so important to an integrated bureaucratic community were generally denied the Indian bureaucrats. [43]

[42] *Ibid.,* p. 168. The quote is from page 228 of Wren's novel, which was published in 1943 by Macrae Smith Company, Philadelphia.

[43] See Greenberger. *The British Image of India,* especially Part I, "The Era of Confidence, 1880–1910," for an interesting perspective on British perceptions of their relations with Indians.

The upper tier, however, was not entirely impenetrable to Indians. Education in British schools and universities and the adoption of British social graces, eating habits, and clothing, when combined with demonstrations of academic excellence and "good character," could gain exceptional Indians entry into the ICS and a measure of social integration with their British colleagues. Because a modest number of Indians achieved ICS status prior to independence, it was possible for a system of distinct tiers, whose origins had strong racist overtones, to perpetuate itself in a setting where race no longer governed access to different tiers. Traditions of recruitment, training, social life, and supervision are sufficient to retain the distinction between those who can be trusted and those who cannot.

Third, the basic characteristics of the compliance system in British Indian administration date from the nineteenth century. Attitudes toward subordinates, understanding of motivation, and ideas about supervision and control have all changed very substantially in the west in the interim. Many nineteenth-century notions, outmoded and reformed in the British cultural transformation to an industrialized society, have been perpetuated in the Indian context. It is important to remember, for example, that it was not until the beginning of this century that the concept of personnel management—the deliberate use of means to organize and control the work force of an enterprise—began to replace the harsh, threat-based supervisory style so effectively evoked by Dickens in his novels.

Reinhard Bendix argues that the existence of an internalized work ethic among the lower classes of nineteenth-century England was an important factor in the transition to a relatively noncoercive work order:

> It is probable that in England the ethic of work performance developed among the masses of workers out of the combined legacies of craftsmanship, the Puritan ethic, and the rising ideology of the individual striving and success. But it is important to add that these legacies had become effective among industrial workers (and that to a certain extent the workers had become adapted to the disciplines of factory work) *prior* to the growth of modern, large-scale industry.[44]

[44] Reinhard Bendix, *Work and Authority in Industry: Ideologies of Management in the Course of Industrialization* (New York: John Wiley and Sons, Inc., 1956), p. 205.

Bendix documents the transition from a traditional loyalty of servant to master and apprentice to craftsman to a more formal bureaucratic pattern of relationships. The notion of responsibility of the upper classes for the well-being of the poor began to fade in nineteenth-century Britain, with widespread ramifications for the nature not only of social policy, but of institutional relationships as well. The sense that a man of the upper class acted *in loco parentis* for his subordinates was progressively replaced by the view that every man was responsible for his own well-being and that with foresight, thrift, and moral restraint, self-improvement was available to all. The evangelical tradition was reawakened to a mission of preaching social and moral virtues to the poor.[45]

It is in this domestic context that the vigorous and influential denigration of Indian character by men such as James Mill, Charles Grant, and William Wilberforce should be seen. Whereas the transition to an impersonal and individualistic pattern of authority relationships in England was eased by the presence of an established work ethic among the lower classes, the apparent absence of such an ethic within Indian society was seen, in British eyes, as clear evidence of the moral and spiritual bankruptcy of Indian society, culture and religion.[46]

Whereas the British employer assumed the desire and capacity of his British subordinates to achieve higher states of moral and character fitness, in the Indian context the perceived pervasiveness of Hindu depravity made such transformations seem unlikely. The enormous significance of this difference in attitude is pointed out by Bendix when he compares the patterns of British development with those of Russia, where, as in India, an internalized lower class work ethic was absent. The parallels with the British pattern in India are striking:

In England the depravity of the poor was rarely mentioned without reference to the good qualities which every self-respecting man can develop, and demands for submission were couched in terms which made submission synonymous with ideal qualities of work and conduct. There was little distinction between work performance expected of the ideal laborer and the submission expected as a citizen to the authority of government. In Russia, this distinction was fundamental. Employers failed to appeal to the conscience or self-esteem of the workers; and the reliance on fear and coercion

[45] *Ibid.*, pp. 73–116.   [46] Symonds, *The British and Their Successors*, pp. 27–28.

effectively precluded the development of an internalized ethic of work performance.[47]

It is also significant that Bendix goes on to relate this lack of expectation to the limited scope of employer concern for employee behavior:

> The demand for submission was only related to civil disobedience and religious orthodoxy, but not to any other aspect of personal conduct. It may be suggested that the employers acted as they did because their own self-esteem depended on the exercise of authority patterned after that of the landlords and the Tsar. And the officials of the Tsarist government were concerned with the conduct of the people only in so far as the maintenance of public order made that concern necessary.[48]

Thus, a pattern of authority relations that was evolving in one direction in England took a radically different turn in India. A reliance on threats, fear, and punishment effectively retarded the growth of identification of subordinate workers with the agencies of government. The lack of trust implicit in close supervision and repressive control practices was a powerful counterforce to either the assimilation of the British work ethic or the application of the dharmic work ethic to the British administrative structure.

The Community Development Model

The community development ideology is fundamentally western—and more specifically American—in its perceptions and approaches to bureaucracy. As a movement, community development has flourished in a wide variety of contexts and has evolved as a result of a wide variety of influences, but its basic precepts derive from the insights of the "human relations" school of administrative analysis. This approach to administration, pioneered by Elton Mayo at Harvard, was concerned with the means of increasing productivity by paying attention to the psychological and social needs of workers.

Though numerous experiments involving the development of village communities took place in India during the 1930s and 1940s, the one that had by far the greatest effect on the subsequent course of development administration in India was the "Pilot Project," conceived by the Ameri-

---

[47] Bendix, *Work and Authority in Industry*, p. 206.   [48] *Ibid.*

can architect and town planner Albert Mayer, in Etawah District of Uttar Pradesh.[49] Though Mayer was the guiding force behind the experiment, it was operated by the government of Uttar Pradesh and later became the model for the formation of community development bureaucracies throughout the country.

Building on a friendship with Jawaharlal Nehru that had begun during World War II, Mayer proposed—and eventually was asked to direct—a pilot experiment in village development. He made preliminary investigations for the program in 1946 and then returned to India on the average of several times a year for a number of years to oversee the evolution of the experiment. Though he did not, therefore, exercise day-to-day control over the program, he acted as a very persuasive and inspiring mentor with clear ideas as to the spirit, motivations, and goals that should direct its development. He carried on voluminous correspondence with a great many of the officials involved in the project and these not only suggested solutions to practical problems, but also conveyed a clear sense of the philosophy he hoped to see pervade the bureaucracy.

Motivation was the dominant theme of Mayer's approach to bureaucratic operations. His primary concern was to get people at all levels of the experiment psychologically, ideologically, and intellectually involved. The key to such involvement, he felt, was widespread participation in planning, implementation, and evaluation of operational programs.

Mayer equated this participation with what he called "inner administrative democracy." [50] His goal was to replace the highly authoritarian and deferential colonial bureaucratic tradition by one that encouraged subordinates to do much of their own planning and organizing, to provide information and ideas to their superiors, and to develop a sense of responsibility for and involvement in the programs of the experiment. In addition to encouraging both superiors and subordinates to speak freely with each other in order to improve vertical com-

[49] See his accounting in *Pilot Project, India* (Berkeley: University of California Press, 1959). For a history written by the first training officer, see Baij Nath Singh, "The Etawah Pilot Project," in History of Rural Development in Modern India, vol. 1 (New Delhi: Impex India, 1967).
[50] Mayer, *Pilot Project, India*, p. 87 ff.

munications, Mayer experimented with democratic structures. Meetings of village-level works (VLWs) were designed to promote sharing of ideas and problems. A system of rotating the chairman's role among the VLWs was tried in an effort to discourage traditional patterns of unquestioning obedience and deference.

In place of a strict hierarchy of line authority, Mayer saw the field bureaucracy operating in terms of a western metaphor: the team. A team has an implicit authority structure, but that structure remains submerged as the contributions, energy, and enthusiasm of the individual members surge forward to give the unit initiative, ideas, and capacities that go far beyond what could be produced by an authoritarian structure. Mayer wrote eloquently of this idea:

> One of the best conceptions we have, one of the best innovations we have introduced, is the close interplay of all team workers in the field. The feeling on the part of every one of our workers, from the village level workers up, that they really have something to say about the programme, that their positive suggestions and their difficulties are being listened to and valued. This joint planning and this feeling of participation and of personal value is the biggest single discovery of our thinking and work. Properly thought out and practised, it unlocks hidden energies and initiative. These factors in turn react on the village and tend to produce corresponding alertness and participation there.[51]

In this view, the mechanisms for control of field workers are clearly very different from those employed in the imperial or dharmic approaches to administration. The worker, by identifying himself with the goals of the agency, becomes self-motivating. Thus, what is important is to perpetuate and strengthen the psychological tie between the individual and program goals. Several techniques contribute toward that end. Workers are repeatedly told that the work they are doing is of great importance, that they are unusually dedicated people, and that they are a part of a noble institution. They are given a sense of the importance of their own participation and contributions. Supervision is minimal and unobtrusive, encouraging workers to live up to the faith that is shown in them. These techniques all played an important role in the effort to get members of the Etawah bureaucracy to perform their development tasks.

[51] *Ibid.*, p. 88.

Where the emphasis is on independence and self-discipline in the attainment of compliance, however, it is necessary to have objective criteria for suggesting standards and providing goals toward which individuals and "teams" can work. Therefore, as Mayer wrote to Nehru:

> In my recommendations and reports, I tried wherever possible to set targets and to devise objective methods for checking results—not only over-all targets, but specific, fairly detailed targets, both acre-wise and objectwise. The presently prevalent method of preparing a "show" is not only useless but positively harmful.[52]

Targets were not to be centrally determined, however, but rather set by the local workers, who had a sense of what would be reasonable and challenging.

Inner administrative democracy was designed not simply to increase the quantity of work performed in the bureaucracy, but also to change the nature of the work being done. Fundamental to the community development ideal was the conviction that the primary task of the village change agent was not to effect physical change, but rather change in the perspectives, motives, aspirations, and sense of competence of the villagers. Thus the workers had to show the leaders how problems that were perceived by villagers as important could be resolved. The workers had to be able to set their own priorities, take initiatives, and calculate the consequences of their choices. The workers would have technical, financial, and programmatic backstopping in these efforts, but their role was seen as an active and creative one.

Mayer's approach to the village worker's role implied a radical change from the conventional Indian bureaucratic manner of dealing with villagers. The revenue bureaucracy was concerned with extraction of resources from the village and dealt with village resistances by using a harsh and threatening approach that depended on villagers' fears of the arbitrary powers of government to induce their grudging cooperation. On the other hand, the village worker of the community development effort was to identify with and become a friend of the people. The interests of the village farmers were to supersede the interests of the bureaucracy; and by long and hard work, the production of quick visible

[52] *Ibid.*, p. 61.

results, the mobilization of bureaucratic resources, and respect for the cultural traditions of the village, the development worker was to gain the villagers' faith, understanding, and cooperation.

The organizational implications of this approach were extensive and would require drastic changes in existing structural patterns. First, the government would have to see the village as a whole, and be prepared to respond to its multiple and varied demands. Indeed, one of the first articles of faith of community development was that the village worker must be a multipurpose worker. This meant that all village development programs had to be implemented through a generalist who was not a member of any of the specialized agencies.

The "team" of technical specialists, directed by a generalist Block Development Officer (BDO), was seen as a source of broad technical and programmatic support for the generalist village worker, who was called a Gram Sevak. If he discovered that a new variety of rice seed was available and that his villagers were interested in planting it, he was to go to the agricultural extension officer (AEO) for technical advice on the characteristics of the variety and its appropriateness in his setting. The AEO would assist in disseminating planting and growing instructions, in getting seeds, and perhaps in distributing, through the Gram Sevak, subsidies available under government schemes. If the villagers were interested in supplementing their agricultural income through village industries, the Gram Sevak could presumably get help from the Small Scale Industry Officer in training, providing capital for equipment, and lending support in marketing to meet this village need. Thus, the image was one of demands being initially stimulated at the village level and of those demands being met by resources available at the block level.

The Gandhian Model

The impact of Gandhian tradition on the contemporary Indian development administration has been less than that of the dharmic, colonial, and community development traditions. Nevertheless, its impact is clear and it is important to specify its roots. Just as community development perceptions derive from western reforms of the same western bureaucratic tradition that produced the British raj, Gandhian thought derives from the same Hindu tradition that produced the dharmic view

of a bureaucratic society. Many of Gandhi's most influential insights—
those relating to *ahimsa* and *satyagraha*, for example—have had little or no
impact on Indian administration. But his views on the nature of caste
roles and the dignity of traditionally demeaning work, his conception of
selfless service, and his view of duty have all been highly influential in
the establishment of new norms within the bureaucracy.

Gandhi agreed with and advanced many of the Hindu views of
social organization discussed in the section on the dharmic tradition. He
accepted the dharmic view of society as an organismic whole and believed in a cosmic ordering which dictates the duties and rights of individuals. He accepted the view that each man should follow the occupation associated with his caste, but vehemently argued that social and
economic hierarchies were not a part of true and original Hinduism, but
rather the additions of later, misguided theorists. Thus, Gandhi argued
that the Brahmanic calling is in no way superior to that of the physical
labor of the Sudra.

In order to break the pervasive contemporary conception of the rigid
social and ritual hierarchy of caste and caste occupations, Gandhi urged
that, in personal matters, each individual should be his own scavenger.
He tried in this way to give a new dignity to such tasks as the washing of
latrines, the sweeping of streets, and the cleaning of wells. Such sharing
of tasks was a part of the routine in his rural settlements, Sabarmati
Ashram in South Africa and Sevagram in India, and was duplicated both
in other Gandhian centers and in the training programs of the Etawah
Project and later national community development programs. In writing
of village level worker training for the pilot project, the first training officer, Baij Nath Singh recalls:

> The prevailing atmosphere at the training institute was one of camp life full
> of austerity, hard work and self-discipline as in ashrams like Sewagram and
> Sewapuri. The daily schedule started with a prayer at 4:30 or 5 A.M. fol-
> lowed by camp cleanliness by the trainees. They dug and filled compost
> pits, trench latrines, spitoons, garbage baskets and placed the refuse into the
> compost pits and swept the vast grounds clean.[53]

Traditionally polluting tasks were the most spectacular additions to
the lives of trainees. However, the Gandhian emphasis on the equality of

[53] "The Etawah Pilot Project," pp. 189–90.

duty also suggested that agricultural work was a respectable form of endeavor, which should be taken up gladly even by high caste youths who aspired to white-collar government jobs.

Gandhi firmly believed, however, that the Hindu idea of dharma—the balance and distribution of duties and rights within a community—was of fundamental importance because it provided a system that kept competitiveness and greed in check and promoted social order. In referring to the pattern of caste duties and rights he saw as central to this system, Gandhi said that "if we can prove it to be a success it can be offered to the world as . . . the best remedy against heartless competition and social disintegration born of avarice and greed." [54]

Railing against the desire for material gain, the acquisition of wealth, and the striving for high status and highly remunerative occupations, Gandhi argued that "the emoluments of all crafts and professions should be equal to a living wage." [55] Self-restraint in matters of material possessions, as in other matters, was of great concern to Gandhi, and he saw both personal religious growth and the peaceful evolution of village communities developing out of self-restraint.

This view had significant impact on the early role definition of Gram Sevaks. Their actual behavior and motives were established within the parameters of Gandhi's vision. The Gram Sevaks were to be selfless and duty-conscious individuals, prepared to sacrifice material comforts and financial gain in the service of villagers. When the system was established in Madras, it was assumed that Gram Sevaks would make a lifetime working commitment to village uplift in return for "a living wage." No provision was made for their promotion, and their minimal wage rate was assumed to meet their needs during their service.

Thus, selflessness and a willingness to work without any thought of personal benefit were important components of Gandhian thought and became a part of the traditions of Indian rural uplift. Gandhi did not, however, embrace the view that one works only for duty by unquestioningly following the dictates of one's superiors and the traditional demands of one's situation. Gandhi, a revolutionary, believed that the pursuit of truth became the goal of the individual. At a philosophical

[54] *Young India*, January 5, 1921; cited in Anand T. Hingorani, ed., *My Varnashrama Dharma* (Bombay: Bharatiya Vidya Bhavan, "Pocket Gandhi Series," no. 12, 1965), p. 8.
[55] Cited in *ibid.*, p. 76.

level, truth bears a close resemblance to dharma, but for Gandhi, truth is something that each individual must determine for himself. The Gandhian value on the absolute, inner-directed morality of truthfulness and honesty is advanced through his popularization of the story of the ancient Hindu king Harischandra. The story, as told by one of the several Gram Sevaks who chose to recount it as an example of the proper performance of duty, goes as follows:

> Harischandra was a king. He had a wife called Chandramati and a son, Logidasan. He ruled his country very well. His fame spread all over the world and it reached heaven also. Everyone knew that he would not tell a lie even if he were to die. The Devars in heaven joined together and decided that Harischandra was the only person on earth who would not tell a lie. Visvamitrar, a saint, disagreed with them. He promised that he would prove that Harischandra also would tell lies. He came to earth and watched his activities. He drove Harischandra from his kingdom and killed his son by snakebite. He created many other difficulties for him. He made him kill his own wife. Harischandra did that also. He did not give up his truth and honesty. The saint was not able to find fault with him. The devars praised him. From this we can understand that only truth will succeed.

What is striking about this story is the way Gandhi, in retelling it for his followers, has led this Gram Sevak and other respondents to see it in a revisionist light. The traditional Hindu version emphasizes allegiance to dharma, including the keeping of one's word and the performance of all assigned tasks, irrespective of their consequences. Gandhi's version shift's Harischandra's guiding principle to the inner-determined value of truth.

In other stories perpetuated in the Gandhian tradition, the separation between the traditional sense of dharma as following the dictates of authority and the sense of truth is made even clearer. This is illustrated in the following story told by a Gram Sevak. This story also appears in Gandhi's autobiography: [56]

> An inspector came to inspect the class in which Gandhi was studying. The teacher gave the class some words for dictation. Gandhi did not know how to spell a particular word. The teacher noticed that and told him to copy from the next boy. But Gandhi did not do that. He did not write the word that he did not know how to spell. Though the teacher asked Gandhi to

---

[56] M. K. Gandhi, *An Autobiography or the Story of my Experiments with Truth*, translated by Mahadev Desai (Ahmedabad: Navajivan Publishing House, 1940), p. 5.

copy, he refused to do so and was truthful. I will ask my brother also to be like Gandhi.

What is significant about this seemingly minor doctrinal transformation is that the Gandhian version suggests that the individual can figure out for himself what is right and that it is his responsibility to do so. That does not mean that the individual will or should do what will benefit him, for the Gandhian view still asserts that truth is achieved when men exert self-discipline. But it does mean that the individual should look at and be concerned with the consequences of what he does.

Within the Tamil tradition, the difference between the traditional dharmic and the Gandhian notions of duty is expressed in the terms *kademai* and *poruppu*. As one Gram Sevak put it:

> The work the Gram Sevak does in return for his salary is called his *kademai*. *Poruppu* means to work according to one's conscience, forgetting about the money he is being paid. . . . In other words, to work for the success of a scheme. . . .
> Example: An order was given to me to go to the block office at 9:00 A.M. to meet a visiting superior officer. On the same day, a farmer asks me to come to his fields because his crops have been attacked by pests. It is my *kademai* to go to the office at 9 o'clock, but it is my *poruppu* to go to the farmer's fields. The superior officer will be angry and strike at me like a snake. The farmer will be like a frog and look to me for help. What to do? Whom to see? The snake or the frog?

Conclusion

Out of these four traditions, then, come distinctly different approaches to formal organizations. It is of particular interest to note the dimensions along which the traditions vary, and to suggest some of the patterns of conflict and reinforcement that are likely to arise when they come together in a single bureaucratic environment.

Conflicts between more and less modern approaches to organization are among the most significant patterns that emerge from comparisons of the four models. Especially striking are differences in general goal orientation. For both the dharmic and British colonial models, the emphasis is on the maintenance of balance and order in the system, whereas in the Gandhian and community development models the goal is to bring about change. The implications of this difference are far-reaching.

The nature of duty, for example, is defined differently in the two approaches. Where stability and order are the goals, duties undergo little change and are likely to assume an absolute quality. They can be specified in great detail, their fulfillment requires only routine effort, and little or no initiative is involved in their performance. These principles are well elaborated in the dharmic prescriptions that one not question the rightness or the consequences of one's duty, that one perform all of one's duties, and that one treat all duties as equal in importance. Elaborate rules and regulations laying down precise procedures to be followed are the British colonial tradition's functional equivalent of these dharmic prescriptions.

In both traditions, allowance is made for incremental change. Disputes are mediated by panchayats in such a way as to approximate the dharmic ordering of the village. Issues that do not fit into the routinized procedures of colonial bureaucracy are handed up to the collector for his discretionary action. For the routine activities in both traditions, however, adherence to the letter of a highly elaborated set of rules is the essence of doing one's duty.

The essence of the community development extension worker's duty, in contrast to this absolutism, is flexibility. He must be responsive to the requirements of his particular villages. Since the specifics of his work evolve and change over time as his villages begin to move toward a process of self-sustaining growth, and since the best strategy to achieve that goal will be different for each village, it is seen as completely inappropriate in this tradition to define explicit and detailed rules of behavior for extension personnel. In the Gandhian tradition there is also a clear notion that duty must be rooted in basic principles but applied to specific circumstances. Recognizing the importance of change, the Gandihian ethic places responsibility on the individual for determining the specific actions required of him in light of the setting in which his duty is performed.

A related theme following the traditional-modern dimension concerns assumptions about human motivation and the nature of bureaucratic control. In both the dharmic and colonial traditions there is an assumption that many workers will default in the performance of duty if given the opportunity. The village's social controls are so powerful and pervasive that the threat of danda generally remains hidden, but the need for vigorous enforcement is made clear in writings relating to the exercise of authority in larger settings. In the British colonial tradition, suspicion about the loyalty, integrity, and diligence of lower-level personnel is pervasive. Elaborate control mechanisms and harsh, threatening supervision are seen as essential to the maintenance of the system.

The more modern traditions are characterized by a much greater confidence in their ability to inspire loyalty, integrity, and intelligence in subordinate officials through extensive training and indoctrination. The community development and Gandhian traditions were in fact successfully integrated in Indian extension training programs because both emphasized the importance of ensuring that field workers develop an internalized identification with the program and its goals through the learning of new attitudes, values, and motivations. Central to these ideologies is the notion that the individual, once trained, does not need close supervision but rather reinforcement of his commitment through supportive guidance and encouragement.

Conflicts between Indian and western approaches to organization can also be seen as shaping patterns among the four traditions. Of perhaps greatest importance is the distinctly different approaches of the two cultures toward authority. Western views emphasize the value of unified authority roles which handle both the definition and implementation of policies. In bureaucratic contexts, these roles are defined as being part of a "line" of authority. Central to this approach to authority is the close interdependence between the definition and the implementation of policies. The authority who defines policy is also responsible for its implementation, and good policy-making takes into account the limitations of one's ability to implement the policy, and makes adjustments according to the difficulties one encounters.

Indian notions, in contrast, emphasize the dual character of authority roles. Appropriate policies define proper patterns of relationships in a dharmic ordering of society; implementation through the enforcement of rights and duties is a distinct and essentially independent enterprise.

These and related patterns emerge more clearly as we begin to examine the implications of the interaction among the four traditions for the evolution of bureaucratic structure and bureaucratic behavior in Tamil development administration.

CHAPTER THREE

Cognitive Models and the Evolution
of Administrative Structure

Contemporary studies of comparative administration are inclined to devote only the most cursory attention to structural issues. This is an understandable but unfortunate overreaction to the recent past, when structural issues dominated bureaucratic analysis to the near-exclusion of all other considerations. An altogether appropriate focus on the realities of behavior in organizations has sometimes obscured the fact that structural considerations are inextricably linked to behavioral patterns. This is especially important in comparative studies because ideological, historical, and cultural patterns are important determinants of organizational structures and consequently exert important indirect influences on bureaucratic behavior. And, as the material in chapter 2 suggests, the four cognitive models of organization that shape Tamil development administration conceptualize bureaucratic structure in very different terms.

Since policy makers can manipulate formal structure with relative ease, they frequently look to structural reform as a means for bringing about bureaucratic change. The interaction between conflicting aspects of fundamentally different views of organization frequently produces unanticipated and unintended consequences of structural change that distort or overwhelm the goals of the reformers. By exploring the conflicts in assumptions, prescriptions, and goals of incumbents and reformers, one is better able to understand and explain the consequences of structural change.

Our attempt to sort out the patterns and consequences of cultural evolution in Tamil bureaucracy begins, appropriately, with the examination of two structural issues around which key attempts at reform have been built. The first of these is the classical conflict in the structure of field organization between emphasis on providing coherent generalist administration for a geographic area and emphasis on providing a set of functionally specialized services, which emphasize narrow technical rationality. The second issue concerns the appropriate pattern of interaction between bureaucratic structures and political processes. This chapter deals in turn with both of these issues in the context of the cognitive models of organization that shape their formulation, resolution, and consequences.

Alternative Approaches to Field Organization

The command—or line—structure of a large, formal organization is based on the principle of division of labor. The senior executive breaks his overall responsibilities into several component parts and assigns responsibility for each component to one member of a small group of immediate subordinates. They in turn subdivide their responsibilities among a similar number of immediate subordinates, each with responsibility for his own subspecialization. In this way, orders can pass down a succession of layers in a command structure to eventually reach and be implemented by a massive number of low-level functionaries.

In any organization that has responsibility for a given range of functions within a particular geographic context, the central organizational dilemma is the choice of the best principle on which to base the subdivision of responsibilities at each layer in the command hierarchy. One alternative is for the immediate subordinates of the top executive to be assigned specific geographic territories within which they would be responsible for the full range of the organization's functions. A second alternative is to conceive of the organization's operations as consisting of a set of discrete functions and to assign responsibility for each function throughout the entire territory covered by the organization to one subordinate. The same issue arises at each level in the hierarchy, though it is uncommon to find, in a single administrative hierarchy, more than one or two transitions from one principle—whether geographic or functional—to the other.

The choice between functional and geographic principles of organization determines the number of field structures operating at any level in the system. In a hypothetical organization in which the ratio of superiors to subordinates is one to five, if the two top layers of a structure are functionally organized and the third based on geography, the organization will operate through 25 functionally-defined subdivisions of the five major departments, each with its own field organization. Because of its unique function, clientele, and communications requirements, each subdivision is likely to need a set of field districts that differ in size and location from those of most, if not all, of the other subdivisions in the organization. The resulting profusion of overlapping boundaries and different sized field units can be expected to make problems of coordination between separate but interrelated field structures extraordinarily difficult.

If the two top layers of the same organization are assigned geographical rather than functional responsibilities, it will operate with a single field structure in which each third-level executive will oversee the full range of the organization's activities within approximately one twenty-fifth of its total territory. At that local level a general-purpose administrator may have a wide range of specialists dealing with specific functional issues under his direction. Problems of coordination are minimal because all of the specialists have the same geographic area to deal with and their orders are received through a generalist administrator whose concern is to provide coherence to administration within the area of his geographic responsibility. The disadvantage of geographically based organization is that it is virtually impossible for the generalist administrator to understand and effectively utilize the specialized knowledge and capabilities of his technical subordinates. As a result, the technical expertise of the institution is generally used ineffectively and is subject to atrophy.

Various mechanisms have been employed to compensate for the disadvantages of each system. Perhaps the most ambitious is the structure of dual supervision, an approach that has been tried with mixed success in a number of American bureaucracies. In this structure, the senior administrator establishes two chains of command: one handles operational matters and is geographically organized; the other handles technical matters and is functionally organized. All functional agencies have their own specialized field personnel, but they are required to use standard field regions, and their personnel are under the operational control of the general-purpose geographic administrator. Thus, technical information and directives are diffused through the specialized agencies, but coordination is achieved through the multipurpose geographically organized chain of command. The problem with this structural solution is that field personnel are constantly being put under conflicting pressures from the two chains of command, each of which would like to dominate field operations. Thus systems of dual supervision tend to be conflict-ridden and, unless carefully balanced, often become dominated by one of the two chains of command.

Four Views of Field Structures

The dharmic cognitive model of organization is very clear in its dictate that the geographic principle of organization should be dominant to very low levels. Though functional specialization is recognized, the key to social order is the balance and interrelationship among specializations. Occupationally specialized castes often extend throughout a large geographic area and certain procedures and practices specific to caste functions are regulated through caste panchayats. The patterns of interaction of caste members, however, take place primarily in the context of the individual village in which they live and are regulated by village elders who consider all aspects of village life in resolving disputes that may arise.

The British colonial model of organization also emphasized the value and importance of general-purpose geographic administration. The need to distribute a small number of British civil servants broadly throughout the subcontinent implied that each would be required to cope with a broad range of subjects. Indeed, members of the elite Indian Civil Service were, for more than a century, classic representatives of the "area generalist" administrator. Their training and experience were designed to give them the broadest possible view of their administrative competence and responsibilities. Those with technical specializations were clearly to accept the broader view and more comprehensive understanding of the ICS generalist.

The dharmic and colonial traditions were mutually reinforcing in south India during the early period of the British raj. Thomas Munro, Governor-General of Madras Presidency in the early nineteenth century, was unusually sensitive to Indian notions of government and argued vigorously that the most effective administration would be one that could deal coherently with all aspects of Indian life within a given geographic context. The most striking expression of this principle came in Munro's successful fight with Lord Cornwallis to preserve an integrated administrative and judicial role for the collector in Madras Presidency.

As specialized functional structures came to play increasingly important roles in western administration in the late nineteenth century, the notion of a single general-purpose field organization began to come under increasing attack within India. The widespread feeling that the colonial administration should be alleviating health, educational, agricultural, and allied problems associated with development strengthened arguments for the establishment of separate field operations to provide these services. Thus, during the early decades of the twentieth century, a number of separate departments and ministries were established at the state level and evolved their own largely autonomous field organizations. The technical skills of officers from these agencies were recognized and accepted, but the overall dominance of general-purpose district administration, epitomized in the person of the collector, was never seriously questioned.

Though the ideology of community development contains many features that represent modernizing forces in post-independence India, other aspects of its approach to bureaucracy reject conventional western views of formal organization. Perhaps the most striking example of this is the rejection of the high degree of functional specialization of bureaucratic structures that characterizes most contemporary western public administration. A basic perception of community development theorists is that the village must be dealt with as an integrated whole because its economic, social, political, and religious dynamics are so closely interrelated as to require a single multipurpose agent of change to bring about their modernization. Even the limited autonomy of specialized development agencies in newly independent India was seen as militating against coherent treatment of village needs. The inability of villagers to determine which agency handled a specific problem and to then locate its agent was widely discussed as a key reason for the failure of British developmental efforts. The multipurpose village level worker, as the role was pioneered at Etawah, therefore became the key to community development structure.

Albert Mayer recognized the need for greater technical expertise at the local level than the village level worker was likely to have. His solution was the establishment of an "extension team" of specialists, deputed from their parent technical agencies and placed under the full operational authority of the BDO. Under this system, the specialists would serve as block-level staff resources and a single chain of command for community development services would flow upward from the BDO. The structure of authority for community development would, in other words, be geographically organized from the state down to the village level.

Another feature of community development ideology that has had profound implications for the structural evolution of Indian development bureaucracy is the importance attached to recognizing and fostering the "felt needs" of local communities. In bureaucratic procedure, this concern gets translated into the notion of "planning from below": a concept wherein organizational goals are established not by the top level of planners, analysts, and administrators, but rather by villagers. Under the guidance of the village level worker, each village was to establish its own development goals. Statements of those goals—and the specific resources required to meet them—were to be passed up the bureaucratic hierarchy and, when aggregated at each level, were to provide a set of block, district, and state development goals. The Department of Agriculture, for example, would take the aggregate agricultural figures from thousands of village plans and use them to calculate needs for fertilizers, pesticides, seeds and other inputs. Each of the other departments would perform equivalent functions for its specialized concerns.

Gandhian approaches to development further reinforced perceptions of the desirability of geographically organized bureaucratic structures. Gandhi retained the traditional Hindu notions of the interdependence of occupations in the village settings, and saw a close linkage between economic, social, and political change. Thus, the notion of a multipurpose village worker was fully consistent with his notions of rural development.

The Field Structure of Development Administration

As plans were being made for the establishment of a statewide community development structure in Madras, then, it was clear that extension work would be handled by a multipurpose village level worker, to be called the Gram Sevak: one who serves the village. A structural dilemma existed, however, because all previous development efforts of the government had been administered through functionally specific technical departments, each with its separate field organization. Some mechanism had to be found to integrate the operations of the technical and multipurpose field organizations.

The chosen response to the dilemma was to place the technical specialists from the functional agencies under dual supervision at the block level. They were to be responsible to the BDO for "operational matters" and to their superiors in their functional agency hierarchies for "technical matters." This differed from the Etawah model which, in placing the technical specialists under full control of the BDO, would have effectively eliminated the functional agencies as line organizations with their own field structures.

The compromise choice of "dual supervision" as a resolution of the generalist-specialist dilemma generally receives mixed reviews from administrative analysts. It does provide for the possibility of effectively balancing concerns for geographic and technical rationality, but only through sacrificing clear and unified lines of authority. The conceptually distinct spheres of "operational" and "technical" are in reality closely interlinked, and conflicts over which chain of command has authority to make specific decisions are common in dual supervision systems.

Given commitments to a structure incorporating a multipurpose Gram Sevak and technical personnel operating under dual supervision, conventional administrative wisdom requires that the programmatic demands flow down the operational/generalist chain of command—in this case through the BDO—to the Gram Sevak. The alternative approach of letting the technical bureaucracies become the source of programmatic demands could be expected to produce adverse consequences far greater than those resulting from the conventional generalist-specialist conflict over control of individuals under dual supervision. In such a system, technical program demands would flow through each of the members of the technical block extension "team" onto the village level worker, without any mechanism for their limitation, regulation, or integration. The exposure of the Gram Sevak to such a multiplicity of independent command structures would threaten to produce endemic authority conflict and chaotic program administration.

The community development concept of "planning from below," however, made these various conventional considerations about chains of command seem extraneous and irrelevant. The basic supposition of the ideology shaping the bureaucratic structure was that the primary thrust of development program content and levels would be determined not at the top of a command structure, but rather in the individual villages. Thus the local regulation and integration of programmatic demands that would normally be achieved by the downward flow of those demands through a single generalist chain of command were instead to be achieved by the village plans, which were to be the source rather than the final subdivision of national program goals.

Since the chain of command linking the BDO to the state government was not seen as the channel for program determination and supervision, it developed in a highly attenuated form. A Department of Rural Development was established, but its functions were largely limited to training Gram Sevaks and to maintaining personnel records for them and for BDOs. What limited supervision and control the BDOs were expected to require was to be provided by district collectors. In order to facilitate their supervisory roles, collectors were to be provided with planning and development sections within their collectorates. In the tradition of colonial district administration, however, these staffs were conceived of as essentially clerical in nature and no provisions were made for them to include specialists with technical development skills.

In contrast to conventional hierarchical bureaucracy, then, the community development structure assumed what might be defined as a supermarket model of service delivery in which there were multiple suppliers—the technical agencies—that made goods and services available. Among these services were technical advice, various forms of physical inputs, and subsidies to a set of buyers whose needs were managed through the Gram Sevaks. The Gram Sevaks were, through their village planning efforts, to predict demand, thereby determining appropriate supply flows and inventory levels. Targets, in other words, were both a planning device and an accounting standard against which to measure "sales." The BDO was to be the equivalent of a supervisor of a small chain of supermarkets, consolidating orders, coordinating the activities of salesmen, keeping track of inventories and reporting to a district manager—the collector—on the progress of his units. Each of the technical extension officers was to play a role analogous to that of the salesman for a producer. He was to keep the supermarkets informed of his company's products, create demand and secure large orders, and report on sales and consumer resistance.

These projected roles and role relationships differed greatly from the conventional bureaucratic patterns of imperial revenue administration. Demands, which had always come down the chain of command, suddenly were to reverse direction. Unified lines of authority were to be replaced by a pattern of dual supervision, but the exercise of authority was to be muted by the working together of a team whose leader would not exercise close supervision but would instead provide support, advice, encouragement, and guidance. Thus, by reducing the authoritative role of superiors, the potential for conflict between alternative chains of command was to be minimized. Finally, the conventional bureaucratic pyramid, in which orders passed down from an agency head to regional subordinates, thence to district officers, and finally to field agencies, was to be turned on its head. Each Gram Sevak was to be the peak of his own small pyramid; demands for development needs for his villages were to filter down into the line channels of numerous technical agencies, and the actual inputs required to sustain development efforts were to converge on the village through the separate efforts of those agencies.

The earliest, and in many ways the most significant, casualty in the confrontation between the structural prescriptions of the community development and Gandhian ideologies on the one hand and the behavioral prescriptions of the dharmic order and colonial bureaucracy on the other was the goal of planning from below. Its failure to become effective in the first year of operation seemed, in part at least, to be a natural casualty of the birth traumas of a great new enterprise. The understandable rush to get programs into operation resulted in early demands for village plans from Gram Sevaks. Since the proper preparation of such plans involved long-term consultation at the village level, realistic responses could not be prepared. Under pressures from their superiors, the BDOs prepared "paper plans" created by the block staffs. These were submitted to the district, consolidated, and then forwarded to the state. Often, "schematic budgets"—prepared in planning offices as guidelines that villages, blocks, and districts were to modify according to local desires and needs—were copied slavishly in the preparation of local plans.

Even more important, the targets that came down through the administrative hierarchies reflected the results of central plans much more than they did the plans—whether paper or real—submitted in the names of villages, blocks, and districts. In interviewing Gram Sevaks in the state of Andhra Pradesh in 1954, S. C. Dube found that "time and again in the course of their training they were told that plans will grow up from the village people, whereas in reality they had the frustrating experience of finding that invariably the plans came from the top and had to be carried down by them to the village people." [1] Within a short time of its introduction, the process of planning from below was, for all practical purposes, abandoned.

The failure of planning from below reflected much more than organizational birth pangs, however. Fundamental conflicts in concepts of authority, motivation, and control were involved. The understanding of these conflicts and their behavioral consequences is the subject of chapter 7. Here, however, it is sufficient to point out the specific consequences that arose from the attempt to adopt a structure designed to accommodate a supermarket model of service delivery for use in a pattern of hierarchical determination of service delivery operations.

The consequences of a process of central program and target determination can perhaps best be understood by imagining what would happen if a supermarket manager, instead of being able to make his own orders for supplies from salesmen, were suddenly required to accept whatever goods those salesmen wished to impose on him, and if his performance, instead of being measured by the excess of sales over the cost of supplies and operations, were suddenly measured by the percentage of supplies he was able to sell. Clearly such a change in parameters would have a major impact on the marketing and pricing strategies of the supermarket manager, as well as on the strategies of the salesmen and the supplying firms.

For the Gram Sevak, then, the technical extension officers suddenly became sources of program demands, which were expressed as targets. The staff of each technical department began developing a multiplicity of specialized programs with overall targets, established in part on the basis of rough estimates as to what might be achieved, but largely on the basis of their own budget allocations. These overall targets were passed down the technical chains of command and were subdivided at each level

[1] *India's Changing Villages: Human Factors in Community Development* (London: Routledge and Kegan Paul, 1958), p. 165.

among geographical areas of responsibility through a complex process of bargaining. At each level officials would argue the limited capacity of their territories to absorb such a program in order to keep their targets low.

At the lowest level of the hierarchy, then, the subdivided targets for all of the programs of all of the technical departments were turned over to the Gram Sevak for implementation. As a result, his work load and the effective plan for his villages were determined through a set of discrete bargaining processes that bore no relationship to each other, to the capacity of the Gram Sevak to implement them, or to the overall needs and interests of the villages.

The Structural Linkage of Administration and Politics

The early failure of planning from below in Indian community development brought about a public reevaluation of a central issue in administrative structure, which resulted in the only major modification of the administrative order between 1953 and 1973. At issue was the proper structural linkages between the public bureaucracies and the political institutions of a nation. Clearly the notion of planning from below had not been put into practice with sufficient attention to the linkages that were to join together the efforts of the Gram Sevak and local political institutions. A growing public awareness of this failure led the Planning Commission to suggest the creation of a "team" to study Community Projects and National Extension Service, established under the chairmanship of a distinguished civil servant, Balvantray Mehta. An understanding of the structure that emerged from this study is enhanced by a review of the main structural issue involved, as it is seen in four administrative traditions.

In the dharmic tradition there is no strict differentiation between political and administrative spheres at the village level. Panchayats, as dharmic decision-making bodies, are made up of respected elders of a village or caste and their decisions are implemented through the actions of the citizenry as a whole. Information regarding events and the perception of those events by various forces in the village social structure constitute the political participation on which that decision-making is based. In the attempt to maintain balance and order within the community, the primary emphasis of decision-making is on regulating the distribution of benefits—goods and services—within the system. Since neither secular economic growth nor planned social change were common features of dharmic village life, there was little practical concern for or interest in proposals or analyses involving "development" or "growth."

During the period of colonial rule, many features of village life continued to be regulated internally. On an increasing range of issues, however, government administration shaped village patterns. Taxation, education, bureaucratic employment opportunities, and access to agricultural benefits grew in significance as government-regulated activities. The basic structuring of these programs, however, was developed in administrative—and in some cases British political—circles that were far removed from the spheres in which village farmers operated. This did not mean, however, that village residents were either disinterested in, or powerless to affect, these incursions on their traditional patterns of interaction.

Denied the power to shape the programs, they concentrated instead on shaping the way individual cases were handled in program implementation. Unable to lobby with lawmakers in the interests of their caste, village, or occupational needs, they intervened with lower-level functionaries to divert resources in their direction and to avoid the excesses of the government's extractive endeavors. Attempts to secure favors, special consideration in employment, and remission of tax levies became commonplace. Elaborate channels of access to the key centers of power in the bureaucracy developed and a thriving pattern of local politics centered around the control and manipulation of these channels.

Local linkages between village communities and public bureaucracies were important not only to the subjects of administrative fiat, but to the overseers of the bureaucratic machine as well. The collector of a district was always in danger of losing control of his administration to the external loyalties of his subordinates, and personal contacts with his subjects provided a critical check on the behavior of the district bureaucracy. The collector was expected to travel extensively. Much of his time was spent in listening to the complaints and problems of village people and in issuing orders that would modify the actions and inactions of his subordinates.

The advent of community development programs had limited impact on these patterns. The Gram Sevaks who came to the villages lacked both the social status and the experience with local agricultural and social conditions that would have made them persuasive agents of change. Efforts to involve villagers in planning and development efforts failed not so much because the villagers were inactive or disinterested in local affairs, but rather because the concerns of the Gram Sevaks seemed to have little to do with the distributive issues that exercised the political sensitivities of the local residents.

The Balvantray Mehta study team diagnosed the source of the community development program's failures as being one of inadequate local political control over the state-run development bureaucracy. It proposed that a structure of local self-government be created to supervise the bureaucracy's block-level operations. In this way, the Mehta team argued, local participation in planning of development programs would be stimulated. A. H. Hanson summarized the thrust of the report quite concisely:

> Basically, its argument was simple to the point of naivete: community development was in the doldrums because the people's participation can only spring from a sense of responsibility; therefore the people themselves must be called upon to exercise responsibility, through their own democratically-elected organs.[2]

Championing the return to traditional Indian roots of self government, the team claimed that the best way to stimulate and structure such participation would be to revive the traditional institution of village panchayats. In a creative effort to modernize a traditional institution, the team recommended the establishment of a structure of panchayati-raj—rule by panchayats—in which elected village councils would carry out village-level planning and the panchayat presidents within a development block would form a Panchayat Union Council to supervise and direct the development planning and implementation of the BDO and his staff.

The British had made numerous earlier attempts to build on the panchayat tradition, but in each case inadequate understanding of the tradition and attempts to involve the villagers in issues of little interest to them—or in issues that were already being effectively handled by exist-

---

[2] *The Process of Planning: A Study of India's Five-Year Plans, 1950–1964* (London: Oxford University Press, 1966), p. 433.

ing institutions—led to the stillbirth of modernized panchayats. The Mehta study team may have had little better understanding of the tradition than its British precursors, but it did foster the birth of a healthy set of new institutions by recommending that they be given control over local expenditure of development funds.

In specific terms the report presented by the Mehta Team suggested a three-tier system of local government. The first tier would operate at the village level and would be based on revitalized and modified village panchayats. The second and most important tier was to operate at the block level. Presidents of the panchayats within the block (around seventy in number in Madras) were to meet together as a panchayat union council, choose their own chairman, and through him and in their own monthly meetings provide direction and leadership for the block's development programs. Most critically, the committee recommended that this council should be responsible for all development activities within its jurisdiction and that it should have access to the revenues—including government grants—necessary to carry them out. The third tier, operating at the district level, was to have primarily coordinating and administrative powers.[3]

Though the Mehta Report was only advisory in nature, most states moved rapidly to implement its main recommendations. Madras passed a new Panchayat Act in 1958. It followed the guidelines of the Mehta Report, though it created at the District tier a development council that had only advisory powers. The power of the block level tier, known as the panchayat union council, was clearly spelled out.

> The Government shall . . . entrust to the panchayat union council . . . the execution in the panchayat development block of the National Service Extension Scheme of Community Development, including in particular, all measures relating to the development of agriculture, animal husbandry and village industries organized on an individual or cooperative basis.[4]

Thus, the BDO—and the block staff—suddenly had a new set of relationships to work out. This structural innovation further complicated

---

[3] Committee on Plan Projects, Government of India, *Report of the Team for the Study of Community Projects and National Extension Service/Balvantray Mehta Committee.* (3 vols.; New Delhi, 1957).
[4] Law Department, Government of Madras, *The Madras Panchayats Act,* 1958 (Madras, 1966), p. 41.

the command structure for local development administration and added new sets of pressures to those already faced by extension personnel. In theory, the village panchayats and the panchayat union council were to relieve the block staff by assuming responsibility for local planning and implementation. In fact, however, the concerns of the Mehta Team for stimulating growth and development were foreign to the interests of politically active villagers. It was perhaps predictable that they would become much more actively concerned with manipulating the distributive consequences of financial and program resources flowing into the local community development administration than in generating overall development plans.

The key relationship was the one linking the BDO to the chairman of the panchayat union council. This elected official, by virtue of his demonstrated support from village panchayat presidents, was likely to be a political 'force of considerable local influence, with allies in a political party that could exert influence on his behalf at the district level. The BDO—and his block team of extension officers and Gram Sevaks— would have to be responsive to the interests and demands of the chairman, in part because of his formal powers, and also because of the political influence he might well be able to exercise over administrative decisions. It was as if the supermarket manager, struggling to get rid of products imposed on him by his suppliers, were put under the authority of the mayor in matters relating to who should be favored in the distribution of his products.

Thus, the block extension team added new titles and new types of interests to the already lengthy and varied descriptions of official and nonofficial superiors to whom they had to be responsive. This, in turn, further complicated the problems of extension performance faced by Gram Sevaks and the block extension officers, the problems of supervising extension operations faced by line officials in the rural development hierarchies, and the problems of program definition and program reform faced by the planning staffs in the state offices of the technical ministries. The organizational structure produced by the interaction of four cognitive models of organization defines the character and intensity of the behavioral problems facing incumbents in the structure.

 PART II

Four Models, One Program:
An Overview

The broad parameters shaping bureaucratic action are established by 'the definition of formal structures. Though structures are devised with the needs of specific programs in mind, numerous promising structural options can generally be formulated. As the preceding chapter shows, the option fixed upon by development planners in India incorporated features of four different traditions that were frought with potential conflicts. Resulting pressures on individual bureaucrats led to the proliferation of unanticipated behavioral patterns that seemed to impede, rather than foster, social and economic change. It was to correct these patterns that panchayati-raj was introduced. This mechanism, designed to increase responsiveness of the bureaucracy to local interests, intensified the ambiguity and conflicts in authority relationships that were already plaguing the administration of development programs.

The responses to these problems can, in some measure, be predicted simply from our understanding of general organizational dynamics. It is clear, for example, that the Gram Sevaks, faced with potentially overwhelming demands, are going to search out various means of insulating themselves from the pressures of their work, and that their superiors are going to respond with the use of more elaborate methods of supervision in order to better achieve the goals set for them.

But such analysis is likely to leave many important questions unanswered. What means of insulating themselves will the extension agents adopt? How will they be supervised? What will be the consequences for the way in which they deal with their villages? What information on the program will reach the planners? How will they respond? Will planning from below be reestablished in some form? Will the structure be redesigned so as to provide mechanisms for the regulation of program demands being imposed on local extension agents? Or will the community development effort become immobilized in an ever-tightening cycle of greater extension agent insulation which both stimulates, and is intensified by, patterns of closer supervision?

A full understanding of the answers to these questions is certainly not yet within our grasp. An awareness of and sensitivity to the cognitive models of organization used by those operating in this bureaucratic context, however, helps us to understand, and eventually to predict, how they respond to the opportunities and problems facing them. The fact that we are dealing with complex interactions among cognitive models, not only within the society but frequently within the cognitive processes of individuals, complicates the analytic task enormously.

Before attempting to disentangle the structural, cultural, historical and ideological roots of behavior in the bureaucratic world of Tamil Nadu, it is useful to explore what actually happens when a specific program is put into operation in a specific locality. Part II describes what happened in North Arcot District of Tamil Nadu when the state bureaucracy decided, in 1967, to try to double the acreage planted in ADT–27, a recently developed high-yielding variety of rice. Most of the material in these three chapters reflects my personal experiences in gathering data on this program. Its focus is on the experiences, perceptions, and concerns of the participants in the program from the planners in Madras down through layers of bureaucracy to the farmers who actually planted the crops.

This focus helps to prevent the development of three types of mistaken impressions, which can easily be drawn from an exclusively analytic treatment of this social reality.

First, a narrative focus helps to preserve some sense of the relationship between the idiosyncratic and the patterned. The analytic focus of this study is designed to elucidate patterns in behavior, emphasizing the common roots of attitudes, values, and perceptions from four traditions that shape the behavior of those involved in development administration in south India. As the descriptions in part II illustrate, however, the behavior of individual participants is also substantially affected by the specifics of their own backgrounds, independent of these traditions.

Second, the valuable analytic exercise of attempting to distinguish between, and separate out the elements of, the four traditions threatens to obscure the ways in which all four traditions frequently impinge on the cognitive sensibilities of individual bureaucrats. Responses to these frequently conflicting sets of prescriptions involve difficult individual efforts to develop coherent and satisfying world views. Often they succeed only in reconciling surface manifestations of deeply seated inconsistencies. Occasionally they evolve truly creative syntheses of diverse traditions. A focus on individuals and the specifics of program implementation points up the human dilemmas and achievements involved in processes of rapid social and economic change.

Finally, the narrative of part II serves as a caution to those who might conclude from the analysis that effective public bureaucracies are prerequisites for rapid social and economic change in India. Though many limits of this particular bureaucracy became apparent and comprehensible in the course of this study, critical administrative failures were compensated for by the effective performance of other institutions in the society. When the extension activities of the development bureaucracy were immobilized by the displacement of efforts into administrative rituals, communications processes through caste and family spread information about new varieties of rice with great speed and effect. The transmission of knowledge was deficient in technical detail, and long term prospects for growth are certainly dimmed by bureaucratic inadequacies, but the resilience of other institutions remains an important consideration in any calculations on the stimulation of development in south India.

CHAPTER FOUR

The Cultivator and the Collector: Two Views of Agricultural Development

"The first time I heard about ADT–27 was about two years ago. I was the ladies' representative on the Panchayat Union Council, which represents about sixty villages in this area. At one of the meetings they told about this new variety of rice and also that loans would be given to people who grew it. Through attending those council meetings I learned everything."

Nadesa Udaiyar, the village headman, and Periyasam Pillai, the village recordkeeper or *karnam*, nodded in agreement with her assessment of the council. As Sunderambal continued to talk, one tried to imagine her in a council meeting. Fifty years old now, she dressed simply as befitted a widow, but her face showed a liveliness, determination, and self-confidence that were unusual for a woman in a small and remote village of south India. Several months earlier, when I was about to meet Sunderambal for the first time, Nadesa Udaiyar had told me of her with the pride of one seeing his own village well-represented before the council, made up of leaders from sixty surrounding villages. "She talks very confidently and well," he said. "The Village Level Worker and the leader of the other villages are afraid of her. During the Panchayat Union meetings she was the only member who would ask questions of all the government officers and show their faults."

Sunderambal's influence is not solely a matter of character and an ability to speak well. Born of a well-to-do family from a town fifteen miles distant, she married into the best family of Marusoor, a village of 1,000 residents. Her husband was the son of Rajagopal Mudaliar, the preeminent village leader during the first decades of this century.

Though her husband has now been dead for 25 years, Sunderambal retains much of the prestige—and a sizable share of the wealth—of her husband's family.

The family's influence has been extended in the generation of her children as well. One daughter was married to a contractor in the prestigious Nilgiris Hills, and a second was married into the wealthiest family of a village five miles from Marusoor. She referred to this son-in-law as she continued her account of how she had come to try ADT–27, the new rice strain being promoted by the Agriculture Department of Madras State. "Sunderamurthy saw the ADT–27 plot of Arni Kirshnan which is alongside the road just before you get to the town of Arni. We talked about this plot and I insisted that he get details because it might be profitable for us. So then in the *sownavari* season [from May through August] of 1966, he planted ADT–27 and later told me that if you put more manure according to the instructions, the yield will be good. During this time I also began to hear a great deal about ADT–27 on the radio. The following season, in January of this year, I was visiting Sunderamurthy and he told me to take the extra seedlings from his nursery and plant them on my lands. I planted one acre of ADT, but since I was new to it and only used a small amount of organic mixture and fertilizer, the yield was not good. This season the Gram Sevak came around to ask if I had planted ADT–27. When I told him I had, he told me to put fertilizer mixture to a cost of Rupees 150.[1] I asked him to help me get a loan. Since I am a woman, he did everything for me. He took the papers to the recordkeeper and then to the Taluk headquarters and back to the Panchayat Union office so that I didn't have to go anywhere myself. It was very kind of him, though I must say he has been very nice to me ever since he came to this village two years ago."

Nadesa Udaiyar had also commented on the attention he received from the Gram Sevak, though he candidly added, "The Gram Sevak comes to see and help those people in the village who would be in a position to complain about him to his superior officer at the Panchayat Union."

Nadesa now told about his own contacts with ADT–27. "I go to Arni by cycle almost daily. Most of the time I go on business. Today for

[1] One Rupee = $.133⅓; Rupees 150 = $20.

instance I went into the taluk courts to help settle a village land dispute that was taken to court. Sometimes I have to help a person from the village get what he needs from the government offices. I had heard about ADT–27 on the radio, and then I saw it in Arni Krishnan's fields, along the road to Arni. Also, the Agricultural Extension Officer told me about it some time ago. Since it seemed to be giving good yield in Krishnan's plot, I tried it last season. The results were not good, though, because I did not use enough manure. I am planting it again this year on one-and-a-half acres. Nearly thirty other farmers are also growing it on my advice."

I was interested in learning more about the role of the Gram Sevak in Marusoor. To the recordkeeper, the important thing about him is that he is the son of a recordkeeper in a village some thirty miles to the east. "Since his father owns lands and his two elder brothers have good jobs, it really isn't necessary for this boy to be working at all. If he is short of cash, his father sends him money and rice from his native village. For this reason he doesn't have to demand money from us when he helps us get loans or fertilizer permits.

"This was not the case with our previous Gram Sevak," Sunderambal adds. "He did require payment in return for his services. Of course this fellow will ask us sometimes to buy green manure seeds or other items we don't want in order to help him fulfill his targets. But then he is helpful to us in getting things that we want from the government."

"Does he also give you useful advice about your crops?" I asked.

"He doesn't really do that," Nadesa replied. "He lives in Arni and visits the village two or three times each week. He stays only in the village, however, and doesn't go out into the fields."

While Nadesa was talking a government jeep drove up and stopped in front of the recordkeeper's house. Though the arrival of any motor vehicle was an unusual occurrence in Marusoor, no one moved to greet the visitors. Indeed, the conversation on the porch of the recordkeeper's house continued without a break. The man who emerged from the passenger seat of the jeep wore the shoes, white trousers, and white bush shirt of a government officer. He called out in our direction to ask if the *karnam* were present. Slowly, Periyasam uncoiled from his squatting position, stepped into his sandals, and walked out to the jeep. As we continued our conversation on the porch the government officer spoke intensely to Periyasam, occasionally raising his voice, clearly delivering something of a lecture. A few men came out of their houses and stood at a distance from the jeep, replying occasionally to the officer's statements with short lectures of their own, directed at no one in particular. Having concluded his discussion with Periyasam, the officer approached the house and introduced himself as the land conservation officer for that part of the state. As his headquarters were in a town more than a hundred miles to the west, I asked what brought him to Marusoor. He explained that a government soil conservation scheme included a large part of the unirrigated lands of the village. By leveling the land and improving drainage, the value of the land was being increased, but the villagers were not at all cooperative. There had been repeated thefts from a small meteorological station that had been set up as a part of the scheme, and recently a rain gauge had disappeared. The village leaders would do nothing about it, so he had come this time to warn them that the whole village would be fined and punished if the rain gauge were not returned.

When the Soil Conservation Officer had returned to his jeep and his driver was beginning to renegotiate the rutted lane which is all that separates the two rows of houses, conversation shifted to the kinds of things the government does in Marusoor. "The Soil Conservation Scheme," the recordkeeper said, "is a good scheme. When it was started several years ago the officials came and said it would be a voluntary scheme. Some of the people from the village who had land in the area didn't cooperate and so the government made the scheme mandatory. The tractors came in and cleared off the land. It has been helpful to most of the farmers, but a hardship for others."

When asked what other reasons government officers have for coming to the village, Nadesa replied, "Mostly to make collections. Both revenue and development officers frequently come to collect for various funds and schemes. There are small savings schemes, electrification schemes, district welfare schemes, and so on. Just in the past month the *tasildar*[2] came to collect for the International Tamil Congress fund, but I told him I didn't have any money at the time and couldn't afford to buy a ticket. He tore off a Rupees 25 ticket and handed it to me and told me I

[2] A *tasildar* is the senior revenue officer for a Taluk, which is a subdivision of a district and contains approximately 300,000 people.

didn't have to pay immediately. He came back about a week later, but I said I didn't have the money, and then when he came back the following week, I gave him the Rupees 25."

I reminded Nadesa of an earlier visit I had made to the village the day following a benefit dance spectacular presented in the district head-quarters, 35 miles away, by a popular dancer and movie star, Padmini, for the District Welfare Fund. "The afternoon of the performance," Nadesa related, "the Block Development Officer [3] and the Taluk revenue officer drove into the village. They went around to the houses of all of the influential people of the village and told each of us how much we had to contribute. I had to give Rupees 75, some others had to give Rupees 50, and others even more." Nadesa went on to say that Chokkanatha Mudaliar, the sole surviving son of Rajagopal Mudaliar, had been asked to buy a Rupees 250 ticket.

"By then it was after four o'clock and there was no way we could get a bus to Vellore so, even having paid for the tickets, we couldn't see the performance."

Why, then, had they bought the tickets? "Being revenue officials," Sunderambal explained, "they know what we can afford to pay. If we own land, we don't dare make the revenue people angry with us. Since Sokkanatha also owns a rice mill in Arni, he has to be especially careful."

As another visitor arrived, the conversation again continued without interruption. The Gram Sevak, a tall and slightly built young man of 25, had agilely disengaged his ankle-length lower cloth from his bicycle as he dismounted, leaned the cycle against the house, and gone directly into the small room off the porch that the recordkeeper uses as his office. The recordkeeper joined him and pulled from a high shelf a large ledger book. The two of them examined it at length, searching for the land ownership records needed for the verification of a pending loan applica-tion. When their work was finished they returned to the porch and rejoined the group that was discussing the problems of getting loans from the government. When the question arose as to how much it would cost to obtain a loan of Rupees 500 to buy a pair of bullocks, the Gram Sevak said that a typical Gram Sevak might get from Rupees 10 to Rupees 25 for his services and that the recordkeeper might get another

[3] The Block Development Officer is in charge of development work within a sub-division of a Taluk.

Rupees 25. Periyasam Pillai interrupted with a personal disclaimer: "I am very honest in my dealings with the villagers and I don't take money from them. But, of course, to acquire a loan for Rupees 500 one would have to make two trips on two different days to Arni. As recordkeeper, I only get Rupees 68 per month and do not have any traveling allowance. Therefore, if I make these two trips with a loan applicant, I ask that he give me Rupees 10 for a travel allowance."

The conversation followed the course that the loan papers would have to take, through clerks in one office to an officer, and then up through another set of clerks to their officer. The conclusion was that one would be fortunate to get the loan in a reasonable time without paying at least Rupees 150 to the various government servants through whose hands it had to pass.

Sunderambal suggested that "since our recordkeeper is well known, if we take him it probably costs us less than it would people from other villages. It isn't right for government servants to get money from people for doing their duty, but we are as much to blame as they are. In former days they used to be paid, not because they asked for it, but because the village people offered it to get quicker service for their requests. Then, as this became a common practice, government servants began asking for it also."

But if it costs 30 percent of the loan just to get it, why do people bother? Nadesa Udaiyar replied: "If a person takes what remains of the loan and gives it as loan to other people in the village at 12 percent interest per month he still has enough to pay the government interest and make a large profit besides."

Now, villagers could occasionally be seen walking down the street toward the fields. The period of intense midday heat was passing and farmers were beginning their return to work. I asked if I might take my leave and saw the heads around me sway from side to side in the traditional sign of assent.

The three streets of Marusoor are laid out in roughly the shape of a lower-case "h." The recordkeeper's house is near the middle of the short leg, and as one continues on down the street toward the base of the leg one passes Sunderambal's house on the right and the Panchayat President's house on the left just before one comes upon the wide expanse of paddy fields, which begin at the village edge. Returning up the long leg of the "h" one sees some thirty houses on either side of the lane, each whitewashed and well maintained. The lack of disparity in size and upkeep suggests a relatively equal distribution of economic resources in the village, but even more, a conscious attempt to minimize the overt and most visible signs of poverty and wealth.

Along the streets of Marusoor, there are approximately 170 houses, of which 70 are divided, sheltering the separate households of two brothers or other close relatives. The larger of the houses, perhaps 50 in number, open into small central courtyards, part covered, part open. Here the families eat, sleep, relax, and entertain close friends. Off the courtyard are two, three, or four rooms, used for cooking, keeping household items, and storing food grains, seeds, pesticides, fertilizers, and agricultural implements. The marks of wealth and prestige are not in the size of the courtyard, the quality of the building material, the richness of the furniture, or the brightness and airiness of the house. In these features the houses are remarkably uniform: small courtyards are trimmed by whitewashed but dirt-smeared adobe, rooms are bare of furniture except for a small plain bench and an occasional cane chair available for nonvillage visitors, and the deeper recesses of the central court are barely reached by the light streaming in under the low eaves.

The presence of a table-model short-wave radio is a mark of affluence achieved by only five or six families in the village. More commonly, prestige is reflected in the display of framed family and group photos. Large picture calendars distributed by businesses testify to the extensiveness of one's contacts.

Nadesa Udaiyar's house is toward the end of Marusoor's long lane, on the right side, set back from the other houses that line the lane. The house would be typical of the better dwellings of the village were it not for the profusion of photos and picture calendars in evidence. Eleven photos—mostly of family, but some showing Nadesa as a member of a village committee or the Panchayat Union Council—and 26 current calendars line the wall. Though most of the calendars are from merchants in Arni, others are from towns and cities hundreds of miles away. There is no radio in the house. It is only the photos, the calendars, and the careful grooming and quiet self-confidence of Nadesa himself that suggest the special position of this household in the village.

I sat with Nadesa Udaiyar in his house, sipping the buttermilk his wife had brought us. I would return to his house at the end of my days of interviewing, and would be served a small meal that was at once a gathering of friends, the rendering of a social courtesy, a symbol of his status with a foreigner, and a restatement of his acceptance of and sanction for my inquiries.

After the meal, I would begin the drive back to the district headquarters. Deep ruts mark the lanes of the village, but as one ascends the slight incline at the border of the village, the lane assumes the characteristics of a narrow road and strikes out straight across the broad plateau. The fields on either side are planted in peanuts whose maturation is now dependent on the vagaries of the monsoon rains. Barren most of the year, these fields stand in stark contrast to those on the lower side of the village where the year-round verdant lushness of young paddy stocks is vivid testimony to the crucial place of irrigation in the landowner's economy.

Farmers are working in their fields alongside the road while villagers are walking or cycling to or from Marusoor. Less than a mile from the village the road meets, at right angles, a larger road, still one lane wide and dirt surfaced, but a little wider and less rutted. A small coffee stall on the corner provides refreshment for the traveler who awaits the bus to Arni. The village of Arayalam is along the road to the left as one goes north toward Arni, and the passing traveler sees only a few stucco houses with red tile roofs and a small but substantial cement structure which is the village panchayat office. It is this building that the Gram Sevak uses as a base in his visits to the villages around Arayalam. Marusoor is not a village of special importance or interest in this area. Its population of 1,056 is somewhat below the area's average village size of 1,300.[4] Though agricultural wealth is difficult to measure, it is generally agreed that Marusoor is unremarkable in this respect. It is not mentioned in discussions of the more wealthy villages of the area, and the more-or-less reliable irrigation it receives from an adjacent pond and numerous wells places it substantially above the poorer villages. Marusoor is striking in its demographic makeup. Though it is a relatively small and somewhat isolated village, 54 percent of its males are literate as compared with

4 See *North Arcot District Census Handbook* (Census of India, 1961, Part X, Volume IX) Vol. 2, pp. 275–76.

37 percent in the taluk. And, whereas 18 percent the district's men who earn their living from agriculture are laborers, in Marusoor the percentage is only 7. Finally, the pattern of castes in Marusoor is not the intricate, multicaste complex that anthropologists have led us to expect in the Indian village, but it appears to be one that is common in this area. All but six of the 240 households in the village are Agamudaiyars, a caste of modest importance and status in the district. The rest belong to various serving castes. The adjacent hamlet of Poosinippadithangal (population: 43) is made up of untouchables, who provide agricultural labor for the village.

In many ways the most important characteristic of Marusoor is its proximity to the town of Arni. Though only the sixth-largest town in the district, Arni is an important local center of commercial and administrative activity. Buses bound for the town regularly pass through Arayalam, and the person who has access to a bicycle can reach Arni in half an hour. Hours, or even days, go by without the passage of an automobile, but oxcarts, bicycles, and men and women on foot are almost always in view along the road. Ruts become shallower and, as one comes closer to town, asphalt paving replaces the metalled dirt.

There were always several residents of Marusoor who wanted to ride with me as far as Arni and they invariably pointed out the fields of Arni Kirshnan as we passed them. The fields were remarkable not only for their extensiveness, but also for the quality of the crop and the spacious amenities—a storage house and electric irrigation pumps. Soon after one enters the town of Arni, the car slows to a crawl, threading the maze of bullock carts, bicycles, pedestrians, and stray animals moving between the lines of small shops. A brightly painted building of modern design and construction is pointed out as being Arni Krishnan's house, one of the few two-story residential buildings in the town.

As we reached the central square of Arni on one of these journeys, I stopped the car to let my passengers off and to pay a call on Arni Krishnan. Above a small stall, perhaps six feet wide, I saw a Tamil sign which read, "K. M. Krishnaswamy Naicker, Traditional Medicines." The floor of the stall was set two feet above the level of the street, and squatting cross-legged on a small pad was a gaunt man in his forties, immaculately dressed in white lower cloth and the full, white, high-necked shirt that is traditional among the rural elite of Madras. I watched for a few minutes as Krishnaswamy chatted with one or two friends sitting just outside the stall, barely breaking the stride of conversation as he sent his young assistant after an item in the rear of the store, wrote out a receipt, and handed over merchandise and change to a customer.

Having recently been introduced to Krishnaswamy as a friend of people he knew in Marusoor, I found it unnecessary to go through the lengthy process of establishing my credentials as a legitimate and sympathetic student of local life. After a brief exchange of ceremonious pleasantries, we began to talk about his experience with ADT–27. He had first heard of this new variety, he explained, from a young man by the name of Shanmugam who had been an agricultural demonstrator in Arni at that time. That he should refer to a government servant by name was striking, because officials are almost always referred to by title (after two years of regular contact with the Gram Sevak in Marusoor, for example, Sunderambal still didn't know his name). Krishnaswamy explained, "Shanmugam is a distant relative of the proprietor of an important bakery in the district headquarters and I also am a distant relative of the same man. As a result Shanmugam came to see me when he was posted to Arni and developed the habit of spending his free evening hours sitting around my shop here. Though he wasn't officially concerned with ADT–27, he knew about it and told me about the results it had given in trials. I asked him to get seeds for me and then planted it in June of 1966. According to his recommendation I used heavy doses of manure and got more than twice the normal yield per acre. The government people came and took photos of the crop and a lot of people asked me questions about what yield I would get and where I had gotten the seed. I sold some of the crop as seed to various people who asked me."

The interesting question was why Krishnaswamy, unlike other farmers, had taken the risk of planting this new variety. He had no ready answer. He had never before tried anything new like this. He thought, however, that he was more willing than others because if his experiment failed he would still not be in financial difficulty. He got most of his income, he suggested, from a rice mill and some more from his shop. Total failure of ADT–27 on two of his fifteen irrigated acres would not represent a serious financial loss to him.

The road north from Arni toward Vellore is fully paved and broad enough for two small cars to pass without either being forced onto a shoulder. The traffic, however, remains predominantly bullock carts, cycles, and pedestrians. Even buses pass along the road more frequently than private automobiles. Most of the fields along the road lack irrigation facilities and are dry most of the year.

The Jagir of Arni was, before independence, the semiautonomous territory of the descendants of Vadaji Bhaskai Pant, who had acquired the 180 square miles in reward for military services rendered during a seventeenth-century Maratha invasion of southern India. Arni Taluk is now the smallest of the eleven administrative subdivisions in North Arcot District.

The taluk was a traditional and important jurisdiction in British revenue administration, having in North Arcot District an average area of 426 square miles and an average population of over 250,000. For purposes of developmental programs, the post-independence district has been divided into thirty-six development blocks, having average populations of about 87,000. Though most taluks are divided into three or four blocks, Arni, because of its small size, has only two. The headquarters of the block in which Marusoor is located is a mile off this main road, seven miles northwest of Arni. It is to this block headquarters village that the panchayat president of Marusoor comes to the monthly panchayat union meetings. It is also here that the farmer must come to transact much of the business of obtaining loans, permits, pesticides, and seeds from the block office.

The 11 taluks and 36 blocks of North Arcot District are coordinated from Vellore. As one enters the city, some 25 miles north of Arni, it appears little different from one of the many towns in the district, and rarely as one moves through the city is that impression belied. Only its physical extensiveness suggests that Vellore is a city of over 100,000 and only the occasional appearance throughout the city of nondescript buildings bearing signs of specific government offices suggests that Vellore is an administrative center. The streets are quite as narrow as those of Arni and the shops as small. There are few overt signs of change or modernization in Vellore. The most notable exceptions are the modern theatres, which meet the ever-expanding demand for the showing of gaudily advertised Tamil films, and the new buildings of a prominent Christian Medical Hospital.

The largest and most imposing structure of the city is the Vellore Fort, an ancient structure that has survived the centuries with remarkable grace. Sprawling in front of the fort walls, within a hundred yards of the main market areas of the town, is an expanse of barren ground from which dust and heat seem to rise in equal measure. From the opposite edge of the town, barren and rocky hills rise steeply out of the valley. The widely accepted local belief is that the heat of Vellore is so intense and unbearable because the sun's rays are absorbed by the hills and reflected into the city as from the walls of an oven.

One of the roads entering Vellore from the south passes through Officers' Lines, the area in which, during the days of British rule, most British officials had lived. The houses are larger and more spacious than those in town. Some now serve as business establishments, others as residences for more wealthy families of Vellore, and a few remain the official residences of senior officials in the civil service, now occupied by the British officials' Indian successors.

One must look closely at the gates on the left side of the road to spot the small plaque which states simply "Collector's Bungalow." Set back some fifty yards from the road, and almost entirely obscured from view by large stands of trees, is the house in which resides the senior government official in North Arcot District. The house is large and spacious, with a circular drive under a portico and expansive porches in front of the main entrance. The present Collector finds he must close off some of the upstairs rooms because his salary will support a much smaller retinue of servants than would that of the English collectors of an earlier day.

Passing on through the narrow thoroughfare of Vellore, the most impressive building in sight is the headquarters of the North Arcot District Supply and Marketing Cooperative Society, a large structure which houses the society's offices, some of its retail distribution facilities, and the only indoor auditorium of any size in the city. Known officially as Rajagopal Nilayam, in honor of P.S. Rajagopal Naidu, the society's founder and president, the building frequently brings renewed recognition and honor to both the society and its leader by virtue of the official conferences, meetings, and performances held there.

Directly across the street from the cooperative headquarters is the old District Board building. Set well back from the road in the middle of a large walled compound, this building housed, during the days of British India, the offices and meeting hall of the District Board, an early experiment in limited local control. Now it is the office building for the Planning and Development section of the district government.

The main seat of district government, however, is another mile down the main road, deep within the protective walls of the old fort. Here are the offices from which the Collector and his staff perform their traditional duties of revenue collection and general supervision of the district. Here also are the headquarters of the district police establishment, the main district courts, and the taluk offices for Vellore Taluk.

For the central administrative apparatus of a subdivision of a single state, the profusion of buildings and offices seems somehow too large and too bureaucratized. But for the administrative apparatus responsible for the well-being and development of nearly 3.5 million people, it seems somehow too small and diffused to be adequate to the task.

North Arcot District is one of twelve predominantly rural districts on the plains of Tamil Nadu. Its population of over three million people is somewhat greater than the average for the state's districts. As in most of the districts, agriculture is the dominant economic activity, engaged in by 62 percent of the working force. The vast expanse of Tamil Nadu, from North Arcot in the north of the state down to Kanyakumari District in the south is a broad plain sweeping down to the sea from the hills and mountains that dominate the central and western lands in this southern extremity of the sub-continent.

The appearance of the land—and the wealth it produces—is determined primarily by the availability of water. In the delta region of the Cauvery River in Tanjore District, vast expanses of lush paddy fields dominate the landscape during most of the year. In Salem District, on the other hand, where only one-quarter of the cultivated land is irrigated, rice accounts for only 11 percent of the total area sown, and the vast majority of the land is planted in other cereals and pulses that depend on the uncertain monsoon rains for moisture. Not only are the yields of these other grains much lower than those of rice, but the market price for them is lower as well. As a result, the product from an acre planted in rice has normally been worth at least twice, and frequently four or five times, that of the produce from an acre planted in the other traditional grains of Madras.[5]

Among the twelve agricultural districts on the plains of Madras, North Arcot has the fifth highest percentage of sown area planted in

[5] This generalization is based on analysis derived from calculations of average yields and prices contained in *Season and Crop Report of the Madras State for the Agricultural Year 1963–64 (Fasli 1373)* (Madras: Director of Statistics, Government of Madras, 1967).

rice. The district has a favorable rainfall pattern and generally good soils, as well as an extensive system of wells and irrigation ponds—known as tanks—which provide reasonably reliable irrigation to 45 percent of the cultivated land in the district. North Arcot has no major year-round river system. The broad bed of the Palar River runs across the northern part of the district, but it is dry eleven months of the year. The majority of its water flow runs underground. An intricate system of canals traps what rainwater there is in a widespread net of tanks distributed throughout the district. These tanks provide water to over half of the irrigated land. Most of the remaining irrigation comes from more than 170,000 large open wells. Varying in size from ten to eighty feet in circumference, depending on the rate of underwater percolation, these wells are one of the striking features of the regional landscape and are of increasingly great importance to its agricultural economy.

North Arcot is somewhat above the average of Tamil Nadu districts in terms of the composition and value of its agricultural products. It ranks third in terms of both the per capita and the per acre value of its crop output. Only four districts have a larger share of their cropped area devoted to rice and three have a larger percentage of agricultural land that is irrigated. On most indices of agricultural productivity, North Arcot is grouped together with its two neighboring coastal districts, Chingleput and South Arcot, and ranked below Kanyakumari (a small and wealthy district at southern tip of India) and Tanjore.

Though typical of an ecological setting in which much of the rice produced in Tamil Nadu is grown, North Arcot sustained an agricultural growth rate of 8.2 percent per year over the twelve-year period ending in 1965.[6] This statistical indication of rapid increases in productivity—one of the highest district growth rates in the country—is surprising to the casual observer of agriculture in North Arcot. It is instructive, therefore, to see just how that growth has been achieved. Increases in the yields of various crops have been responsible for about 25 percent

---

[6] The basic (uncorrected) statistical indices on which the following analysis is based were developed through the joint efforts of the Economic and Statistical Advisor of the Ministry of Food, Agriculture, Community Development and Cooperation, Government of India, and the US Agency for International Development officials in India. I am deeply indebted to Dr. William E. Hendrix, then of AID, for sharing the raw data with me. I have reconciled inconsistencies in the indices, but the possibility of some error remains. Responsibility for the use and analysis of the data, of course, rests exclusively with me.

of the increase in output value. The cultivation of new land has resulted in 10 percent of the increase, and an additional 5 percent increase has been achieved by raising the yield of previously cultivated land.

The great bulk of the growth—over 60 percent of it—has resulted from changes in the pattern of land use. In 1952, 35 percent of the cultivated land was planted with low-yielding cereals and pulses. Twelve years later that figure had dropped to 16 percent. During the same period, the share of cultivated land devoted to rice rose from 22 percent to 42 percent.

It is difficult to know exactly what circumstances were responsible for this rapid change in cropping patterns, but probably the most critical factor was improved irrigation. Until the late 1950s, water from the wells in the district was brought to the surface by either human or bullock power. The advent of widespread rural electrification, however, created another alternative. Large numbers of electric pumpsets have been installed during the past ten years, under both private purchase and government-sponsored loan programs. This has made possible the more efficient use of irrigation water, allowing the farmer both to irrigate his own fields more fully and to sell surplus water to neighboring farmers lacking adequate irrigation facilities.

The introduction of the electric pumpset into North Arcot District appears to have brought about the first major change in production patterns during this century. Figures from the turn of the century show acreages planted in rice to be roughly comparable to those of the 1950s.[7] The total land area cultivated had expanded under the pressure of a growing population (population density increased from 365 to 677 people per square mile over the period) but the new lands were marginally productive, and only low-yielding cereals or pulses could be grown on them.

Yields also remained remarkably constant during the first half of the century. The North Arcot District Manual, published in 1881, suggests that the average yield per acre of rice was probably around 1,000 pounds

[7] See Madras (Presidency), Gazetteer of North Arcot (Madras, 1903). Since the old district, as it existed in 1903, was soon bifurcated with the new boundaries of North Arcot including eight taluks from the old district and two from more southerly districts, it is impossible to develop fully comparable statistics for the 1903 and 1950 data. Comparisons of seven taluks whose borders have remained essentially constant over the period form the basis for this statement.

at that time.[8] By 1954 the figure had risen by only about 10 percent. These meagre results in the improvement of yields do not, however, mean that changes were not taking place during the first half of the century. As early as 1913, a Paddy Breeding Station operated by the Madras State Department of Agriculture began studies on the genetics of rice plants. At least five substations were opened in later years, and by the mid 1940s, perhaps a hundred new varieties of rice had been released for commercial use.[9] Reliable figures on the use of these varieties are lacking, but they appear to have been tried on a wide scale and the best estimate is that one or more of them were adopted on perhaps 75 percent of the rice growing lands of North Arcot District by the end of World War II.

The increases in yields produced by these new varieties were, however, hardly spectacular. Increases for most varieties were estimated at 10 to 25 percent, depending on land conditions, availability of water, and the extent of fertilizer use. Other possible innovations of the period produced yield increases that were also marginal. The production techniques subsumed under the rubric of "the Japanese Method of Paddy Cultivation" would produce somewhat higher yields but with additional labor. Limited applications of fertilizer also increased yields, but the varieties available at the time had low tolerances for fertilizer and above a modest level of application the additional cost of the fertilizer quickly outran the value of the additional yield it produced.

In the mid-1960s a number of separate developments came to fruition in such a way as to dramatically change this situation. Work of the International Rice Research Institute in the Philippines produced a new variety, IR–8, which promised yields of from twice to four times those of varieties normally grown in Asia. On Taiwan other new varieties were producing yields that, while lower than those of IR–8, still represented increases that were spectacular when compared to earlier gains. About the same time, field tests began on a variety developed at Adathurai, one of the rice research substations in Madras State. As a part of an Indo-Japanese collaboration, the researchers at Adathurai experimented

[8] Arthur F. Cox, compiler, *A Manual of the North Arcot District in the Presidency of Madras* (Madras: The Government Press, 1881), pp. 312–13.
[9] S. Y. Krishnaswami, *Rural Problems in Madras* (Madras: The Government Press, 1947), p. 186.

with crosses between some of the best varieties developed in Madras and some of the higher-yielding dwarf Japanese varieties.[10] Field trials on the most promising result, a variety that was to be given the name ADT–27, indicated that yields throughout much of Madras State could at least be doubled by the use of this highly fertilizer-responsive variety. Meanwhile, in northern India, a variety of experiments with Mexican wheat and hybrid maize were beginning to make clear that these varieties, too, could produce startling results under Indian growing conditions.

Around 1965, C. Subramaniam, the Indian Minister for Food and Agriculture, and B. Sivaraman, his senior civil servant, had decided to begin a major drive to popularize these exotic new breeds of food grains in India. This decision was taken in the face of considerable opposition and ridicule because one feature of the varieties was their short—or dwarf—stalks, and it was widely believed that Indian farmers would not be open to varieties that did not produce tall stocks. In late 1965 the various state departments of agriculture began limited and controlled promotion of the varieties that appeared to hold the greatest promise for their growing conditions. In Madras, primary attention was given to ADT–27. By the end of 1966, it had become clear that if this variety were planted with reasonable care in almost any season on almost any irrigated rice land (only highly alkaline soils are unsuitable), and with even moderate doses of fertilizer, the results would be no worse, and in all probability far better, than those obtained with traditional varieties. In these early trials, undertaken on the fields of "progressive farmers," the average yield in North Arcot District was between 3,800 and 4,100 pounds per acre—well over twice the average yield for the district.[11] The state Department of Agriculture decided it could conservatively project a 67 percent increase in yield for each acre shifted from a local variety of rice to ADT–27.

Elsewhere in India, the experiments, while not unqualified successes, were sufficiently impressive to justify the course that Subraman-

[10] See "The Rice Revolution," an interview with Dr. M. S. Swaminathan, Director of the Indian Agricultural Research Institute, New Delhi, *Times of India*, April 6, 1969, for a description of recent progress in the development of improved rice strains.

[11] US Department of Agriculture and US Agency for International Development, *Accelerating India's Foodgrain Production 1967–68 to 1970–71*, (mimeographed, December 1967), pp. 15–17.

iam and Sivaraman had set. As the potential for high-yielding varieties of food grains was becoming clear, two other developments were reaching critical junctures. First, the full psychological impact of two disastrous agricultural years was beginning to be felt. The frustrations of a national failure in agriculture were intensified by the general economic recession that resulted. The humiliation of dependence on the United States for massive shipments of food grains to minimize starvation was heightened by American threats that further aid would be conditional on changes in Indian food policy advocated by the World Bank and American specialists. Second, the fourth general elections were rapidly approaching—to be held in February 1967—and the position of the ruling Indian National Congress was generally felt to be precarious.

The clear signs of success of the high-yielding varieties, the frustrations from economic decline and dependence on the United States, and the election—by then just four days off—probably all contributed to the decision of the Indian Government to announce, on February 10, 1967, its intention to push ahead with a crash program to increase agricultural production by extension of high-yielding varieties. The results of the strategy, the Government promised, would mean an end of food aid from the United States by 1971.

Targets for this expanded program were established and then passed down through the agricultural bureaucracy. North Arcot District's share of the first season's new target for coverage in ADT–27 was 20,000 acres, double what had been attempted the previous season. It was to look into the progress being made toward this goal that I had gone to Marusoor and that I attended, shortly after the Marusoor trip, a meeting of the District Collector's High-Yielding Varieties Committee.

I had learned from experience that it was safe to arrive fifteen or twenty minutes late for most administrative meetings held in North Arcot, but that one did so at his own peril when the Collector was to be present. As a result, I arrived at the District Board building a few minutes before the 10:00 A.M. meeting time. The large hall above the offices of the collectorate's planning and development section was already filling up with officials from around the district. I recognized some of the 36 BDOs, the four Revenue Divisional Officers (RDOs—each of whom is responsible for administrative matters in three or four taluks), and the three DAOs. In addition, there were representatives present from the cooperative society and the district cooperative bank, and one or two other agencies that were peripherally involved in the high-yielding varieties program.

The room was dominated by a large desk, elevated on a platform and located toward one end of the hall. Covered by a printed cotton material, the desk had on it a handsome desk set and lap board—the Tamil government officer customarily leans back in his chair and works off the board, which is propped between his lap and the edge of his desk. Off to one side of the desk a covey of clerks was scurrying around a table stocked with official files, searching for particular documents and arranging them in new piles. The various officers were sitting in hardback wooden chairs, arranged in rows on either side of a central aisle, facing the large desk; the most senior were near the front, the more junior and the less self-confident were scattered among the numerous empty chairs toward the rear. So many of those present were wearing white trousers and open-necked white shirts that it seemed as if they were in uniform.

I took a seat next to one of the three District Agricultural Officers (DAOs), and we began talking about the visit we had recently made together to the village of Dusi, on the eastern border of the district. I was particularly interested in Dusi because it had been visited and commented on by at least four authors during the past sixty years.[12] The impression I had gotten from these accounts was of a village that had once been dominated by Brahman landlords who, with the advent of increasing opportunities for urban life, had largely deserted the village. The pressure of a growing population on limited land had, these accounts suggested, been depressing the economic level of the village. I was consequently surprised to find that Dusi was a center of activity in the ADT–27 program. In discussions with farmers I encountered on a tour of village paddy fields I found that most of the men were themselves planting ADT–27, many of them for the second season. My impression from these talks was that the extent of ADT–27 cultivation in the village was largely the result of the activities of one man, a wealthy lawyer from

[12] See Gilbert Slater, *Some South Indian Villages* (London: Oxford University Press, 1918); P. J. Thomas and K. D. Ramakrishnan, *Some South Indian Villages, A Resurvey* (Madras: University of Madras, 1940); Census of India, "Descriptive Memoir of Dusi Village," in *Census Handbook, North Arcot District, 1951;* and Jacques Dupuis, *Madras et le nord du Coromandel* (Paris: Librarie d'Amerique et d' Orient, 1960).

a traditionally dominant Brahman family who was the public prosecutor for the district. Though an absentee landlord, the lawyer returned regularly to Dusi on weekends to oversee his lands. Several years ago, I was told, he had brought ADT–27 seeds from Tanjore to plant on his own lands, and the practice had, by the time of my visit, spread throughout much of the village. The DAO confirmed the importance of the lawyer in these developments, though he suggested that the seeds had come from Tanjore via the Agriculture Department. He emphasized, however, that a man such as the lawyer was a great help in his work because he could be counted on to plant a demonstration plot of a new variety, and to do it properly. During the current season, in fact, he was one of the few farmers in the district introducing IR–8 on his lands. I was interested in learning more about how the DAO proselytized for ADT–27, but rumors were circulating through the hall that the arrival of the Collector was imminent.

The Collector entered the room through a door behind his desk that was reserved for his use only. He was followed by his personal attendant, a short man wearing a ceremonial turban and a red and blue shoulder sash to which was attached a large brass shield proclaiming 'The Collector of North Arcot." The assembled officers rose as the Collector came through the door and stood until he was seated at his desk. In his middle thirties, the Collector was younger than all but a handful of his subordinates in the room. He was tall and strongly built. He wore the same style white trousers and bush shirts as the others but somehow they looked fresher, brighter, and more casual on him.

The informal and unassuming manner in which the Collector opened the meeting contrasted with the formality and ceremony that had surrounded his entry. He spoke in the precise British English of the higher Indian Administrative Service (IAS), quietly saying that he wanted to check on the progress of the HYVP to date. He had, he noted, a report on the status of target fulfillment in each of the blocks and the situation, though better than it had been two weeks earlier, was still not satisfactory. "For instance," he said, "in Arcot Block——" Suddenly, toward the rear of the room, a man popped to his feet. The Collector addressed him directly: "You have approved loans for less than half of the loan scheme allotment. What is the problem?" The man stammered something about his Gram Sevaks being off on special assignment. The Collector, with apparent impatience, replied, "This just isn't good enough. All the loan funds available should be approved by now."

The Collector glanced again at the report form in front of him and quickly focused on another displeasing figure. "In Walaja Block, . . ." he began. The Arcot BDO sank to his chair as another man on the other side of the room rose. This series of individual confrontations with BDOs continued for a quarter of an hour when the Collector abruptly broke off in mid-sentence, focused his attention on one of his RDOs, and said, with barely controlled anger, "I want you to pay attention to what I am saying. You know where you stand with me." The sense of unease I felt increased to almost unbearable proportions in the silence that followed. After half a minute had passed, the Collector broke the focus of his glare and said quietly, "This is not a social gathering, after all."

The concern with inadequacies in the approval of loan applications was eventually replaced by concern with inadequacies in the distribution of fertilizer to block distribution points, and then by concern with the inadequate supply of pesticides. The pattern of exchange between Collector and BDO, however, varied hardly at all. Occasionally the Collector would indicate that he required additional figures, and the attending file clerks would scurry around the stacks of files until they located the appropriate document. Periodically the Collector would address the RDOs, to say that they needed to take greater interest in these matters. At length one of them rose and said that this was the first time they had been told of these matters. The Collector turned toward the men standing around the file table, and singling out the oldest and most senior of them, his personal assistant (PA) in charge of planning and development, said, "That is because you didn't invite the RDOs to the earlier meetings. I made it clear," he went on, "that the RDOs were to come and I don't understand why they weren't invited." He then returned his attention to the RDOs. "You can have my PA explain why you were not here at earlier meetings."

When the inadequate target achievements had been disposed of, the Collector made a brief statement expressing the sentiment that, although some progress had been made, the program was still behind schedule. He made a final special appeal to the RDOs to review the program and see that the schedule was implemented on time. Then he rose—the entire gathering rose with him—and left the room, his personal attendant at his heels. Immediately the officers began gathering up their papers, chatting with their neighbors much as students would do when released from a class. The several officers who had received especially frequent and severe rebukes from the Collector seemed unaffected by the experience. They joined cheerfully in conversations and neither received nor seemed to expect any demonstrations of moral support or disapproval from their peers.

The Collector has three offices. One is in his bungalow; a second, his traditional revenue office, is in the fort; and a third, for planning and development affairs, is in the old district board building. It was to this third office that he retired at the conclusion of the staff meeting and it was there that I sought him out. After making my presence known to the Collector, his personal attendant showed me in and then returned to his post at the outer door of the office.

The Collector was in a relaxed mood, talking with a young IAS trainee who was getting his introduction to district administration in North Arcot. There are strong bonds uniting the members of the elite corps of IAS officers, and the Collector probably felt more at ease with this young man than with any other person in the district. The two of them were talking about the trainee's experiences in the various posts which he had held in the district. He was next to act as a BDO for a month to familiarize himself with the development activities at the block level. When I asked the Collector how he felt about the general standards and performance of the BDOs he had working for him, he replied, "As in any group, there are a few bad apples, but on the whole they are very good. When I really want to get something done I can always count on them to put out a lot of effort and get the results. For instance, as you know we had a benefit dance performance recently for the district welfare board for which we sold tickets all over the district. I wanted to make it a big success so I pushed the BDOs hard to sell as many tickets as possible. They worked very hard and, as a result, we collected over ten lakhs Rupees [a million Rupees, or about $133,000]. As you may have noticed, even the Chief Minister commented on this. So I am quite satisfied with the BDOs."

I noted that one of the major problems of any administrator was finding out what happened out in the field, and that this must be especially difficult when he had the development work of 36 BDOs to look after. The Collector agreed that this was a difficult problem. "The major difficulty," he said "is that my staff members are not willing to express themselves freely about the nature of difficulties that arise. There is a kind of psychosis of fear. These people have worked for a variety of superiors, some of whom want them always to be agreeing and not raising difficulties. When I first came to the district they spent four months trying to find out how I wanted them to respond. They should be free to say, 'Sir, we can't do that because of these problems. . . .' But there is a human factor that prevents this. So I have to rely on other methods of getting information.

"There are, for example, the periodical reports that the BDOs send in on the progress of various schemes. From these I can see if the funds for various programs have been spent. If they haven't, that is a clear indicator that the program is not going well. I also can check from these reports to see if the amount of area targeted for agricultural programs has actually been planted and if the necessary number of farmers has been brought into the program.

"Then, I am careful to listen to the views of nonofficials because they don't have any special interests to protect. For instance, I frequently have a few progressive farmers from around the district attend the HYVP committee meetings. Last year it was through them that I learned that the fertilizer for ADT–27 wasn't reaching the local distribution points soon enough. This year, I've been pleased to hear them say that they didn't have any serious objections to the way the program is operating. Also, of course, I ask you what is happening around the district because you don't have any special interest to protect.

"Probably most important, though, is what I find out when I go out on camp to various parts of the district. I'll go out, for example, and visit plots of land where ADT–27 is being planted. I'll leave the choice of the plots up to the block staff. It has a good effect on the program to go to a good plot. People think that if the Collector goes to a particular plot, then there must be something important there and they will investigate it; their attention will be drawn to it. This gives a sense of priority to the program. Then I will always talk to the President of the Panchayat Union and get his ideas. Again, in talking to him I project what is important and define our goals and priorities. I'm going out on camp next week to look at some developments in the HYVP in the southern part of the district. Why don't you come along?"

I agreed to make the trip and then excused myself, leaving the Collector to hear the problems of the several officials who were patiently waiting for a signal from the attendant to enter the office.

CHAPTER FIVE

Extracting Work: Contrasting Styles in Extension Supervision

Not long after the Collector's HYVP Committee meeting I spent some time in the area of Ranipet, the headquarters of the District Agricultural Officer who is responsible for the village of Dusi. Ranipet forms, along with the two adjacent towns of Arcot and Walaja, an important town complex for the northeastern part of the district. Straddling the broad Palar River bed, they are at the point where the main road from Madras separates into two branches, a southern one following the Palar toward Vellore and a northern one which leads into the adjoining state of Andhra Pradesh and then onto Bangalore, the second-largest city of India's deep south.

Like many government offices dispersed throughout the district, that of the DAO had been built as a residence and then modified to meet its administrative functions. Tables were set in every spare area. Seated at each of them was a young clerk, sandwiched between stacks of files on the table and towers of files in closets behind him. The lack of attention to any but the most serious maintenance problems was apparent. The architectural style featured dark, interior rooms, each lighted with one or two low-watt exposed bulbs. The whitewashing solution used on the walls produced a pale dirty-looking yellowish-brown finish. The overall appearance was one of deterioration, decay, and disinterest.

I was shown into the DAO's office, a spacious room separated from the rest of the headquarters by swinging double doors. A large man by Tamil standards, the DAO was jovial and self-assured. We talked for a few minutes, and then two other visitors, a leading ryot (farmer) and a panchayat union chairman, were ushered into the room. Conversation turned to events in their locality and soon the DAO was reaching quietly

for files from a tall stack on his desk, flipping nimbly to the page requiring action, reading briefly, then affixing his initials at the bottom, rety-
ing the ribbon that held the papers together, and reaching for the next
file. As his three visitors talked, he disposed of perhaps thirty files,
working unobtrusively behind his lap board, adding a comment or story
to the conversation from time to time. Certain that the chairman had
come to intercede with the DAO in behalf of the farmer, I sought an
early excuse to take my leave.

After I had finished my interviewing, had dinner, and was beginning to go over my day's notes in the comfortable lodgings of the govern-
ment-run tourist bungalow, the DAO rode up on a motor scooter. There
was a striking contrast between this man—traditionally dressed in ankle-
length wraparound lower cloth, and full cut high-necked shirt, with a
religious medallion on a chain around his neck, and his forehead smeared
with purificatory white ash—and the man in bush shirt and white
trousers who had been sitting behind a desk several hours earlier. Here
he had an impressive dignity in his bearing; in an office he was in an environment that was very familiar but somehow still foreign.

The DAO came, I learned, from a prestigious Brahman family of
Tirunelveli district, in the south of Tamil Nadu. He had studied one
year toward a degree in mathematics, but then switched to agriculture.
He had hoped, upon graduation, to do advanced research work in Delhi,
but his family had him married and saw to it that he settled into a stable
government position. He was now 39 and, during seventeen years in the
department of agriculture, had seen service as an extension officer, as a
teacher and director at training schools for extension workers, and as a
BDO, before becoming a DAO.

When I asked him what he thought it meant to be a good DAO, his
reply focused on two characteristics. "He must be helpful to the farmers
and he must complete the government schemes in a successful way.
Now, to be quite frank, that means fulfilling targets. My superiors judge
me by my success in fulfilling my targets and in keeping my paper work
up to date. One kind of DAO will keep the list of targets always in front
of him and push his subordinate AEOs to fulfill their targets. By departmental standards he will be a good DAO, but as far as the people are
concerned the only evidence of his having been in the division will be on
paper.

"When I leave this post, I think people in the area will say that I have done a good job and made many contacts with the farmers. That is not to say that I don't threaten AEOs and push them to fulfill their targets. I do plenty of that too. But if some farmer I know well comes for peanut seeds or for a new variety of paddy seed for himself or a friend, I'll tell the concerned AEO to give him special attention and to make sure he gets the technical advice and the inputs that he needs. Then, of course, at the end of the month, the AEO will try to tell me he spent so much time with these fellows that he didn't have time to fulfill his targets."

But how, I asked, had he, as a DAO, gone about getting ADT–27 started in his district? "I first came to this post," he noted, "in August of 1965, so that by January of 1966, when the program got started in this district, I had a pretty good idea of the area. In my previous experience in teaching posts I had developed good qualities of talking with farmers in a convincing manner. So I went around to various panchayat union meetings and talked about ADT–27. Also, I visited a number of progressive farmers whom I had gotten to know."

I asked the DAO to tell me who some of the specific individuals were who planted ADT–27 at his encouragement that season. In a list of about twenty names, one especially attracted my attention: Govindaraj Mudaliar of Nesal village. During a visit I had made to Nesal, I had discovered that Govindaraj was the village panchayat president, an important political leader, and the elder brother of Sunderamurty, Sunderambal of Marusoor's son-in-law. It was my interest in learning about how ADT–27 had been introduced into Marusoor that had led me to visit Nesal. Sunderamurthy, I had learned, had grown the variety on the advice of Govindaraj, who, in turn, first heard of ADT–27 when he attended a panchayat union meeting in Arni at which the DAO talked about the new variety. He obtained seeds and planted them on one acre but the results, he had told me, were very disappointing. At this point in his story, however, Govindaraj had become reticent, so I was interested in hearing more about it from the DAO.

"Govindaraj," he began, "got a yield of a little better than 500 pounds per acre that first season, but that was because he failed to use any fertilizer. He came to me and told of the poor yield he had gotten and I convinced him of the importance of using large quantities of fertilizer with ADT–27. Also, I promised him he would be able to get enough fertilizer. Later I met him at the BDO's office in Arni. He was trying to get a loan, but the BDO said that since the Nesal cooperative bank was in arrears, it was not possible to give him a cooperative bank loan. So I wrote a letter saying that I was very particular that this man grow ADT–27, and that it was important that he be given a loan. I sent Govindaraj with the letter to the secretary of the district cooperative bank and he later told me that within three days he had gotten a loan for Rupees 1,000. Since he did use heavy doses of fertilizer in the next season, he got very good results from his ADT–27 crop and is now growing it on most of his irrigated land. There are some hard feelings between him and me now, though, because I told him I would purchase his ADT–27 for seed to be used in Tanjore District. The seed testing laboratory rejected his seed as being substandard, however, and so, after making several excuses, I finally had to tell him that. He was very unhappy and ended up writing a letter of complaint to the Agriculture Minister who happens to be a member of his political party."

Very frequently in their conversations with me, government officials would mention the difficulties they had in, as they would put it, extracting work from their subordinates. The DAO described his techniques for handling subordinates. "First of all," he said, "we have punishment powers over the AEOs, but this process is slow and takes up a lot of my time. Moreover, the person being punished will stop working during the proceedings. I can get better and quicker results by transferring the fellow to the most undesirable and out-of-the-way block with the harshest BDO.

"The AEO doesn't have problems with going out to the farmer and telling him to use a particular variety and a certain dose of fertilizer. Anyone can give advice like this. The problems are in the paper and administrative work. A new AEO, for example, may not know how to get fertilizer for a farmer with only an authorization form. He may be afraid to come to me because he will think, 'It is my duty to know this. If I go to the DAO he will be angry with me.' So he will just hold off on the application and not do anything. In a week or two I will get a letter from the bank asking me where the authorization form is and I will have to go down to the AEO's block headquarters and get mad at him and then explain to him.

"Frequently these fellows need to be guided in a proper way. That is, if an AEO comes to me with a problem, I will get angry with him for fifteen minutes because he has not done his duty. Then I will settle down a little and casually ask him what his problems are. In this way he will learn not to be afraid to come to me. He will think, 'The DAO will get angry at me for fifteen minutes, but then he will listen to my problems and help me.' "

Before the DAO left that evening he invited me to join him the following morning at a meeting of the staff in a nearby block. The development block headquarters buildings, unlike the buildings that house most other government offices, have been specifically designed for their purpose. When the community development program was expanded to cover virtually the entire state during the 1950s, a block headquarters building design was approved and all blocks within the district were allocated funds to erect these structures. Thus, one can generally drive into the headquarters town of a block and very quickly locate the block office.

This particular town was the headquarters of an early experimental block in North Arcot. The block office building, set behind a thick wall with large gates, had a number of doors opening the length of a front exposure. In the unlandscaped front yard stood a government jeep—a symbol of status for the BDO and an object of desire for those around him—and the ubiquitous life-size statue of Gandhi. Squatting on the porch of the building were several farmers waiting for the attention of one of the staff members.

The DAO and I were directed into the office of the BDO. The contrast between the agricultural officer—jovial and self-assured—and the BDO, a small man who seemed threatened by any unexpected intrusion, was striking. At the recent HYVP Committee I had heard the Collector criticize, ridicule, and threaten this particular BDO in front of his colleagues. He had made no effort to defend himself. Knowing that he faced many serious difficulties in trying to fulfill his targets, I asked the BDO why he did not tell the Collector about the difficulties he encountered in implementing the program. "It is not my duty," he replied, "to tell the Collector the difficulties. It is my duty to fulfill the targets. He will say that if I am not capable of doing this work then I am not fit for the post of BDO. Though there are difficulties, we must get results in the end somehow. Even if people do not want many of the schemes, it is my duty to convince them. That is the nature of the community development program, to get across the many schemes."

The scheduled hour for the staff meeting was now well past, and the BDO suggested that we go to the meeting room after a courtesy call on the Panchayat Union Chairman, who had an office at the other end of the porch. We entered the office and found three older men, one behind a desk, the other two on a facing bench. Their dress was traditional, as were their manners. The BDO's uneasiness in simply making the necessary introductions was apparent. He now had to show appropriate deference to these ill-educated village leaders who ten years ago he could have treated "in the official manner"—haughtily and with disdain. His success as a BDO was now, however, greatly dependent on his relationship with the man behind the desk. As Chairman of the Panchayat Union Council, that man influenced, and sometimes controlled, the authorization of funds for many projects.

If a chairman chose to do so, he could tie his BDO in procedural knots by delaying or killing council resolutions. He could—and frequently did—also demand special attention, privileges, and projects for his personal followers, often in contravention of government rules. The BDO who could not work out a modus vivendi with his chairman was in serious trouble. Besides his powers in the block, the chairman was generally also an important regional politician with powerful contacts in his party's hierarchy. Through these contacts or independently, he could generally arrange the replacement of his BDO by a more malleable—or skillful—one. Virtually every BDO realized that special attention to the chairman's sense of prestige and status was indispensable to his own success. As a result, courtesy calls such as the one we were paying were a standard part of a visit to a block headquarters when the chairman was in the area.

This particular Chairman—despite his traditional clothes, his ignorance of English, his lack of education, and his low standing in the traditional hierarchy of castes—was clearly in control of the encounter. Once he had established the legitimacy of my visit to his own satisfaction, we talked about his village and the agricultural situation there. At the first diplomatic opening, however, the BDO suggested we proceed to the staff meeting. We left the three local politicians in the office and went off to the council hall.

As we entered there was a flurry of activity as those already in the room rose to their feet. The BDO, the DAO, and I took the three chairs set behind a head table, facing rows of chairs on either side of a central aisle. In the first few rows on the left side sat about a dozen men, mostly young, all wearing trousers and shirts. These, my experience indicated, would be the extension officers, generally college educated, and each responsible for a specific aspect of the block's program. The first several rows on the right side were vacant, but farther back, grouped against the wall, were seven or eight more men, in their early twenties, wearing the traditional wraparound lower cloth and white shirts. These, I knew, would be the high-school-educated Gram Sevaks. In the back row of this group might also be one or two agricultural assistants or gardeners, young men who demonstrate to farmers the approved methods for fertilizing and spraying their crops. Toward the back of the room, on the left side but well behind the extension officers, a group of young women hovered together in giggling embarrassment. These were the maternity assistants and the two Gram Sevakiyas—Village Level Workers for women's affairs.

The presence of a DAO at a block staff meeting was unusual and his seniority gave him the dominant role in the proceedings. After a brief exchange with the AEO, he turned his attention to the Gram Sevaks. Only five of the ten assigned to the block were present. Four of those absent were on special assignments to checkposts, which attempted to control movement of grain between taluks, and the fifth was on leave.

The DAO began by asking one of the Gram Sevaks how many farmers in his villages were enlisted in the HYVP. The young man rose from his chair and replied that he had himself only returned the previous day from a month's assignment on checkpost duty and hadn't had time to get that information. The DAO remarked that it was the Gram Sevak's duty to have that information and that he should somehow have gotten it. He continued to interrogate the young man for several minutes, demanding information about the number of acres planted in ADT–27, the amount of money that would be needed for loans, and the amount that could be obtained through the cooperative bank. The Gram

Sevak stood meekly at his chair, replying to each question that he didn't have that information. The DAO terminated his questioning in disgust and went on to a second Gram Sevak, with whom he repeated the same pattern. Indeed, four of the five had been in their villages only one day after returning from checkpost duty and were unable to answer any of the questions. The fifth, though he provided the figures, was roundly berated for having failed to achieve the levels of performance that had been set for him.

After the last of the Gram Sevaks had resumed his seat, the DAO told them that there was no excuse for their having failed in their duty. He demanded that they report to him by the following evening with all of the information on the status of the HYVP in their villages. He reminded them of, and threatened to use, his powers of punishment, then rose and left the meeting.

Soon after the staff meeting, I returned to the block in order to spend some time with the AEO, a young man by the name of Shanmugam. Unlike the other extension officers in the block, the AEO had his office in the local agricultural depot rather than in the block headquarters. In this, as in most of the blocks, the depot was temporarily in rented quarters pending the completion of a special building adjacent to the headquarters. The building to which I was guided for my meeting with Shanmugam had once been a residence. The entranceway was dark and murky, leading into a dimly lighted room cluttered with agricultural implements, bags of grain, and boxes of pesticides, as well as the desks and stacks of files normally associated with a government office in India.

I accepted Shanmugam's invitation to inspect the depot, and let him tell me about the things he thought would interest me. Like most government employees I talked with, he seemed anxious to demonstrate his professional competence and to describe the organizational features of his job. He pointed out the various implements, types of pesticides, and varieties of seed that were available to local farmers, mentioned the scheme under which each was distributed, and frequently the target that he was expected to meet. When I questioned him about specific schemes, he focused on the way they were structured: the targets, the type of loan available, the subsidy provided, and the prescribed type of extension work. Problems of implementation I had encountered elsewhere were ignored or glossed over, not, I had come to decide, because of an unwillingness to discuss them, but rather because most government employees had, after long experience, come to the conclusion that their superiors and others who visited offices were much more concerned with the appropriateness of the form and structure of a program than with the effectiveness of its implementation.

As our brief tour of the depot ended and Shanmugam and I sat down on either side of his desk, I asked him about the green manure program. Seeds of short-duration plants with verdant foliage, he explained, were sold to farmers at a subsidized rate. They were told to plant the seeds on fallow land and then plow the plants into the soil for fertilizer before the next crop was planted. He then explained what seeds he had and what his target was for each type. I mentioned that the AEOs I had talked to all agreed that farmers didn't like the seed and that the only way they could meet their targets for this program was to tell farmers that their loan applications would be approved only if they bought a certain quantity of green manure seeds. I asked him how the farmers in his block responded to this kind of treatment.

There was a pause as he grasped the implications of the question. He did his best to repair the theoretical form of the program. "Since many of the farmers are illiterate," he said, "it is sometimes necessary to compel them to take up the schemes. But in this way they learn the benefits of the schemes and the next year they will take them up happily."

"We must," I replied, "have been talking to different farmers. The ones I know don't even bother to plant their green manure seeds." Stifled laughs came from several points in the room and I suddenly realized that our conversation had become the focus of attention for several clerks and farmers sitting at desks in the dark shadows on the other side of the room.

Shanmugam made no further attempt to rescue the shattered green manure program, and I refrained, somewhat to his surprise, from criticizing him for having failed to somehow do his duty despite all the practical difficulties.

When asked how many schemes he had to implement, Shanmugam had no ready answer. After looking at the 21-page report form he submitted monthly to the DAO, and the list of agricultural schemes initiated by the block under the supervision of the Rural Development hierarchy, however, we concluded that he was responsible for perhaps 30 to 35 schemes. Many of these schemes, however, subsumed several distinct operational programs. The promotion of five new varieties of different food grains, the loan program, and fertilizer distribution to support the promotion were considered a single scheme. Recognizing the impossibility of implementing all of the schemes, would it not be wise to eliminate some of them, such as, for example, the green manure scheme?

"The ryots," he noted, "are not taking any interest in the green manure scheme." He thought for a moment and then warmed to this subject: "Yes, I think it would be all right to terminate that scheme. We should have only essential schemes." But what does "essential schemes" mean? He thought again, and then replied, "Essential schemes means schemes for crops that are needed by most of the people. That means paddy, sugar cane, bananas, coconuts, chilies; all of the crops which most of the people eat."

We talked then about the problems of achieving targets in the various schemes, and Shanmugam brought up the problem of control over the Gram Sevaks. They were supposed to be used exclusively for agricultural programs, he noted, but in fact the BDO would use them for whatever he wanted. I asked him how he handled the Gram Sevaks when he did have control over them, suggesting that some people thought praising subordinates for doing their work in a proper way was a good idea while others seemed to think it was not.

"It's better not to praise a person directly," he replied, "because if you do that he won't work hard. That's human nature. If you praise him, he will think 'Well, I've already worked to get a good name and now that I have earned a good name I don't have to work hard again.' You must always tell the subordinate that he is not quite up to the mark. We don't work for praise, we work only for duty's sake. That means we should fulfill our targets." There was a moment's pause. "There should also be some benefit to the farmers."

Not long before this interview I had given out a questionnaire to a number of government employees, including those in Shanmugam's block. In one of the questions I asked what story the individual would tell to his younger brother if he wanted to give an example of proper performance of duty. I asked my respondents to tell the story in their own words. Shanmugam had written:

King Dasarathan ordered his eldest son Raman to go to the forest for fourteen years and told a younger son, Bharathan, to rule the country. Raman went to the forest with his wife according to his father's order. When Bharathan came to know about it, he requested Raman to come back and to rule the kingdom, but Raman stayed in the forest for fourteen years since it was his duty to obey his father's words. I will explain to my brother that to obey father's words is duty.

As we now sat in his office, I asked Shanmugam why he had chosen to tell this classic story of Hindu mythology from the *Ramayana*. "Because," he replied, "in that story Raman went to the forest though he did not want to, only in order to implement the promise of his father. Obedience to father is the most important aspect of our duty. In government service, it is obedience to our superior that is the most important part of our duty."

Shanmugam, at the age of 31, had 10 years of experience in the agriculture department. His native place was a Hindu farming community fifteen miles from his present post. He is a member of the Vannia caste, the largest single caste in North Arcot District, and one traditionally recognized as among the lowest of the agricultural communities. The 1881 district manual, noted that:

> The Vannias have, apparently, recently raised a claim to be considered Kshatrias [second only to the Brahmans in the traditional Hindu hierarchy], which is ridiculed by all other castes. They, however, quote several common stanzas in which acknowledged Kshatria kings are called Vannia, Pillai, or Naicker [common Vannia titles], and point to their sacred thread and the mantrams which they have always repeated morning and evening. Other castes declare that they are a link between Sudras and outcastes, and that an unscrupulous Brahman, after investing one of them with the cord, taught him the morning and evening mantram. Their pretensions certainly seem modern, and the manners of most are rude. They allow widow remarriage, make divorce extremely easy, and eat flesh without scruple.[1]

Vannias later organized a caste association to further their status pretensions, increase their educational opportunities, and strengthen their political positions. With the advent of elections by universal suffrage after independence, the Vannias became increasingly central to the calculations of any politician in this part of Madras State. Though the caste as-

---

[1] Arthur F. Cox, compiler, *A Manual of the North Arcot District in the Presidency of Madras* (Madras: The Government Press, 1881), p. 280.

sociation has been unable to hold the caste together as a voting block, local Vannia leaders have continued to grow in political importance and the caste has been moderately successful in its attempts to raise its status.[2] During recent years the educational level of its members has been rising substantially, and they have been moving into more prestigious occupations.

Shanmugam's father was a small landowner in a Vannia hamlet of a predominantly Moslem town; he was somewhat more wealthy than most people in the village, but apparently not a caste or village leader. Shanmugam studied in the local Moslem high school, where Tamil was the medium of instruction until he was 13. I asked if this college degree were not unusual.

"I am," he replied, "the only degree holder from my hamlet, due to my having good luck. Because of my high marks in the exams I was able to get a government scholarship to a college in Vellore. After two years there I got an advanced scholarship to the state Agricultural College where I got my B.Sc. in 1957. Without the government scholarships I would never have gotten beyond my high school certificate. After my graduation I worked as a AEO for a year and then was a seed farm manager for three years. I went back to the Agricultural College for a six-month training course in soil conservation, and after a six-month field assignment there I spent four years as Assistant Soil Conservation Officer working on a dry farming scheme south of Arni. To qualify for a promotion, however, I needed two more years experience as an AEO so I got this post several months ago."

I noted that he had been in Arni at the time the HYVP had been getting started and asked if he had had any connection with the program. "I was officially responsible only for the dry farming scheme, but I took a lot of interest in the High-Yielding Varieties Program too. There is a very good farmer in Arni, K. M. Krishnaswamy Naicker by name, to

[2] The story of the Vanniya caste organization, the Vanniya Kula Kshatrya Sangam, and of Vanniya politics in general has been extensively reported on. It provides the major example used by Lloyd I. Rudolph and Susanne Hoeber Rudolph in their pioneering study of "The Political Role of India's Caste Associations," *Pacific Affairs* 33, no. 1 (1960), and figures prominently in Lloyd Rudolph's, "The Modernity of Tradition: The Democratic Incarnation of Caste in India," *American Political Science Review* 59, no. 4 (December 1965) and in Rudolph and Rudolph's recent joint effort, *The Modernity of Tradition: Political Development in India* (Chicago: Chicago University Press, 1967).

whom I first introduced ADT–27. At Voorhees College I had a class-mate who was distantly related to me. He, in turn, was related by mar-riage to the proprietor of the ASA Bakery in Vellore. When ASA [the bakery owner] learned I was going to Arni, he introduced me to Krish-naswamy Naicker who is somehow related to him. Whenever I went to Arni I used to spend a lot of time with him and in his shop. I told him about ADT–27 and helped him get some seeds. When he was ready to plant them I told him about the full package of practices. He followed my suggestions very closely and got good results. He accepted my ad-vice, I suppose, because he trusted me and knew I wanted to help him, but also because he is quite an educated man."

The AEO is a part of two hierarchies. As part of the "team" of block extension officers, he is subject to the authority of the BDO, and as an agricultural specialist he is subject to the technical supervision of a DAO. His two bosses are interested in different programs and frequently place contradictory demands on his time. For most AEOs, however, loyalty lies with the Agriculture Department and there is a strong sense that a good AEO must be able to manipulate his BDO and the Gram Sevaks into carrying out the Agriculture Department's schemes.

Each DAO coordinates the work of his twelve AEOs primarily through a monthly staff meeting. Most extension officers leave their headquarters villages and towns early in the morning in order to make bus connections, spend most of the day in the meeting, and then return home late in the evening. In addition to the DAO in Ranipet, two others operate, one out of Vellore and the other out of Polur, a town of about 20,000 people, thirty miles south of Vellore. The road from the district headquarters toward Polur passes just to the east of an extensive out-cropping of steep and rocky hills that cover much of the western half of the district. Along the eastern side of the road are long stretches of dry, parched land interspersed with occasional fields of rich green paddy. Polur is off the two lane highway and is reached by a short, narrow dirt track. Within fifty yards of the highway the track is flanked by stucco houses that barely leave room for two bullock carts to pass each other. The path winds for a hundred yards through the town, then turns abruptly to the left and opens into a small square rimmed by shops and dominated by a two-story building housing a photographic studio and, as an unassuming sign indicates, the "Office of the District Agricultural Officer."

I had driven down to Polur one morning at the invitation of the DAO, to attend a staff meeting. As I entered the building my eyes required a few moments to adjust from the hot and dusty glare of the outside to the dimly lit office room. Slowly two rows of desks, which extended the length of the narrow, long room, came into focus. At each desk sat a young man, and behind him on the wall was a small sign with a letter-number combination that identified the clerk and the subjects for which he had responsibility.

Behind the first desk on the right sat a man in his fifties, painfully thin, with several teeth missing from his mouth, and with carefully drawn thin vertical lines painted on his forehead. He epitomized the Brahman who, thirty years ago, had learned the rudiments of English and then become a clerk in the vast bureaucracy that administered India for the British. Slowly he had made his way up in the hierarchy, survived the transition from imperial to national bureaucracy, and was now an office manager, overseer of the dozen clerks in the room.

After introductions were made, I asked him to explain something of the office organization to me. The letter identification for each clerk, he began, represented the section in which that clerk works. "A" Section, for example, would be concerned with accounts, auditing, physical verification of depot stocks, preparation of pay, and related items. An office assistant would be in charge of the section and would have a clerk to assist him. I asked who would be in charge of the HYVP. He called out in a loud, commanding voice, "C–3." Far down on the other side of the room a young man put down a pen and slipped from behind his desk. As he reached the front of the room, the manager explained, "This is C–3. He is responsible for the HYVP, engineering schemes, the crop yield competitions, vegetable development, and related schemes."

C–3 explained that he was currently preparing a periodical report on the HYVP for submission to the Department of Agriculture. The figures from the reports submitted by each AEO were entered onto a large sheet of paper and then consolidated. The report was already overdue and the clerk showed me the file of advance reminders and subsequent reminders he sent to the AEOs as well as the ones he received from the Department of Agriculture. Each report consisted of figures relating to acreage and numbers of farmers enlisted for each of several varieties of food grains. The last item was an open-ended question asking the responding officer to indicate any problems encountered in the implementation of the program. This is a standard part of reports submitted to superior officers, and the fiction that no substantial practical difficulties were being faced seemed, on the basis of the reports from these AEOs and others I had seen, to be the normal and expected reply.

A large stock of files occupied one corner of C–3's desk. I chose one at random and asked if we might look at it together. Apparently pleased that anyone should take interest in the mechanics of his job, the clerk pulled the file from the stack. A knowledge of English was a requirement for his position and a symbol of his status as a government employee. Though communication with the AEOs was in Tamil, reports and correspondence to the Department of Agriculture were still in English. Like most clerical employees, however, C–3's knowledge of English was largely limited to the memorized key words and phrases that were standard elements in the bureaucratic vocabulary. After initial exchanges, we increasingly used Tamil to tie together English nouns.

The file, a thick sheaf of rough papers held on a legal-sized cardboard backing by flaps and a ribbon tied in a bow, contained correspondence on the High-Yielding Varieties Program. Several dozen sheets of paper on the top of the file were held together by a length of string, which was poked through a corner of each paper as it was added to the file, and then tied. A second section of the file was reserved for notes to be written to other clerks or to officers, and a third for drafts of correspondence which were being prepared for approval.

C–3 pointed out the mail clerk, who showed us the procedure he follows when a letter comes into the office. He gives it a serial number, enters particulars about the letter in a logbook, and determines whether it should be added to a preexisting file or should be the subject of a new one. He then routes it to a particular clerk. When the letter is actually handed to the clerk, the mail clerk obtains the initial of the receiving clerk for his logbook, thus relieving himself of responsibility for the letter. When C–3 receives, through the mail clerk, a piece of correspondence that requires an official response from the office, he prepares the file for the attention of the officer to whom it is addressed. In routine matters this may involve the preparation of a draft reply in a conventional format. In a more complex case, he might summarize the contents of the letter and suggest the general lines of the response.

The file would then go to the manager, who would review the work of the clerk, add any comments of his own, and then either return it to the clerk for correction or send it on to the officer. In larger offices there might be several supervisors between the clerk and the final decision-maker. Each would add his own note, frequently repeating material in other notes and commenting on the ideas of the notes that preceded his own. One Indian administrator, commenting on the tradition of note-writing in the civil service, has written: "One's note on a file is one's 'contribution.' It is futile to say that one has discussed the matter with one's subordinate at length, made enquiries and satisfied oneself fully; unless one has added one's own note one runs the risk of being consid-ered to be a person who signs, without reading, what someone else has written." [3]

The officer who finally gets the file is presumed to have read the let-ter and the notes, after which he writes a note of his own, indicating the nature of his response. The file goes back to the subject clerk for drafting and then returns back up the hierarchy, always being logged in and out of the personal registers of the clerks. When the draft reaches the officer in an approved form it is then sent down to the fair copy clerk who sees that it is typed up. The typed copy goes back to the officer through the manager and, if reasonably accurate, is generally signed. The final let-ter is then put in an envelope, sealed, stamped, and signed and dated again by the officer.

As C–3 and several other clerks who had gathered around proudly pointed out, this system, known to all as the Tottenham System—after the British Indian Civil Service Officer who developed it—provides a complete record of every piece of correspondence in the office and the accountability of each clerk. It is possible to determine how many files a clerk disposes of in a week, and if a file disappears it is a simple matter to follow the progress of a file through the annotations in the personal regis-ters of each clerk who handled it until one shows no acknowledgment from the person next in line to receive it.

The Tottenham System is ideal for the scholar who is interested in administrative patterns. It is possible, as one student has done in the

[3] Ramaswamy R. Iyer, "Understanding Our Bureaucracy," *Indian Journal of Public Adminis-tration* 12, no. 4, p. 711.

state of Kerala, to re-create the written arguments, disagreements, and actions that went into the resolution of any particular issue.[4] Not infrequently, of course, the written record is but the rationalization for actions taken for officially unacceptable reasons, but such an approach does reveal the attention to convention that dominates the slow but inexorable movement of a file toward final disposal.

As I became familiar with the intricacies and complexities of the Tottenham System, I became increasingly impressed by the relative speed with which work was made to pass through it. Each clerk worked slowly, frequently understanding only vaguely the English he was reading or writing, frequently unaware of the results he was supposed to be achieving, but with a single-minded devotion to form and procedure. The stacks of files on his desk never seemed to grow smaller, but new files did slowly replace the old, and cases of entire stacks being lost for extended periods of time seemed much rarer than the disarray of the office would have led one to expect.

I found that by using the name and title of an official when writing to a government office—instead of the title only, as is the tradition—I could get my letters to bypass the first step through the office hierarchy; "personal" letters are taken directly to the desk of the addressee. There were, nevertheless, occasions when I would receive a letter that was written four days before a meeting to which I was being invited, signed a week after the meeting, and mailed two days after that. The personal accountability which the Tottenham System made possible was, however, undeniable and my understanding of this fact was a clear source of satisfaction to C–3 and his colleagues.

A narrow, winding cement staircase outside the clerical office led upstairs to the DAO's office. The officer was sitting behind a desk reading through a file. In front and to the side of his desk were five old wooden benches and behind was a display board which also acted as a partition, separating the office from the rest of the large room, which appeared to be unused. On the display board was a graphic portrayal of a recently completed local campaign to get farmers to spray their peanut fields against a ravaging caterpillar infestation. Each of a dozen small snapshots showed different stages of the campaign, with descriptive captions couched in the vocabulary of Everett Rogers, an American sociol-

[4] K. Kesava Panikkau, *Community Development Administration in Kerala* (Ph.D. Thesis, Department of Politics, University of Kerala, September, 1966).

ogist who has analyzed, categorized, and named the consecutive stages in the successful promotion of a new pattern of behavior.[5]

The DAO rose to greet me as I entered. We had met in his office once before, and talked about his visit to the United States a year earlier. He had spent a summer visiting farm families and county agents, mostly in Missouri, and then joined with eleven other Indian agricultural officers for a year's course in a Master's Degree program at the University of Missouri. He had, he told me, been very much impressed by the kindness, openness, and friendliness of Americans; and this was clearly reflected in his exuberant, informal, and self-confident mannerisms and the Americanization of his speech. What he had learned in America also made him less pessimistic about the rate of agricultural change in India than were his colleagues. Whereas they compared the Indian farmer with an idealized image of the rational American who immediately takes up a new idea simply because an extension agent recommends it, this DAO saw the Indians taking to new varieties perhaps even more rapidly than American farmers accepted hybrid corn.

He felt that the greatest impact of his visit to America, however, had been his introduction to the principles of what he called scientific administration. What he had in mind, I discovered, was primarily a way of dealing with subordinates that was, to him, revolutionary. "Before I went to the U.S.," he had said, "I used to feel that the administrator had to drive the man below him to get things done. In our society people respect those they fear, those who have power, and those who inspire awe, so we have used the fear complex, with threats of punishment to get things done.

"At Missouri I took a course in 'Interpersonal Competence' that completely confused me for the first few weeks. Then slowly I began to understand what the professor was talking about. In that course I learned the importance of involving subordinates in the objectives of our programs. I now try to listen to their work problems and their personal problems and to get them personally involved in the programs. Frankly, during the first three months I did this with the AEOs I got no response. They took me for granted and thought that, since I was not being harsh, I was following a weak-kneed policy.

[5] See Everett Rogers, *The Diffusion of Innovation* (Glencoe, Ill.: The Free Press, 1966).

"In one block recently, the AEO, in connivance with two other people, illegally sold six hundred bags of peanut seeds. When I discovered this I suspended all three of them immediately. People were very surprised when I took firm action because they thought I was following a weak-kneed policy. By now, though, I have gotten good cooperation with most of my subordinates.

"The AEOs are really looking for leadership and I do try to provide it for them, not only in setting a good example for their work, but also in problem solving, in dealing with farmers, and in correspondence. I would rather get behind in my correspondence to superiors than in my correspondence with the AEOs. I try to encourage them to take decisions. If they make honest mistakes I will back them up. For one small example, if they make grammatical or spelling mistakes in their reports I will generally not emphasize their faults by correcting them.

"Also, I try to do some staff development during each of my AEO meetings, taking one or two small subjects at each meeting. One time I had them jot down what they thought the ryots think of them and then we discussed what the image of the AEO should be."

The DAO was now, however, preparing for his staff meeting and our conversation was limited to brief, almost ceremonial, exchanges. At length he pressed a button on his desk, and a small man, the office peon, came running up the stairs. The DAO told him to see if the AEOs had all arrived because it was time to start the meeting. During the next ten minutes the twelve AEOs, and several additional young men of parallel status who were working as special assistants in the DAO's office, came up the steps and sat down on the small wooden benches. I was reminded of a traditional old schoolroom with students looking up at the teacher, who was seated behind a large desk. The meeting had been called for 9:30 sharp, and already, at 10:45, the heat was becoming intense. Occasional hints of a breeze reached the AEOs from the single ceiling fan, which was located directly above the DAO.

The DAO began the meeting by explaining that they would discuss some ways of fostering innovation. Speaking in English—perhaps out of courtesy to a foreign visitor and a sense that officials of this level should be comfortable in English—he talked briefly about the nature of innovation. He spoke of awareness, interest, evaluation, and adoption; of innovators, early adopters, and laggards. I again recognized the categories developed by Everett Rogers in his studies of innovation, but doubted that the terms would have much meaning for any other members of the audience. The DAO asked which group the extension officer should work with most extensively. There was a painful silence. He repeated the question. Silence. Singling out one of his subordinates, he repeated the question a third time. The AEO got up and stood mute in front of his bench. After two further attempts to find someone who would speak to the question, he provided the answer himself and tried a new subject. On the third question he got the rudiments of an answer from one AEO, and slowly, partly in Tamil and partly in English, the meeting proceeded through a painful, formal, and largely academic discussion of innovation. Each time an AEO would stand to answer, the DAO asked that he speak from his seat. The extension officer would sit down, the DAO would repeat the question, and the AEO, as he started to answer, would instinctively stand up again.

The DAO then introduced a bright and intense looking young man who, he informed us, had recently been posted as the soil chemist at the district's soil testing laboratory. This man was important, he noted, because it was necessary that every farmer expecting to plant ADT–27 the following month have his soil tested first.

The chemist began a prepared speech in English, stating that every AEO should have a soil map of his block, which could be inspected by touring superior officers. He then went into considerable detail about the procedure each Gram Sevak should follow in collecting a soil sample in order to ensure that a random sample of 25 points within each 25-acre section be included in each bag sent for analysis. Next, he suggested that it was important for each farmer to know the chemical makeup of his soil so that he could choose scientifically the fertilizers to apply to his land. He noted that, since soil conditions change rapidly, the map would have to be remade every two or three years. "We need," he concluded, "to pass on this information to the farmer and somehow convince him. It is our duty to see that the farmer is educated properly."

The DAO suggested that this program might require more time and effort than the extension staff could spare at that particular time (my own calculations suggested that the soil map would require that a minimum of 175 samples be taken from about 4,500 holes by each Gram Sevak). One of the AEOs added that it was already impossible to get the

Gram Sevaks to do their work. This point of view was clearly perplexing and distressing to the soil chemist. "It is," he repeated, "our duty to prepare this map." The DAO replied that it was much more important that the land of farmers growing ADT–27 be tested first, and as a gesture of conciliation the chemist agreed that work on the soil map might be put off for a couple of months.

The DAO then asked if any of the twelve AEOs would have any problem in sending 100 samples each—taken, presumably, from 2,500 randomly selected holes—to the soil testing laboratory during the following two weeks. There was total silence. A few of the extension officers managed small nods indicating that they wouldn't have any difficulties. The soil chemist, clearly embarrassed, hesitantly suggested that, since his laboratory could only process samples at a rate of 250 per month, a smaller target might be better. The DAO relented and fixed the new target at 25 samples per AEO, inquiring two more times whether there would be any difficulty in meeting the target. A subdued silence brought the session with the soil chemist to an end and the extension officers, wilted by the heat, bored by the proceedings, and sore from prolonged contact with the wooden benches, adjourned to nearby shops for their noon meals.

The afternoon session of the staff meeting was taken up with a series of assignments. The DAO would take a file from the top of a stack on his desk, discuss the scheme, criticize the AEOs whose past performance on the scheme had been particularly deficient, and then indicate what he wanted done: a list of the names of farmers growing ADT–27 and the acreage to be grown by each to go to the Collector within nine days' time; preparations for a crop competition which, although now far behind schedule, must be carried out so as not to disappoint the farmers. As the list of assignments grew longer, the heat more intense—by this time the overhead fan had burned out and even the hints of relief had died out—and the effects of a large rice meal became more apparent, the AEOs leaned farther forward on their benches in attempts to brace supporting elbows on relatively stable legs.

At length, the DAO became aware of the inattention and the passive responses to his standard question, "Are there any who can't do that?" In a sharp tone of voice that could no longer be ignored, he emphasized that it was very important that the AEOs pay full attention.

They should all, he went on, have been taking notes on what they had been promising to do. Slowly they withdrew pens and blank paper from their file pads and began perfunctorily writing out the remaining assignments.

On the road home I detoured slightly to take one of the extension officers to his block headquarters. "How did you feel about the meeting?" I asked. He nodded his head in a way that conveyed both resignation and acceptance. "It seemed to me," I went on, "that the assignments given by the DAO were far more than any AEO could possibly complete."

"Somehow," he replied, "we must do them."

"But what will you do if you can't complete all of them?"

"Somehow we must do them."

Shortly before the date set for my trip to the southern part of the district with the Collector, I dropped by the offices of the planning and development section to get some information about the area we were going to visit. Immediately to the left inside the door was a large office belonging to the Personal Assistant (PA) to the Collector for development projects. When his office was not filled with politicians and petitioners trying to exert their influence over the decisions of the Collectorate, I generally stopped in to pay him my respects.

We had often talked of the differences between families in America and India because he had a strong sense of the value of traditional family loyalties in India and was very skeptical of—and perhaps a bit frightened by—the frequency of divorce and the limited nature of filial responsibility in the West. On this visit he told me something about his own background.

He had been born fifty years earlier into an agricultural family which lived in a village of about a thousand people. When he was three years old, he related, his father had left the village to take work in Singapore. His father stayed there until his death, 25 years later, and though he did send money back for his children's education, he made only one visit back to his family during that time. The PA went, successively, to a village grade school, a high school in a nearby town, and then the equivalent of a junior college. From there he went to a large Christian college in Madras and won a B.A. After a year in law school he applied for government service and obtained a post as assistant inspector

of cooperative societies. Slowly he worked his way up in the administrative hierarchy, first to senior inspector, then to extension officer for cooperation, and later still to BDO. After ten years experience as a BDO
he had been appointed the previous year as PA.

"To be a good PA to a collector," he explained, "one must maintain
the office properly and dispose of papers correctly and efficiently. We
have to dispose of 1,500 files in this office every week. Most of them are
minor and routine, but they must be dealt with in the correct way.
About eighty or ninety of the files are important enough to go to the
Collector and on those I have to write my note and put them up to him.
Occasionally these involve making new suggestions, but that is not an
important part of the job. Mostly it is a matter of commenting on suggestions or requests in the files.

"One part of my job that has become much more difficult recently is
the evaluation of projects in the district. We used to have two PAs for
this office, each of us handling 18 of the 36 blocks. Now, however, the
government has cut back our personnel and I am responsible for the entire district. Whereas I used to visit my blocks regularly, I now must
judge their work on the basis of the periodical reports that are sent into
this office. These reports show the progress, in terms of the funds spent
on each scheme, and also the physical achievements in terms of the
targets. If the achievement is very low in a particular block I will call for
an explanation from the BDO and then punish him."

I asked what he did when a BDO said that the target was too high.
"There could," he replied, "be no mistake in setting targets. They are all
carefully figured out and rationally decided. It is not possible for a BDO
to say that targets were too high. It is his duty to somehow fulfill the
targets."

I suggested that some people were of the opinion that there were really too many programs being implemented and too many targets to fulfill, though other people I talked to seemed to feel that the number of
schemes wasn't excessive. "The number of programs we have is not for
me to say," the PA responded. "That is a decision that must be made by
senior officials and politicians. It is our duty only to implement the programs."

Although I recast my question in several different forms, the PA
repeatedly insisted that it would be presumptive of him to suggest an an-

swer. At length he said—albeit reluctantly—"If a senior officer asked me for my personal opinion, I would say that we must do everything. We can't do one thing and then another. We can't have fertilizer, pesticides, and irrigation, and not have seed until a later time. Also, we can't increase agricultural production first and then have family planning later. We must do everything at once. Everything is all important."

As he began to warm to this subject, a small group of local politicians entered the room and sat down in the several chairs around his desk. Their interests were clearly of a confidential nature, and after introductions and brief pleasantries were exchanged, I excused myself and moved into the inner offices of the planning and development division.

Seated behind large desks around a long and narrow high-ceilinged hall were perhaps six men. These were the administrative supervisor of the division and the section heads. Behind this office, in a large converted meeting hall were perhaps fifteen more clerks, grouped in lettered sections according to their specific responsibilities. To get the information I wanted, I went to the desk of Ramakrishnan, the section head concerned with agriculture. An alert young man who appears to be in his late twenties, Ramakrishnan is, in fact, forty years old. His father was a Brahman school teacher, and when Ramakrishnan finished high school his father managed to get him a post as a typist in the district office. A combination of intelligence and hard work had been responsible, I suspect, for his rapid rise through the ranks of typist, lower and upper division clerk, and section manager. He had just received official word that he was shortly to be promoted to the position of administrative supervisor for the entire planning and development section.

Right now, however, as head of the subdivision concerned with agriculture, animal husbandry, fisheries, and town panchayats, he was the senior person on the Collector's staff who was concerned primarily with agriculture. His own view of his position, however, was that of an administrative expediter whose job was to move files rapidly and faultlessly through the clerks in his section. His own career, he felt, would have advanced more rapidly had he been in the prestigious state revenue cadre instead of the district bureaucracy.

The district's senior agricultural specialists are the three DAOs. Their primary responsibilities, however, are to the state Agriculture Department, which has its headquarters in Madras, and to the subordinate Agriculture Department cadres working under them in the blocks. Ramakrishnan is the agricultural specialist on the Collector's staff and the DAOs are the senior line officers in charge of the departmental operations in the district. The Collector can draw on the technical knowledge of the DAOs as he wishes, but there are no formalized procedures or standing committees at which he would be likely to engage with them in any kind of extended substantive discussion. The responsibility of each DAO for a specific third of the district and the location of two of them at considerable distances from the district headquarters reduces the Collector's opportunities to draw on these men for technical advice concerning the agricultural situation in the district as a whole. Any such information that the Collector does obtain is as a result of his own personal interest and initiative, and the DAOs in North Arcot felt fortunate indeed that the current Collector had established—and actually convened with some frequency—a District High-Yielding Varieties Program Committee. He had also been instrumental, along with P.S. Rajagopal Naidu, the President of the District Cooperative Society, in activating a committee for the planning and coordination of fertilizer distribution in the district.

Despite his lack of background in agriculture, Ramakrishnan was able to give me a general description of the program that I was going to be visiting with the Collector. Deep in the southern part of the district is an area of some 15,000 acres, which is irrigated by water from the Sathanur Dam. The dam had been built nine years earlier and during subsequent years water had been released for irrigation purposes on the first of December and then closed by April. Farmers owning good land in this region were thus able to get one predominantly rain-fed crop during the heavy monsoon from August through November, a second irrigated crop from December through March, and a third crop, watered by a second monsoon, from June through August. Depending on the quality of his land and the arrival and appearance of the monsoon, the farmer had to choose, during this last season, between leaving his land fallow and planting paddy, peanut, or a hardy cereal. Normally the bulk of the land was in peanut because of its limited water needs, the small amount of work required to plant it, and the high price the crop could fetch in the markets. The situation was different this year, however, because a series of events had led to the decision to release an additional allocation of water from June through September, creating the assured water supply necessary for an extra paddy crop.

One factor bearing on this decision was that the two previous agricultural years had been, on an all-India scale, largely disasterous in terms of food grain production. Retail rice prices had risen precipitously in a period of general inflation. At the time of the general elections of February 1967, the ruling Congress Party in Madras State had been attacked strongly for having allowed the price of rice—the most critical and frequently the largest single item in the budget of nearly any lower-class south Indian family—to rise to unprecedented levels. The most effective opposition party, the Dravida Munnetra Kazhagam (DMK), hoping to increase its position to that of a strong minority contender, made election promises to cut rice prices to about 60 percent of their prevailing levels.

Much to the surprise of political analysts and the party's leaders, the DMK, operating in a strikingly successful electoral alliance with several other parties, suddenly found itself the majority party and in the embarrassing position of being expected to make good on its promise to nearly halve the price of rice. After initial indecision, the DMK began selling rationed quantities of rice at the promised price in the two urban areas of the state where its strength was the greatest, incurring an enormous budgetary deficit in the process.

The need for increasing rice production without raising the price the government paid to the farmer became, as a result, critical for the new government soon after it took office. A report prepared by the Commissioner of Food Production suggested that, among other things, water from several irrigation projects, including the Sathanur Dam, might be used more efficiently for this purpose. Using ADT–27, which besides yielding well has a short growing period, an area of perhaps 8,000 acres could be transformed from rain-fed peanut land into irrigated paddy land by the simple expedient of releasing the surplus water in the Sathanur Reservoir beginning in the middle of June.

On June 8, the government decided to implement this proposal and almost immediately the Collector made arrangements with the Cooperative Society to deliver substantial quantities of fertilizer into the region. He also instructed the three DAOs and several of the BDOs to temporarily transfer a number of AEOs and Gram Sevaks into the area. The extension workers had the task of moving into an unfamiliar territory and, in a very short time, convincing farmers that they should discard plans to plant peanut and instead contract for water from the project and plant ADT–27. The officials' task was somewhat facilitated by a general familiarity with ADT–27 in the area, but was complicated by the economics of the situation. Rain-fed peanuts clearly would yield a lower profit than ADT–27, but would also require much less labor than the rice crop. Moreover, the very availability of irrigation water opened up the possibility of planting an irrigated peanut crop—one that would yield profits almost equal to those of a rice crop while requiring much less labor and not involving the risks of a new variety in a new season.

The Collector was making his visit in order to see how well the mechanics of distributing fertilizer, seed, and credit were being handled, but also in order to get a sense for the effectiveness of the extension effort. The Sathanur Project House is on the outskirts of Thiruvannamalai, an important temple town nearly sixty miles south of Vellore. Built for the comfort of touring senior officers, it is an attractive and spacious bungalow set in a pleasantly landscaped compound. When I arrived at 9:30 A.M., a group of twelve district officials was already present and awaiting the Collector's arrival. The DAO from Polur pointed out the RDO responsible for the area, two engineers from the project, two BDOs in whose blocks the special HYVP program was being implemented, and two tasildars responsible for revenue collection in the two taluks of the project.

At 9:40 the Collector arrived in a small but immaculately maintained sedan, followed by his personal staff in his touring jeep van and a standard jeep. He moved swiftly from the jeep, greeted the attending officers with a quick smile, and went directly into a small room of the bungalow and requested that it be prepared as a temporary office while he washed. In a flurry of activity a table and chairs were arranged and files were lugged in from the jeeps in large, locked metal containers. The Collector's personal attendant, fully attired in turban and shoulder strap, was at his post, and the clerks from the planning and development section were standing by in an adjoining room.

Within a few minutes the Collector was behind the table, pressing a call button, obtaining files, and summoning officers. The DAO and the RDO entered the room and took seats facing the Collector, who began by asking what progress had been made in getting farmers to plant

ADT–27 and use project water. The RDO stood up and replied, after an embarrassed pause, that he thought probably around 4,000 to 4,200 acres were being planted in irrigated ADT–27. How, the Collector wanted to know, had he arrived at those figures? They were estimates, the RDO replied, based on the amounts of fertilizer and seed distributed and on observations that the RDO and DAO had made in touring. The Collector said that he had given adequate advance notice of his visit so that the officers should have been ready with accurate figures on the status of the program. The RDO replied that it was very difficult to get figures because of an unusual feature in the locality. As many as six villages, he pointed out, shared a single recordkeeper. The DAO added that some of the Gram Sevaks had been taken away for training and, since some transplanting was still going on, it was very difficult to get final figures.

"What good are these excuses?" the Collector demanded. "I have come to review the progress of the program. You should have this information prepared. I did not come here on a holiday." Having dismissed the excuses as irrelevant, the Collector then returned to one of them and demanded of the RDO how it was that he had allowed some of the Gram Sevaks to be sent out for training just at the height of the sowing season. The RDO replied that the Collector's PA had passed orders for the transfer. The Collector said that was an unwise thing for his PA to have done, and that the RDO should certainly have opposed it. As the conversation went on, the RDO let it be known that three additional Gram Sevaks were to leave that afternoon for training and the Collector immediately sent him out to call the PA and have the orders cancelled.

The Collector spent what remained of the morning in reviewing the programs of a succession of officials. His tone shifted from one of open and rough criticism of the RDO and BDOs—over whom he had direct administrative control—to one of more reserved and distant questioning of the DAO and project engineers—presumably members of the Collector's development team, but under administrative control of their technical departments.

The Collector asked me to join him for lunch in a spacious hall which had been prepared as his dining room. He had, he told me, a standard noon meal when he was out on camp. A delicious combination of northern and southern Indian preparations, the meal was served with quiet efficiency while we talked.

I asked the Collector about the adequacy of his staff. "It is very difficult to handle the wide variety of programs I am responsible for with the staff I have," he began. "The clerks really lack a concept of what these programs are all about. As a result, though I have the clerks put up drafts to me, I usually have to redraft much of them myself. I don't so much mind the problems they have with writing correct English, but they frequently aren't able to grasp the requirements of a situation. I have sometimes thought that this may partly be a problem of language, but mostly, I think, it is a question of training. There is really no one in the development division that has the capacity for thinking through what is needed in a particular program. Of course that isn't too critical because, at our level, we are mostly just implementing programs that are set up at the state level.

"Another problem that I mentioned to you before is that most of my staff members don't feel free to express their ideas openly. This comes, I think, from our administrative traditions. These people naturally have a concern for themselves and they don't want to anger me. I try to set them at ease. I indicate that I am interested only in a frank expressing of business views, not in their families or personal problems. In this way I build their confidence. Many of these people have had years of experience in the field; far more than I have. They are great repositories of experience, so I consult with them in order to profit from their experience and learn about the difficulties. The RDOs, for example, have great experience and knowledge. On the other hand, with their experience and hard work in the ranks, they become concerned mostly with the smooth working of the system. They are like the turbulent river when it reaches the plain: it becomes quiet and calm.

"Also, most of my staff have worked under many difficult superiors so they have become more cautious. There is this great willingness to agree. They would rather agree than set out the difficulties and present their objections. They are afraid of rubbing their superior the wrong way. I try to make them feel relaxed and give them a feeling of partnership in these programs. I find that this is the best way of doing things. This kind of dialogue leads to them feeling free to express themselves."

I asked how he felt, based on what he had learned during the morning, about the progress of the program in the local area. He replied that it was really probably too early to tell. The problem was difficult because the officials and extension agents could exert very little control over the farmers who wanted to get the benefits of growing a cash crop like peanuts. "We have worked hard to get the local officials, even the revenue officers and the local politicians, to address village meetings and put pressure and convince the people that they should change to paddy. We can threaten them that they will be charged a penalty rate if they use water for peanuts, but there is actually nothing we can do about it. After we have a rest, though, we can go out and see for ourselves."

When the most intense heat of the day had passed, the Collector's party set out. I joined the Collector, his driver, the DAO, and the BDO of the first block we were to visit in the lead jeep sedan. Following behind in an open jeep were the AEO, the tasildar, and other officials. After traveling south and west on a main road for some five miles, we turned sharply west onto a service road running along the bank of the irrigation project's main canal. The Collector pointed out with some irritation each field he noticed in which there were signs of peanut plants sprouting. The DAO and BDO countered by calling his attention to larger fields where paddy was growing or was about to be transplanted.

Within a few minutes we reached a village road where some twenty to thirty farmers had gathered. The Collector got out and walked over to the group, his entourage quickly arraying itself behind him. The village recordkeeper spoke briefly, telling what he had done in an effort to get farmers to plant ADT–27, then introducing several leading farmers who had done so. The Collector asked about resistance to ADT–27 and a gaunt man angrily replied that he was planting peanuts and didn't see that it was any business of the officials to force him to plant paddy. The Collector made some remarks about the importance of food grain production to the nation, and one of the bystanders commented that this fellow was a troublemaker anyway. Soon we were all back in the jeeps and going along the canal road.

At several other places along the three miles of road we stopped to talk with groups of farmers who had gathered to meet the Collector. After the initial inquiries about the status of the program, individual farmers would invariably bring up personal complaints or problems that they had with the actions or inactions of local officials. Disputes about water rights, land boundaries, and taxation were presented to the Collector. He listened to each petition, heard the story of other parties to the dispute, and then assured the petitioner that appropriate action would be taken. One of the clerks was, meanwhile, rapidly writing out notes on the proceedings.

Just as the last scheduled meeting was coming to an end, an old lady prostrated herself in front of the Collector and asked for his mercy. She related the story of her husband's death and of her financial plight as a widow. The Collector listened patiently, asked several questions, and then ordered the tasildar to make certain that this lady was given a parcel of vacant government land. As the officials moved off to the jeep, the clerk scurried over to the lady and demanded her exact name, address, and other particulars that would make it possible to identify her in the Collector's records.

Back at the project house, the Collector met with his officials individually and in small groups, indicating his dissatisfaction, issuing orders, and demanding more satisfactory performance in the future. Soon after the last of the officials had left we went in to dinner.

I knew that the Collector came not from Tamil Madras, but from a region of Mysore known as Coorg. The tribal Coorgis are a traditionally martial people who have adapted very successfully to westernization, exploited the richness of their own region, and moved into positions of power and influence throughout the south of India.[6] I asked him more about his own background. He had, he told me, been brought up in the city of Madras, where his father was a senior police official. He obtained a B.A. from Madras University, and then went on to get an M.A. in economics. He wanted to take the IAS examination, the key for entrance into the most elite occupational corps in India, but he was then, at 20, still too young. He spent one year in a law course and then took the IAS examination, which he passed on his first try.

The IAS recruit spends his first year in a training course in the hills of north India, learning the mechanics of Indian administration, developing a strong esprit de corps, and absorbing and internalizing the norms of independence, analysis, self-sufficiency, and internal motivation and direction that set the IAS officer at such a distance from others in the Indian bureaucratic apparatus.

After this introduction to the IAS, he was initiated into the realities

[6] On Coorg, see M. N. Srinivas, *Religion and Society Among the Coorgs of South India* (London: Oxford University Press, 1952).

of district administration in Madras State. He spent a year of training in North Arcot, acting for periods of up to a month in the capacity of BDO, tasildar, and other key roles in the subdistrict administration. A further part of this training involved a study of the economy and structure of a village in the district. He took his first regular assignment as a subcollector—the equivalent of an RDO—in one of the southern interior districts of Madras State. After a year and one-half he was transferred to the city of Madras, where he spent three and one-half years as a deputy secretary and later a joint secretary in the department concerned with state protocol, public services, elections, and general administration.

In 1965, the Collector was sent to England for a one-year course in international administrative studies at the University of Manchester. There, in the company of some eighteen other administrators from throughout the developing world, he studied problems and techniques of administration and visited a number of governmental and quasigovernmental institutions both in Britain and Europe. Within a week of his return to India he was posted as Collector of North Arcot. Now, at the age of thirty, he had held, for a year, responsibility for the well-being of some 3.5 million people.

Up to that point, he related, it had been an exciting year. Within two months of his arrival the district had been hit by a severe cyclone, and he had had the responsibility of organizing and directing emergency relief and redevelopment efforts. He had seen—and survived—the most dramatic political shift in the history of Madras when the DMK dislodged the Congress Party from the centers of power in the state. He had organized the most successful District Welfare Fund benefit ever held in North Arcot and had received special recognition from the Chief Minister of the state for his efforts.

"Doing a district," he said, "is something that a person really must go through. You can read about the experience in books, but to know how it feels one must actually have the experience. I have known other IAS officers with ten and fifteen years experience who have never done a district and it puts them at a disadvantage in the service. I am fortunate to have had this chance. It is an exciting experience because there are so many opportunities and challenges.

"People frequently say that the influence and power of the Collector in Madras State have declined, but my own view is that the reverse is true. Perhaps my statutory authority is less than that of my predecessor of twenty years, but the scope of my responsibility is wider and there is greater opportunity for exercising initiative. It is in the area of development programs that the new role has opened up.

"My responsibilities as Collector are of three types. First, I am the district officer for the Revenue Department. As such I must see to the collection of taxes, procurement of foodgrains, allocation of chemical fertilizers, and to other matters controlled by the Board of Revenue. Second, I have general jurisdiction over the district. I do not need to be concerned with the day-to-day operations of the different offices in the district, but if special problems come up—especially problems involving disputes between different district officers—I must deal with them. Third, where special programs or projects arise, I can use my initiative to see that they move smoothly and swiftly.

"It is in this third area that the role of the Collector has expanded. There are now many development programs that I can devote my attention to. There is a very delicate line between taking initiative and leadership in these programs and interfering with the day-to-day operations of the concerned officers. Much of the work is setting priorities for attention and seeing that coordination and cooperation are properly effected. For example, the District Welfare Fund benefit performance was an enormous undertaking. We collected over a million Rupees and had one of the most popular dance troupes in the whole state. I mobilized my staff to carry out the arrangements for ticket sales, seating arrangements, extra electrical supplies, police service, and extra transportation from various towns in the district. The whole thing went off very smoothly and was a great success.

"As you know, I have also given a lot of attention to the HYVP. In the committee meetings I have tried to get the DAOs to set up plans of operation starting from fifteen days before planting time and then working backward and forward, figuring out what inputs they will need at each point. People at the state level recently said that our district has the best fertilizer distribution system of any district in the state, but it is still a serious problem. During the last year we had all of the paper allocations made, but some of the fertilizer still did not reach the villages in time for planting.

"This year I have tried to get the Cooperative Society, my own staff, and the Agricultural Department people to plan together well in advance and I think the results have been much better. During one meeting I had recently with some progressive farmers I was very pleased to hear them say that they didn't have any serious objections to the way the program was operating. Of course there will always be some complaints, but this time they were not of a serious nature. That means that most of the fertilizer is getting out to the villages in time for it to be used.

"Actually, there are almost no pressures put on me to give special attention to any particular programs, or even to any programs at all. The RDOs assume much of the responsibility for the routine revenue collection activities. Of course, if problems of special difficulty come up I want to see the files and pass orders on them. I could just spend much of my time unproductively and I would not be penalized particularly. The IAS officer, unless he is grossly incompetent or hopelessly corrupt, can do little to speed up or retard the advancement of his career. Our promotions are based almost entirely on seniority. We are expected, though, to have a concept of what is important and to be able to set priorities. After all, the characteristic of a good administrator is that he be able to set priorities."

When dinner was over the Collector returned to his office where, on a table to the side of his desk, were three neatly arranged stacks of files. His daytime schedule was so filled with official meetings, ceremonial responsibilities, traveling, and meeting individual petitioners—one morning a week was set aside specifically to hear the personal pleas of any ordinary citizen who had the resources to get to the Collector's office—that the only time he had to dispose of files was from after dinner until midnight. I sat for the better part of an hour, watching him and occasionally talking with him as he worked his way through the first stack of files, reading a letter, glancing through the comments of his subordinate clerks and assistants, and then writing out his own instructions.

One could not help but feel the impact of the venerable tradition of the imperial district officer: the administrative procedures were virtually unchanged, the symbols of authority preserved, and the pride in going out on camp undiminished. A hundred years earlier this night halt in the far reaches of the district would have taken place in a lantern-lit tent and the journey would have resumed the following morning with a slow, hot horseback ride to a nearby village. In 1967, the Collector, refreshed after a relaxed sleep in spacious quarters, broke "camp," and returned to his bungalow quickly and comfortably in a chauffeur-driven automobile.

CHAPTER SIX

Planners and Planters: the Views
from Madras and Marusoor

The offices of the Madras State Department of Agriculture are in an area of Madras city bordering the seacoast. Occupying a wing of what was once a palace, the buildings are marked now by little of the splendor and pride that must once have surrounded them. The visitor has to find his way into a large compound and around to the side of the building, where a small portico and a simple signboard mark the entrance to the Agriculture Department. A flight of stairs, covered by a jute carpet that is worn through from the daily trudging of clerks and officials, leads upstairs to a great hall.

Crammed into every available space on the main level is an assortment of desks, barely visible beneath the forest of stacked files. As one seeks out the narrow lanes that provide access to the other side of the room, however, the appearance of massive chaos is broken down into individual units of order. Each desk, lined up as squarely with its neighbors as its unique size and shape allow, has its own clerk, with his own orderly stacks of files, quietly and deliberately performing the procedures in which he has been trained. At the back, a narrow winding staircase leads to a balcony which runs the length of the room, where the same scene is replicated on a smaller scale. Surrounding the army of clerks on the main level are rows of offices, partitioned off to provide a degree of privacy. Just outside each of the swinging barroom-style doors that lead to each office, diminutive men in turbans sit on small stools. They announce the arrival of visitors to the officers inside, carry messages to clerks on the floor, and make trips to the nearest canteen for coffee.

This setting had been my introduction to the world of Indian agricultural administration. On my first visit I had talked at length with the Joint Director of Agriculture for Intensive Programs. The Director of Agriculture, I learned, was an IAS man who was expected to bring to the position the skills of an administrator and the breadth of vision of one with wide experience in government. He was assisted by some six specialist joint directors who provided him with the technical skills and advice necessary to run the department. There were joint directors for Commercial Crops, Extension Operations, Agricultural Engineering, the State Seed Farms, and Inspection, in addition to the one responsible for Intensive Programs.

I was at first puzzled by the Joint Director's western name, that he seemed more at ease speaking in English than in Tamil, and by his generally western demeanor. He later explained that, though he was from a Tamil Brahman family, both of his grandfathers had been converted to Christianity. He used his Christian given name in the traditional Tamil manner: with the two preceeding initials representing his place of origin and his father's given name. His father had received an engineering degree and then gone to Malaya to work for the railways. He himself had been brought up there and had gone to English-language schools with English instructors. The family returned to south India when he was ready to begin his college work, undertaken in a Tamil-language college. He managed to pass his introductory years, he told me, because he had learned some formal Tamil from having listened to his mother read the Bible. He then wanted to do his degree in literature, but his father was intent on his taking up a profession. He didn't meet the ten-year residence requirement for medical school and he didn't like animal husbandry, so he ended up in agriculture because it was the only other professional course taught at the local college in which he had any interest.

By 1957 he had reached the level of deputy director and was in charge of a regional office, which coordinated the work of several DAOs. In 1959 he was selected for a one-year training course at Cornell University under a program sponsored by the Ford Foundation. When his year of training was up, the Foundation chose him to act as Project Officer for the Tanjore Package Program, which it had proposed and was financing. He spent four years in Tanjore and rapidly gained a reputation among the agricultural specialists in the Foundation as being a most effective administrator. He was responsible not only for getting the organizational structure moving but also for starting (in 1964) a seed multiplication program that made possible the large-scale dissemination of ADT–27 in 1966.

From his position in Tanjore, he came to the Joint Directorship for Intensive Programs in the entire state. He had responsibility for the Tanjore project and two other programs that developed as by-products of that experiment. The Intensive Agriculture District Program (IADP) was an attempt to extend the idea of the package program and its staffing pattern in a somewhat diluted form to four additional districts in the state. The HYVP soon became the major substantive component of both the Tanjore and IADP projects and an important program in other districts as well. At the time of my visit, the Joint Director was busily engaged in taking advantage of a German offer for collaboration on an intensive program for potato development in one of the rich hill districts of the state.

I was struck by his interest in, but distance from, the practical problems of program implementation in the districts. He was aware that credit was not being used for production purposes, that panchayats were not assuming leadership of community-wide production programs, and that farmers were not using recommended dosages of fertilizer.

These seemed, however, to be incidental bits of intelligence on the periphery of his actual duties. As I watched him over the course of several days, arranging for the distribution of fertilizer and pesticides throughout the state, negotiating with the central government over the following year's target levels for the state, and considering with German specialists the technical requirements for the potato program, it became clear that this was not the point at which communications from the field were handled and related to program planning.

During one of my visits I asked the Joint Director what happened to the periodical reports submitted by the DAOs. He referred me to his assistant, a man of DAO rank, who in turn sent me to the head clerk for the Intensive Programs section, who actually processed the reports.

The previous month's report had just been completed and the clerk explained to me how it had been prepared. On the 11th of that month an advance reminder had been sent out to all the DAOs, informing them that their consolidated report would be due four days later. On the 23rd a Most Urgent reminder was sent out to those who had not yet submitted their reports, and within four days each of the forty DAOs had submitted his report. The clerk then went on to point out that he had discovered discrepancies in eleven of the reports—errors in addition, defects in format, inconsistencies, etc.—and these he had returned for resubmission.

When they were cleared up, it took a section clerk the better part of two days to consolidate the reporting categories from the twenty reports and prepare a state-wide report. The Head Clerk then reviewed each DAO's report for target deficiencies. Where the deficiency was only marginal he would do nothing, but where it was serious he would draft a letter of criticism and exhortation over the name of the Joint Director. I was by then familiar with these highly stereotyped letters and the disdain with which the DAOs received them.

I was also aware that the monthly report, though it was the most important and extensive, was only one of a number of periodicals the DAOs had to file. It is extraordinarily difficult to come by an entire listing of these reports, but in one file on the subject which I later found, it was said that DAOs were required to submit a total of 81 separate periodical reports, in addition to their major monthly report. It is in the filing of these additional reports that the most noticeable delays take place. Even in the offices of well-organized DAOs it is standard to find reports that are one or two months late, and in cases of the most obscure items, I have seen urgent reminders calling for the submission of a report due more than a year earlier.

Having observed the heavy time demands that the system of targets and reports places on every level of the development bureaucracy, I inquired about the reasons for and value of the system. The assistant to another of the joint directors explained that the Legislative Assembly of the state required certain figures which were compiled from the reports and that the government of India also required reports on achievements of plans. Moreover, he emphasized, the Department had to watch over the progress of its schemes and the reports provided its primary source of information. These were reviewed, he noted, and if progress on a scheme was not up to the mark a note would be sent to the DAO in question and an explanation requested. If it proved to be adequate the incident would be allowed to pass, but otherwise, the assistant assured me, the DAO would receive a letter telling him that he must do better in the future.

I was also concerned with the role of targets in the bureaucracy's operations. I spoke about this problem to the assistant to the Joint Director for Intensive Programs, who had been an extension specialist at the state agricultural college for five years before coming to his present position. Though he assured me that he valued extension work, he explained its limitations: "India is in a great hurry to get development and that means implementing a vast number of schemes quickly. The question," he said, "is how to carry on all of these schemes if we don't have targets. If we take away the targets, how will we extract work from the subordinates? If you remove targets and allow them only to do extension work, then how would the targets for all the schemes get achieved?

"For example," he went on, "if I am given a target of two tons of seed to distribute within one or two months, there will be no time to carry out a proper demonstration and follow the extension methods. So I will go to the farmers, remind them of how I have helped them in the past, and then ask them to please help me by buying some of the seed and trying it. If necessary I would get them something they needed, such as an iron plow, only if they would buy the seed. We have the right to force it on them because of our hurry to develop. There is so much to do because we cannot neglect any crop."

Concerned that I have a sense for the breadth of departmental programs, he arranged an appointment for me with the Joint Director for Commercial Crops. The Joint Director seemed intense and businesslike behind his neat desk. His angular face and horn-rimmed glasses gave him an appearance similar to that of a well-tanned western executive. Trained as a horticulturalist and specializing in spices, the Joint Director had served both in Madras as State Horticulturalist and in the Government of India's major agriculture research center. His enthusiasm for his subject was such that a simple general question would prompt a lengthy discussion of his many goals and projects. "Commercial crops," he pointed out, "are tremendously varied in Madras. My job is to formulate schemes for the development of all these crops in various areas of the state." He mentioned a number of such crops and then discussed the schemes that were already in progress or in the planning stage for each. He mentioned at length that there were also a number of crops not grown in Madras that could usefully be introduced, and then he went on to describe his plans in this area.

In response to a suggestion that the resulting number of schemes must be very nearly unmanageable, he acknowledged the problem but said that it was impossible to limit the number of schemes because of the vast variety of crops and areas in the state. This set him off on an extended monologue about still another crop he felt was inadequately developed in the state and for which he had formulated a number of new schemes that were already being implemented.

When I looked over some of the proposals I found that they helped to explain several things of interest about the agricultural programs in North Arcot. First, the projects all assumed that the bulk of implementation would be carried out by existing extension staff. However, many of the proposals called for special staff assistants to work out of the offices of DAOs and oversee the programs. The special assistants had been added one at a time as new projects developed. Assignments to specific DAOs depended in part on the area or region for which a specific project was designed and, undoubtedly, on other factors as well.

More striking was that programs for each crop were planned independently and without reference to other crops and programs, and that targets were also assigned without consideration being given to the importance of other crops. This helped to explain why programs for the development of both peanuts and rice could be competing for the same land in the Sathanur Dam area and why the Collector was, at a meeting sometime later, to threaten a special DAO for peanut development with expulsion from the district if he were again found promoting the development of peanuts in the area.

Several miles north of the Department of Agriculture offices, also along the beach front, stands Fort St. George. This British fortress persists as a symbolic representation of the beachhead from which the British built Madras Presidency—consisting of present-day Tamil Nadu and parts of Andhra Pradesh, Kerala, and Mysore. Once the seat of Presidency Government, Fort St. George is still the center of governmental activity in the state of Tamil Nadu. Just inside the front gate stands a large, whitewashed, columned building in British tropical colonial architecture. It houses the state legislature, cabinet, and some of the senior civil servants. Behind and to the side of this structure are numerous other office buildings in which are located the officers and staff of the state Secretariat.

The Secretariat forms the link between the government (the legislative party and cabinet under the Chief Minister of the state) and the departments that have responsibility for implementing programs. The Chief Minister is supported by the senior civil servant in the state, the Chief Secretary, and each of the other ministers in the cabinet has a parallel supporting Secretariat officer and his staff.

Thus, to learn about matters of fundamental policy and thrust of the agricultural development program in Tamil Nadu, I visited, at Fort St. George, the Secretary to Government for Agriculture and members of his staff. I had met the Secretary briefly during the early stages of my study, when he had been Director of Agriculture. We agreed that it would be useful for me to talk with one or two of his assistants before I saw him, and I was directed to the Deputy Secretary for Food Production.

The Deputy Secretary was a pleasant man in his middle fifties who, I learned, had spent his entire working life of 32 years in this same building. He had been brought up in Madras and managed to get both a B.A. and a Masters Degree in economics. He very much wanted to go next to England to prepare for the Indian Civil Service examinations, but his father was, as the Deputy Secretary described him, too conservative to let him go. So, as a young man of 23, he joined government service at the level of office assistant in 1936. From this essentially clerical post he advanced, after six years, to the position of office superintendent, and nine years later to the post of assistant secretary. Five years later he was promoted to his present rank.

I asked him what he felt were the qualities that made a good deputy secretary.

"The most important thing," he replied, "is that a person should keep the files moving. Then he should know the provisions of the rules and regulations, and follow them. He must be a practical person and not excessively hidebound or academic. Finally, he must have good writing ability."

He then went on to explain that, as Deputy Secretary for Food Production, he was responsible for helping the Secretary establish policy, evaluate and pass on to the cabinet the budget of the Department of Agriculture, handle interdepartmental affairs involving agriculture, and advise the Agriculture Minister on petitions and the implementation of schemes in which he had a personal interest. When I asked whom he dealt with in these matters, he replied that officially his contact was with the Secretary and his subordinates, since official channels went through the Secretary to the Minister, to other secretaries and to the Director of Agriculture. "On an informal basis, however," he added, "we often discuss problems in person or on the phone with people in the Department or in other parts of the Secretariat. Similarly, to save time, the Director and his subordinates frequently go to people in another department and keep us informed. When things are informally settled in this way, the official correspondence on them then goes through the appropriate channels."

When the conversation shifted to the budgetary process and the Deputy Secretary began speaking of "setting priorities," I asked him just what he meant by that phrase. He replied that it meant "arranging schemes in the order of their importance, giving first place to important ones. If there are 94 schemes and we have money for only 90, then we can cut out the ones on the bottom or we can reduce the budget for the ones toward the bottom."

I asked about the possibility of strengthening the most important programs by adding to their budgets. "We could do that," he replied, "but that would be very unlikely because the concerned officers put the full amount required in their requests in anticipation of its being cut. This year, with the added attention to agricultural development, we knew we could move somewhat ahead of last year's budget. So, we were able to add more schemes to make the budget larger."

"You make the budget larger only by adding more schemes?" I asked.

"Yes, of course," was his somewhat bemused reply.

I was rather puzzled by this concept of priorities, which seemed to deal with projects as discrete and unrelated units. "What," I asked, "is the Tamil word for priorities?"

The Deputy Secretary puzzled for a moment and then said that he couldn't think of it. As he sat considering, a voice from an obscure corner of the room replied, "*mudal idam.*"

"Yes," added the Deputy Secretary, "*mudal idam*, first place."

"So when we say that the HYVP has a very high priority, what does that mean?"

"Well, that we give first place to the HYVP in the distribution of fertilizers and loans."

The Deputy Secretary's superior, the Secretary to Government for Agriculture, had entered government service—with roughly the same educational qualifications as the Deputy Secretary—sixteen years after his subordinate started as an office assistant. The Secretary, however, had gained access to the IAS. After seven months' training he worked for several years in three different districts before becoming Collector of a fourth. He then assumed the directorship of a minor department and, after being posted to a second—and this time major—collectorship, he became Director of Agriculture. After two years in that job he was sent to the United States for a three-month advanced management course run by the World Bank. He was made Secretary to Government for Agriculture soon after his return.

I asked the Secretary to tell me something about this new position and what was required to fulfill its duties.

"My job," he began, "is to advise government on all matters regarding agriculture which require their decision. I myself take the decisions which do not need to go to government. The Director of Agriculture is responsible to me, in my capacity as senior advisor to government, for the operation of the Department of Agriculture.

"As to doing my job well, if a problem comes to me, I need to be able to get a quick decision. If a request from a group comes to me, I get satisfaction out of being able to satisfy it quickly. Or, if a personal problem is brought to me, I should be able to settle it quickly."

Since the Secretary had earlier been Director of Agriculture, I asked him what he thought the goals of the Department were. He appeared to be somewhat taken aback. "That's a very difficult question," he noted, pausing at some length before he replied further. "I would say, though, that the goal is to get the ryots of Madras State to adopt methods to increase productivity."

His answer interested me because it seemed in such contrast to the ambivalence and imprecision I thought I had noted at lower levels with respect to the goals of productivity and equity. My impression was that the two goals were frequently in conflict and that, though certain concessions to political demands for equity should certainly be made, the major thrust of the civil servant's attention ought to be on increasing productivity. The Secretary's comment reassured me, and I followed it up with a question about program evaluation.

"In evaluating a program," he replied, "I first consider what kinds of results the program is producing. With all that, of course, we cannot afford to neglect our backward areas. We must consider their potentials."

"And when there is a conflict between the two?"

"Then," he replied, "we must draw a middle line."

I asked about political demands for equity and how he dealt with them, but as he began talking about the problem, it became clear that he saw it not in terms of a conflict between productivity and equity, but rather in terms of the politician's efforts and desires to overcome or bypass the bureaucrat's rules and regulations. "The politicians are, however," he concluded, "the representatives of the people, and many of their demands represent the demands of the people, not their own self-seeking."

The Secretary seemed to share the concern of many of his subordinates that opportunities were being missed in many aspects of agriculture. He noted the problem of the ceiling of Rupees 420 million on scheme subsidies from the Central Government. "The Centre is always proposing new schemes which we are unable to take up because implementing them would take us over the ceiling."

"Some people," I noted in response, "say attention must be concentrated on schemes which will produce the best results; others say that agriculture in Madras is highly diversified so it is necessary to have many schemes to cover all of these areas." How, I wanted to know, did he feel about that question.

"The latter view," he replied, "is certainly correct. It is not possible to have fewer schemes. Perhaps some of the schemes should be put together and be made parts of larger schemes. That would bring greater administrative efficiency."

This view seemed to conflict with the basic approach of cost-benefit analysis, which has long been the presumed operating principle of western bureaucracy and has recently been formalized in numerous ways by systems analysts. The fundamental premise of the approach is that the ratio of costs to benefits for any program provides a measure of the efficiency with which that program uses resources. A business executive is concerned that such an analysis will suggest whether or not a program will yield a reasonable profit. For the government policy maker who is not worried about profitability, a comparison of cost-benefit ratios of different programs provides a basis for making programming decisions that will yield the greatest results from limited budgetary allocations. The approach is controversial in the western world not because of its assumptions, but because of the extreme difficulty of measuring costs and benefits accurately.

I presumed that the Secretary had been exposed to cost-benefit analysis in his World Bank training course and he confirmed that it had indeed been a major component of the program. How, I asked, did he see its relevance for his own work in agricultural policy-making?

"Cost-benefit analysis," he replied, "is not very useful in the situation of developing countries. There will be many programs that won't meet the critical ratio; that is, programs for which benefits won't exceed costs. Still we have to carry on those programs in the early stages of development. We can't worry about the costs and benefits of the programs; we have to get on with all of them."

The converging pressures of the development efforts in the Agriculture Department, the Rural Development hierarchy, and the Collectorate fall on the link between the lowest levels of the bureaucracy and the farmers in thousands of villages. The AEOs are each responsible for at least forty villages in addition to their substantial administrative duties and so have little time for intensive village extension work. Consequently, it is to the Gram Sevak that the bulk of the actual extension effort falls.

My first contact with the Gram Sevak responsible for the village of Marusoor, other than brief and public encounters in the village, had come when he invited me to visit his home in Arni. I took this opportunity to learn something about his background and his views of the village, which we both knew but from differing perspectives.

The house of the Gram Sevak is reached by following a series of narrow lanes leading away from the main road of Arni. As one nears the outskirts of the town, the lane takes an abrupt turn to the right. At the juncture of the angle is located a small single-story dwelling with an adobe exterior and a red tile roof which overhangs a porch. Most of the protected area consists of a red cement slab elevated two or three feet above the surface of the ground. Here visitors can sit by day or sleep in comfort on a warm night.

It was to this porch that the Gram Sevak, a tall and thin man in his late twenties, led me. As we began to talk, an older lady brought out coffee and quickly disappeared back into the house.

Confirming what the recordkeeper of Marusoor had told me, the Gram Sevak described his own family. His father was a village record-keeper with substantial lands of his own, and his brother held the same position in a second village. The Gram Sevak had, after completing secondary school, decided on government work and been employed as a health assistant. Several elder acquaintances who were Gram Sevaks, however, convinced him that he should take up that work. He was accepted into the program and spent two years in training. His first post had been his present one, and he was then completing three years in it. He had married several years earlier, and at the time of my visit had two young children. His wife's mother was temporarily living with them, and it was she who had brought the coffee.

I asked him to tell me something of his normal routine. "I go daily to Arayalam by cycle," he replied, "arriving there about nine o'clock in the morning. Generally I visit two of my five villages in a day, one in the morning and another in the afternoon. I do my office work in the evenings."

After talking about the importance of fulfilling the various program targets, he went on, "We must also identify with the villagers and learn about their problems."

I suggested that this seemed, on the basis of my experience, to be a very difficult thing to do. "Yes," he replied, "when I first came to the village, 75 percent of the people thought that I had come only because it was my duty to advise them, so naturally they did not pay any attention to me. They thought I was coming and going only because I was paid to do so. During the past three years, however, their attitudes have changed and they now listen to me."

When asked what kinds of farmers first listened to him, he replied,

"It was the people with larger land holdings who listened in the early stages."

As I probed further, he indicated that a second factor was literacy, though if a man both had large land holdings and was illiterate he would still listen. "People with less land," he noted, "are afraid that their experiments will fail."

In replying to a question about the most influential farmers in the village of Marusoor, the Gram Sevak quickly named Egambaram Mudaliar (the Panchayat President), P. Nadesa Udaiyar, Chokkanatha Mudaliar (the one surviving grandson of Rajagopal Mudaliar), and Sunderambal. After thinking for a few moments, he named three other men. When asked about the best farmers in the village, he again listed Nadesa, Egambaram, and Sunderambal.

I noted that, since several individuals were both good farmers and very influential in the village, his best strategy for making as much progress as possible on his targets must be to work primarily with those individuals in the hope that they would use their influence to spread the new ideas he brings to the village.

"They are influential people; they can give advice to the people, and the people will follow them with good effect," he replied. "It is still my duty to visit the ordinary ryots even if they will listen better to Egambaram, Nadesa and Sunderambal. It is my duty to change the attitudes of the people, not to just go off and talk to a few of them. We must go more frequently to those who do not listen to us in order to convince them. Those who listen to us do not need so much of our time so we don't have to go to them so frequently."

The conversation turned to some of the specific programs for which he had responsibility. His comments reaffirmed my impression that he had an astonishing number of programs to implement, many of them subsuming several specific targets. His attention did, however, seem to be focused on the HYVP more than any of the others. I asked what he had done about promoting the program.

"Three months ago," he replied, "I went to the Panchayat President and asked him who he thought would grow ADT–27. I then visited each house and every person told me how many acres they were going to grow. From this I made up the list required by the block. Actually, other farmers will grow as well. The target for the village is only thirty acres, but I think about ninety acres will be grown in Marusoor."

When asked to what extent he thought this result had come from his own efforts, he answered, "If no Gram Sevak had been in the village during the past three years, I think five acres, at the most, would be grown this year."

As I got ready to leave, I indicated that I hoped to see him again soon in Marusoor. He would be away, he replied, for about two months attending a Gram Sevak refresher course, but the village would be in the charge of the Gram Sevak who normally had responsibility for an adjacent group of villages. That Gram Sevak, I noted, would be faced with real problems. Since he was already overworked in his own area he would find it impossible to carry out all of the assigned schemes in an unfamiliar area as well.

"He can't just work on a few of the programs because it is our duty to do all of them," the Marusoor Gram Sevak observed. "We can't say that one is more important than any of the others. He cannot spend twice as much time, but he must take care of both groups because that, also, is his duty. It will, of course, be difficult for him to do everything, but he has to do it somehow."

As the *sownavari* planting season progressed, I made a series of visits to Marusoor in order to talk with a variety of farmers about the HYVP. It soon became clear that it would not, in most cases, be practicable to hold private interviews. The presence of a foreigner was a source of considerable interest, and the interviews—generally held on the front porches of different houses—were frequently witnessed by from ten to twenty people. Though their presence limited somewhat the topics that could be discussed, there were some advantages as well. When a farmer was reluctant to talk about a particular problem or tried to distort facts, he would frequently be prompted by one of the onlookers to "go ahead and tell him," or "tell the truth. He won't do anything to you."

Early in my interview, I generally asked the farmer how often he listened to the radio, read a newspaper, or traveled outside of the village. I found that almost all of them listened to the radio at least several times a week. In most cases they went to the small square near the village school to listen to the panchayat's receiver. Though tastes in programs varied, most listened, at least a few times during a month, to an evening program, *Vivasaigulukku,* "For Farmers."

Only a few of the more than twenty farmers I talked to did not make an average of at least one trip per week to Arni or some other nearby town. Many went on business or with certain needs in mind; for others such trips were simply occasions for visits to coffeehouses or a film.

When I asked where a particular farmer had first heard about ADT–27 the response was generally "the radio." Frequently individuals were able to remember and recite back to me figures they had heard on "For Farmers" about yield, fertilizer dosages, and pesticide treatments. As the importance of this program as a source of information became apparent, I began listening myself. The program would generally begin with a series of announcements on the weather and items of topical interest. The major portion of the fifteen minutes, however, was frequently given over to a dramatic presentation, usually in a village setting, depicting a farmer faced with an agricultural problem. There was invariably spirited dialogue between one character who was opposed to a particular innovation and another who was able to articulate the arguments in its favor. Many of the views that were expressed struck me, on the basis of my own interviewing, as being highly realistic. I was also aware that Tamils take a great delight in good drama and suspected that this was a highly appropriate vehicle for the transmission of information about new agricultural practices.

Another common feature of "For Farmers" was the interview with a successful progressive farmer. Though the program originated in Madras City, an effort was clearly made to locate, and interview on the radio, farmers from all over the state. Several of the individuals I talked with in Marusoor had clearly been impressed by hearing a fellow farmer from a nearby area relate his own experience and success with a particular variety or fertilizer.

Though the radio seemed to be the only source of information for several farmers who planted ADT–27 in Marusoor, a number of others who had planted the variety had seen it growing "along the road to town"—on Arni Krishnan's land—or in villages to which they went on visits to relatives. Several farmers mentioned Nadesa Udaiyar as a source of information, but only three—Egambaram, his uncle Chokkanatha, and Sunderambal—mentioned the Gram Sevak and each of them referred to two other sources before they mentioned him.

Even when asked specifically about the Gram Sevak, the villagers denied hearing from him about ADT–27, and most indicated that they didn't get any other kinds of information from him either.

Even though most of the farmers I talked with were probably above the average in sophistication, education, and success, many indicated that they had had little or no contact with the Gram Sevak. Frequently there were titters of laughter from the onlookers when I asked about this government agent. On one such occasion the farmer I was talking to replied, "I have never seen the Gram Sevak. When you ask about him we all laugh because the name means village servant, and he does not do any service for the village."

Nadesa's brother said of the Gram Sevak that "he comes to the village when it suits his convenience; perhaps once to three times in a week. I talked to him most recently last week and asked him for a plow, but he said there was no stock. The Gram Sevak never enters the fields. He goes to the house of the Panchayat President and calls the ryots to him there. As far as I know he has never talked about ADT–27 in the village."

Another farmer made the following comment: "I last saw the Gram Sevak three months ago. He has been here two years. I do not get advice from him, though. If I have a cultivation problem I will listen to the radio, and there they talk about problems different farmers are having and I get advice there. If I have a pest problem, and if I have some money, I will go to a shop owner in Arni and ask his advice about what plant medicine to use."

When I later saw lists of farmers from Marusoor who had received agricultural production loans and fertilizer permits from the block headquarters, it became clear that they were, for the most part, the same few individuals who spoke positively of the Gram Sevak. They were sophisticated enough to understand the requirements for obtaining benefits from the government and wealthy enough to risk trying a new agricultural practice.

My final visit to Marusoor was made shortly after the *sownaavari* season harvest. By that time I had become convinced that the Gram Sevak's estimate of village land planted in ADT–27 was a gross understatement of the actual change that had taken place. This was in marked contrast to the situation of most programs, for which figures usually were sufficiently inflated to make the level of underachievement appear at least moderately respectable.

Of the farmers I talked with on that last visit, most were sufficiently satisfied with ADT–27 to use it again the next year. They were, at the same time, disappointed because the yields they had obtained were well short of the spectacular results they had heard about on the radio. Those who were planting it on their land for the second time were often the most unhappy because, in some cases, their yields had decreased from the level of their first experiments. Nadesa, Egambaram, and Sunderambal, however, were all pleased with their results and were planning to maintain or expand the acreage they would plant in ADT–27 the following year.

These findings confirmed the fears I had developed during the course of my interviews. Though the Department of Agriculture was very explicit in its statements that for maximum yields ADT–27 needs a particular fertilizer mixture in dosages that are very high by local standards, few of the farmers I talked with seemed to have been influenced by these statements. Sunderambal, Nadesa, and Egambaram had all made provisions for additional fertilizer, but most of the others indicated that they were using the same types and quantities of fertilizer that they used with conventional varieties of paddy. The ADT–27 plants were extracting greater quantities of nutrients from the soil and using them more efficiently, but sustained success would require that these nutrients be replaced and supplemented through the use of much larger dosages of fertilizer.

Clearly a revolution in the economic life of Marusoor was not yet at hand. Yet, I left the village that day with the distinct impression that it was approaching more quickly than anyone in the village realized. Almost every farmer I talked to who owned irrigated land with an assured source of water had either already experimented with ADT–27 or planned to do so during a later season. The bureaucracy was still very much wrapped up in its own procedures and traditions, but I saw that even there the demands of its farming constituency were beginning to force its members into new patterns of work and thought.

The last interview I had in Marusoor was with an elderly gentleman who was, in many ways, very conservative. I found, however, that he had planted ADT–27 on his land. As we continued our discussion, I asked him how he learned about new agricultural practices. "I don't," he replied. "I work my fields just as my father did before me. His methods were good and there is no reason to try anything new."

"But," I protested, "you have planted ADT–27, and surely it was not available to your father."

"That is true," he answered, "but my father frequently tried new varieties. I am simply doing as he did. That is nothing new." The heads of the onlookers rocked from side to side in confirmation of the obvious.

 PART THREE

The Dynamics of Bureaucracy

CHAPTER SEVEN

Managing a Field Operation: the Dynamics of Motivation and Control

Bureaucratic Compliance Systems

Fundamental for the study of behavior in any bureaucracy are the interrelated issues of motivation and control. Motivation has to do with the factors that lead individuals to act in a given setting. Types of motivating factors are commonly perceived as being significant in the actions of bureaucrats: a desire for material gain, a desire for ego satisfaction, a desire to avoid mental stress or anxiety, a desire for status recognition, a desire to avoid physical stress or discomfort, and a desire to fulfill internalized social, cultural, or religious norms.

Control is the obverse of motivation. Whereas motivation deals with the forces that lead individuals to act or avoid action in a given situation, control deals with the stimuli that mobilize those forces. In offering a salary contingent on the performance of certain acts, a superior attempts to control—or gain the compliance of—a subordinate by appealing to his (or her) desire for material gain.

The character of a bureaucracy is greatly shaped by the dominant patterns of motivations and control mechanisms that it uses. Etzioni terms the interaction of these two elements a compliance relation,[1] and it is useful to think of the aggregate of a bureaucracy's compliance relations as its compliance system. Etzioni suggests that organizational control can be exercised through the use of physical, material, or symbolic means.[2] He goes on to argue that these means have progressively greater levels of

[1] Amitai Etzioni, *A Comparative Analysis of Complex Organizations* (New York: Free Press, 1961), p. 4.
[2] Amitai Etzioni, *Modern Organizations* (Englewood Cliffs, N.J.: Prentice-Hall, 1964), pp. 59–60.

effectiveness. Physical means tend to force compliance and generate little commitment but great alienation. Material means build up self-oriented interests in conforming and generate moderate amounts of commitment and alienation. Symbolic means tend to convince people and generate high commitment but little alienation. These principles apply, according to Etzioni, "all other things being equal, at least in most cultures." [3]

If each successive means of control provides greater commitment, less alienation, and more effective compliance, then why do not all organizations use symbolic means? Clearly, this relates to the problems involved in getting subordinates to respond to—or be motivated by—symbolic appeals. As Etzioni suggests, there is a general correlation between types of organizations and dominant means used to control their lower ranks. Physical means dominate in prisons and custodial mental hospitals where inmates are present against their wills. Material means dominate in factories and civil service organizations in which routine tasks are performed by personnel interested in financial rewards and security. Symbolic means dominate in voluntary organizations, schools, and religious or ideological-political organizations. [4]

The inclination and capacity to motivate subordinates to respond to successively "higher" forms of appeals depends on more than social role, however. Cultures differ in their evaluations of alternative motives, in their assumptions about basic qualities of men, and in their repertories of techniques for interpersonal influence. Different historical experiences generate and perpetuate distinctive myths about how specific groups of men behave and how they must be managed. And different ideological traditions generate an impressive range of techniques for inculcating new values, commitments, and modes of behavior. Thus a sociologically defined category of worker that might in one setting be seen by superiors as responsive only to physical threat could very well be successfully controlled by symbolic means in a different setting.

The nature and effectiveness of a compliance system is of particular importance in the management of a field organization that depends on agents who are geographically remote from one another. Since conventional physical surveillance is impossible under these circumstances, alternative compliance mechanisms must be used. Frederick Frey has sug-

---

[3] *Ibid.*   [4] *Ibid.*

gested three compliance mechanisms that have been used to maintain indirect control over the behavior of physically inaccessible field agents.[5]

The first, *material incentive control*, is achieved by arranging the terms of a field agent's employment in such a way that it is to his personal advantage to fulfill the requirements of his agency. In isolated areas where government activities are at a low level, for example, a man can be hired as a tax collector and be told that he is responsible for the remission of a specific quantity of tax money every year, the understanding being that he can keep anything he collects above the quota. The tax collector thus has a strong personal incentive to carry out the government's tax collection program as long as he can extract from people in his jurisdiction amounts substantially in excess of his quota. Material incentive control relies on a direct appeal to the motives of material gain. Indeed the mechanism is defined in terms of its motivational basis.

The second compliance mechanism, *feedback control*, is achieved by requiring the field agent to send in regular reports on his activities. His reports can be checked for internal inconsistencies, and physical verifications can be made on a small sample of reported activities. This system's major limitation is the need to translate the activities of the field agent into measurable *quantitative* units. A rural extension agent may be required to report, among other things, how many agricultural demonstrations he has performed, how many farmers he has persuaded to adopt a new seed, and how many acres he has induced them to plant with that seed. Where the work involved has a heavy *qualitative* component, feedback control is frequently unable to provide an accurate accounting of the degree to which field agents are actually accomplishing the agency's goals.

Feedback control can be linked to one or a combination of several motivational forces: the desire for material gain, the desire for ego satisfaction, the desire to avoid mental stress, the desire to fulfill certain kinds of norms. What becomes critical from a motivational perspective is the set of rewards and sanctions that are used in response to more or less satisfactory feedback. Thus, a superlative report might provoke public

---

[5] *Concepts of Development Administration and Strategy Implications for Behavioral Change* (Massachusetts Institute of Technology: Mimeographed, n.d.), pp. 2–14. The following analysis draws on Frey's typology, though modifications have been made both in terminology and in conceptualization.

praise, a financial bonus, a promotion, a reduced set of future targets, an increased set of future targets, or no response at all.

Preprogrammed control, the third type, is achieved by persuading the individual field agent to accept and internalize the goals and methods of his agency. This is generally accomplished through an intensive training program and maintained by newsletters, periodic reunions, refresher training, and other techniques designed to foster and sustain a strong esprit de corps. The agent is sent to the field with general instructions and the hope that his high ideals and motivation will lead him to act in ways that fulfill the goals of the agency. He is not assigned specific quantified targets, but is instead told to work in whatever ways seem to foster the broad goals of his agency, given the situation in which he finds himself. He is thus allowed a great deal of discretionary freedom of action and is encouraged to work toward results that are qualitative, as well as quantitative, in nature.

Only a limited range of motivating factors can be associated with preprogrammed control. The conscious appeal is almost always to the field agent's desire to meet norms he has internalized in the process of his training and probationary work. A variety of techniques are used to encourage the field agent to identify his personal self-esteem and social status with the satisfaction of those norms. A considerable sense of elitism is frequently associated with preprogrammed control. A major source of identification with one's cadre derives from the unusual capacity of its members to perform effectively without any apparent administrative control. The Indian Civil Service was a classic case of a preprogrammed field cadre and its successor, The Indian Administrative Service, has maintained the tradition. The Peace Corps is another example of an agency that has relied heavily on preprogrammed control in the handling of its field workers.

Because material incentive, feedback, and preprogrammed control mechanisms are likely to be based on distinctive motivational appeals, there are rather severe limits on the extent to which they can be combined in the management of any one group of field agents. Preprogrammed control, for example, depends on the desire of the field worker to justify the high degree of trust placed in him as an individual and as a member of his cadre. Feedback control, on the other hand, makes explicit the limitations of trust and confidence which are placed in the field agent. Thus when a field agent who has been preprogrammed suddenly finds himself increasingly controlled by feedback procedures, he finds it correspondingly difficult to maintain the spirit and sense of pride which are essential underpinnings of preprogrammed control systems.[6]

The Evolution of a Compliance System

The four models of organization that impinge on Tamil development administration have distinctive approaches to motivation, control, and compliance mechanisms. The interaction of these models in the evolution of administrative processes has been of fundamental importance in shaping the character of bureaucratic behavior in this setting.

The dharmic tradition idealizes allegiance to duty, but sees man as being constantly tempted to forsake his duty because of laziness or a desire to maximize his short-term material gain. Powerful social controls keep these predilections within bounds in village society, but a more overt and menacing form of threat is necessary when one moves to larger jurisdictions. Danda, the coercive face of authority, is the necessary complement to dharma. Fear and threat are the mechanisms one uses to provoke adherence to duty among recalcitrant and devious subordinates.

The British colonial tradition contains two separate models of motivation and control, one for the top tier of primarily British officers, and the other for lower-level Indian subordinates. The British officer was trained to internalize and value a set of norms that emphasized his honesty, independence of mind, physical vigor, and capacity for decision making. The structure in which he operated reinforced adherence to these norms by assuring him of high status recognition and very considerable material benefits.

There was little sense, however, that Indians would respond to appeals directed at internalized norms. Rather, the British saw their Indian subordinates as being motivated to act contrary to the interests of the bureaucracy by their desire to avoid mental and physical stress and their

---

[6] Etzioni makes a similar point in his *Comparative Analysis of Complex Organizations*. Referring more generally to means used to make subordinates comply, he differentiates between coercive, remunerative, and normative power. He then argues that most organizations tend to emphasize only one means of power because "when two kinds of power are emphasized at the same time, over the same subject group, they tend to neutralize each other." (p. 7)

desire to fulfill the social norms of family and caste loyalty. Powerful sanctions against such actions were, as a result, felt to be necessary to keep their behavior within acceptable bounds. The role of the remote, harsh, and punitive father became the model to be emulated by the British official in the management of his subordinates.

The dharmic and British colonial traditions mutually reinforced each other in their approaches to compliance systems. Dharmic perceptions show skepticism of man's voluntary adherence to duty because self-denial is so central to the fulfillment of personal dharma. British skepticism was based more on widely shared perceptions of laziness and deviousness as integral features of Indian character. The shared expectations that subordinates could not be trusted fostered and perpetuated a pattern of close and openly abusive supervision among both British and Indian officials. Sustaining fear of a remote, powerful, and threatening authority figure was seen to be an essential ingredient in the task of "extracting work from subordinates."

Mechanisms for exacting compliance of field agents in the colonial bureaucracy reflected the dual character of control in the colonial tradition. Collectors were preprogrammed representatives of the elite ICS cadre who were broadly trusted to implement the goals and norms that they developed in training and probationary service. At lower levels in the hierarchy, however, reliance was placed on an elaborate system of feedback control. Checks and cross-checks, as well as frequent physical inspections, were used in efforts to maintain satisfactory levels of compliance. The Tottenham system of record keeping, with its elaborate procedures for keeping track of documents, reflects one aspect of this highly sophisticated set of mechanisms.

A radically different approach to motivation and control permeates the community development tradition. The nature of extension work is not consistent with close supervision and control of field agents through the requirement of detailed quantitative feedback. Rather, the extension worker must be allowed flexibility to meet specific needs of his own villages. Thus, preprogrammed control is the appropriate mechanism for assuring compliance, and the tradition has always emphasized the importance of lengthy training programs. The most effective motivating force for extension workers is believed to be the ego satisfaction that one derives from guiding a dynamic program of social and economic change. It was recognized that enthusiasm would wax and wane, but extension-team meetings, refresher training courses, and other mechanisms were available to revive sagging spirits.

The Gandhian transformation of the concept of dharma has an important impact on that tradition's approach to motivation and control. Duty, in the Gandhian sense, is not the simple performance of traditionally assigned tasks, but rather the pursuit of what Gandhi called Truth. Though his use of that term is ambiguous, Gandhi seems to have had in mind an ordering of society that undergoes change but retains a fundamental harmony. Thus, each individual must endeavor to follow a path of right action that will be consonant with this pattern of development. Gandhi, of course, had his own vision of that pattern, which he propagated broadly in his writings. The ideology thus encouraged the individual to become familiar with Gandhi's world view and then undertake his own pursuit of Truth.

The community development and Gandhian traditions came together in their common concern for training and indoctrination of agents of rural change. Elements of Gandhian thought and practice permeated the community development training organizations.

Intensive training in the precepts and norms of the community development and Gandhian approaches to bureaucracy was thus given to the vast army of young high school graduates who were hired to fill the ranks of the Gram Sevaks. Before assuming their posts they went to training centers for up to two years of intensive education and indoctrination. They were instructed on technical subjects such as agriculture, animal husbandry, and village industries, but they were also infused with the ideals of planned village development, the importance of felt needs, and the role of the Gram Sevak as friend and helper of the peasant. The training emphasized the values of village change, respect for manual work, selfless action, and team effort. Gram Sevaks were taught skills that would presumably be useful in advancing those values and told that they were members of a noble group of trained and dedicated workers. They were made to feel proud of their positions and dedication, and were led to believe that they would be appreciated and respected by coworkers and villagers alike.

Adapting Community Development Processes to the Needs of Feedback Control

The hiring, training, and placement of thousands of new Gram Sevaks within a period of several years represented a major investment not only in a new and exciting development program, but also in an approach to bureaucratic compliance that was revolutionary for India. Young men went out to their block assignments with a dedication, commitment, and determination that had never before been seen in the lower levels of the public service. One to two years of training instilled in them new attitudes toward development and new motivations for undertaking development work.

It was considered impractical or unfeasible, however, to provide extensive training for men who were to fill the middle and upper echelons of the emerging development bureaucracy. The BDOs were to be men who had already gained years of experience in the revenue-dominated district administration of the colonial era. What little training they were given familiarized them with the structure, goals, and ideals of the development effort. DAOs, who were to supervise the burgeoning ranks of AEOs, assumed their jobs on the basis of the seniority they had accumulated in the Department of Agriculture bureaucracy. Both BDOs and DAOs, however, had been trained in, and were practitioners of, traditional close supervision and feedback control of field agents.

Thus, when Gram Sevaks and AEOs met their supervising BDOs and DAOs in the field, their expectations and anticipated working styles were strikingly different. Gram Sevaks and AEOs saw their interactions with the villages as being the primary determinant of their work. The block establishment was thought of as a source of support and as a communication channel. Only in unusual circumstances was it seen as likely to impose constraints. BDOs and DAOs, however, brought with them to the new bureaucratic structure the conventional view of their supervisory role, rooted in the colonial and dharmic traditions.

The structure of the new community development bureaucracy appeared to be ill-conceived from the perspective of the traditional supervisor. The anomalous position of the AEO, whose role was defined as a member of the block "team" under the dual supervision of the BDO and DAO, seemed to threaten the supervisory power of the DAO. The authority of the BDO over the Gram Sevaks was unclear in light of the presence of extension officers who were also of higher rank than the Gram Sevaks, but only partially under the BDO's control. And finally, both BDOs and DAOs were uncertain about how they would be able to exert their supervisory authority and extract work from their subordinates if standards of achievement were to be established from the bottom, rather than the top, of the hierarchy.

The anxieties of the middle- and upper-level supervisors were soon relieved, however, as it became clear that traditional patterns of supervision could still be applied in this new structure. Such integral features of the community development model as targets, reports on extension work, block team meetings, and visits to the field could, they soon discovered, be used as mechanisms of rigorous feedback control.

Though the demise of planning from below may have begun as a result of sincere desires to get the planning process underway quickly, it was accelerated and made irreversible by the need, felt by superior officers imbued with colonial and dharmic approaches to supervision, to have clear standards against which to measure the performance of their subordinates. Target figures, designed to be specific goals which the field worker would himself help to define, rapidly became externally imposed norms against which his performance was to be judged.

In the central offices of the technical agencies, planners began formulating new development programs and assigning targets to the field organization. Soon the initial anxiety of the middle level supervisor about criteria for evaluating his subordinates was replaced by an opposing consideration. His own performance was being evaluated on the basis of his ability to coerce his subordinates into fulfilling their targets. Thus, the more demanding the levels of performance required of his subordinates, the greater the difficulty he would have in achieving a creditable record. So, as an overall state agricultural target came to be broken down into specific targets for Deputy Directors, DAOs, and AEOs, each officer was strongly motivated to minimize the potential of his region and the capacity of his staff in order to keep his own targets to the lowest possible levels.

Targets, then, were not set as a result of what was appropriate to a particular village, but rather as a result of a multistaged negotiation process through which an overall target was broken up into a multitude of

smaller targets. Impressionistic attempts were made at each level to allo-
cate the overall target among the smaller units in proportion to their potential, but the resulting targets were, nevertheless, often inappropriate
to the needs or capacities of specific villages.

The most glaring problems arose, however, when the aggregate of
targets assigned to any one Gram Sevak was considered. When each of
the technical officers on the block team assigned the targets among the
Gram Sevaks, their resulting workload was many times their capacities.
Well over a hundred programs might require implementation, each with
its accompanying educational, organizational, distributional, and record-
keeping components. Some were of real interest and of potential benefit
to the farmers; others held out little prospect of benefit, and villagers
remained indifferent to them.

The relative merit of the programs, however, was not a concern of
the line officer of the colonial tradition. His interest was with extracting
work so as to fulfill targets. In order to achieve maximum response from
their heavily overburdened Gram Sevaks, the BDO and DAOs relied
heavily on the second and third institutionalized structures facilitating
their control requirements.

The periodical report was the second feature of community development administration that was transformed into a tool of intensive feedback control. The field agent operating under a system of preprogrammed control is required to make frequent reports, but their purpose
is to provide information on field conditions, not to serve as a means of
evaluating his work. They are, as a result, apt to be qualitative, discur-
sive, and concerned with program failures and inadequacies, though they
will frequently also contain reports of successful endeavors. In a feedback control system, on the other hand, the primary function of periodical reports is personnel evaluation. As a result, the formats specify in detail the figures that must be provided on achievements made toward a
multitude of targets. Such reports can also be used as sources of information about program success and supply requirements, but the dangers inherent in such use are obvious. When an individual who provides the figures for a report knows that they will be used to evaluate his work, he is
under enormous pressure to falsify his real achievements.

Gram Sevaks writing to their superiors initially for informational purposes soon discovered that their reports were treated primarily as bases for evaluation of their personal performance, and that the evaluation was based on their relative success in achieving targets. The formats on which reports were to be submitted became increasingly quantitative and restrictive in nature, and the character of the reports soon reflected the changing motivational forces operating on field agents. Descriptive, problem-oriented accounts of the trusted representative were replaced by the quantitative reports of the defensive subordinate. The final item on many report forms—"Have you any special difficulty in the implementation of the programme?"—became a token reminder, ignored by almost all respondents, of a type of superior-subordinate communication that was promised in training programs but never effectively achieved in the field.

Twice monthly staff meetings supplemented the control function of targets and periodical reports. Here again, the intended role of these forums as opportunities for open discussion of practical program difficulties was soon almost entirely displaced by the concern of superiors for the achievement of quantitative targets. The presiding officers of such meetings—whether BDO, DAO, or collector—used the occasions to openly criticize and threaten those of their subordinates who had failed to report a minimal performance level. The formal, critical tone of the staff meetings described in chapter 5 was typical of the proceedings. The Polur DAO stood out as a striking exception in his attempt to introduce consideration of substance and work strategy into his sessions.

Finally, "going out on tour" provided a critical supplement to the supervisor's arsenal of control devices. Team leaders in Mayer's Etawah project were expected to visit the field in order to assist and encourage their extension agents. More familiar to the new BDOs and DAOs, however, was the use of such traveling to check on the accuracy of their subordinates' reports. Records were gone over in detail, the presence of supplies under the subordinate's care was physically verified, and performance on specific targets was reviewed and deficiencies pointed out and criticized. Like the Collector on his tour to Sathanur, many officials viewed these field visits as opportunities to symbolize close supervisory techniques and to stimulate their subordinates to more effective action through the desire to avoid further criticism and possible sanction. The

Ranipet DAO was unusual in his attempts to follow up his criticism of a subordinate with an effort to help that subordinate learn how to deal with his administrative problems.

Preprogrammed Workers Respond to Feedback Control

The transformation of the compliance system in development administration from the one envisaged by community development planners to the traditional feedback control mechanisms of colonial bureaucracy radically altered the role of the extension agent. Instead of the incremental efforts to change the attitudes and practices of villagers that were to be at the heart of their extension work, attention had to be focused on achieving highly specific targets: meetings held, fertilizer sold, loans processed, permits issued, and acres planted in new varieties.

Since the use of approved extension methods to inform and persuade farmers of the value of so many schemes was impossibly time-consuming—and in many cases unsuccessful—Gram Sevaks, AEOs, and others involved in the actual implementation of the multitudes of development programs quickly developed three basic strategies for coping with the impossible set of demands placed on them: falsifying or distorting reports; neglecting targets they determined to be of low salience; and using resources under their own control to stimulate farmer participation in unpopular programs. The choice of strategies depended on the nature of the program, the degree of attention it was receiving in the bureaucracy, the motivation of the field agent, and the supervisory enthusiasm of his superior.

The systematic distortion of reports was the usual strategy followed when the chance of their being effectively verified by superiors was low. Activities that were either not carried out or carried out in a perfunctory manner were inflated into significant achievements on paper. AEOs, for example, were expected to conduct Radio Farm Forums each month. They were required to listen with people of a particular village to the evening radio program, "For Farmers," and then discuss with the villagers the relevance of the program's material to their own needs. Though the scheme attracted little attention, and officials in the state Agricultural Information Office did not see it as central to the success of their radio activities, it was still one of the 24 schemes on which the

AEO had to report his monthly progress. The standard method of handling this demand was for the AEO to spend, once or twice a month, a few minutes listening to part of the program in a village where he had to be for other reasons, count the number of villagers listening to the program, and chat briefly with a few of them afterward. He then reported the village, the date, and an acceptable number of participants. That no forum was actually held would not be reflected in the report, nor was the fact likely to be discovered by a superior.

A modified version of this same strategy was frequently applied to acreage targets. When these became matters of special attention, Gram Sevaks and AEOs were required to list individual farmers, their village, and the number of acres planted in a specific crop. Since such lists could be spot-checked by superior officers, reasonable standards of accuracy were generally maintained. Gram Sevaks were supposed to compile the lists as they made their extension rounds. In theory they were to enlist farmers as participants in the program, explain a package of practices to them, and help them fill out "farm plans" containing growing schedules and instructions. More frequently, however, such lists were compiled as the Gram Sevaks were approached by farmers for loans and fertilizer permits which were conditional on the farmer's planting a certain number of acres in the specific variety. Target deficits were made up by calling together small groups of farmers shortly after planting time and adding to one's list the names of those who said they were, on their own initiative, already planting the variety in question. AEOs received reports and lists from the Gram Sevaks and consolidated them; if the total acreage did not meet their targets, they added names from their own lists of individuals who had come to them for fertilizer permits or seeds.

Though targets could not always be completely fulfilled in this way, a large measure of success could be achieved with a minimum of time invested. With the introduction of new varieties that gave dramatically improved yields, the extension agent's problems fulfilling acreage targets were greatly reduced. For the better varieties, reports of full target achievements could generally be compiled from only a partial listing of acres contracted for by individuals who had obtained seed, fertilizer permits, or loans. The extension agents were aware that some individuals would not, in fact, plant the variety for which the fertilizer or credit was given, but the chance that specific evidence of this fact would reach their superiors was quite remote.

Another strategy used by extension agents was to ignore some targets. As the feedback system evolved, they soon came to realize that whereas deficiencies in reports on some targets brought swift and voluble reaction from their superiors, failure to even submit reports on other schemes produced no adverse reactions at all. They then fell into a pattern of ignoring programs their supervisor ignored and emphasizing those he emphasized. Staff meetings gave some clues about which schemes fell into which categories, but even more useful was an elaborate and ubiquitous system of "reminders."

As the numbers of programs, targets, and reports increase within any bureaucracy, the headquarters staff becomes progressively overloaded and, as a result, the processing and analysis of reports becomes less regular, prompt, and consistent. Clerical staffs aggregate figures, analyze discrepancies, and write critical letters relating to programs of concern to their senior officers; they defer actions on less salient programs. Harried clerks and officers in subordinate offices soon discover that delay in filing certain reports will produce prompt demands for immediate submission, whereas delay on other reports may cause no response at all.

Awareness that little or no attention was being given to certain schemes and reports soon began to filter down the hierarchies of Tamil development agencies. The greater the work overload and the frequency of late reporting, the more rapidly this awareness reached the Gram Sevaks. Consequently, it became conventional practice to ignore the initial deadline for many reports. The receipt of an "urgent" and then a "most urgent" reminder, however, made it clear that a particular scheme was being followed closely and that a report had best be made.

In addition to simply not filing reports on some targets, extension agents soon discovered that, when numbers of targets were consolidated onto a single periodical form, some of them were virtually ignored at higher levels of authority, so that gross underachievement produced no complaint from their superiors. On more salient programs, however, moderate underachievement seemed to evoke intense criticism and threats. There was, in short, a de facto scale of allowable underachievement which was a function of program salience. Attention to schemes in terms of that scale made it possible for extension agents to further reduce their actual workloads.

The strategy of selective target fulfillment worked, however, only within a large margin for error. Extension agents had little way of knowing when a particular scheme would suddenly become the subject of the collector's special interest or the concern of a joint director in Madras. Nevertheless, it provided a basis for handling an otherwise unmanageable set of demands and reduced pressure, criticism, and threats from superiors.

The third and perhaps most powerful strategy available to extension agents was the use of resources that were in demand as inducements to farmers to help them with their more intractable targets. Gram Sevaks and AEOs controlled the distribution of seeds, fertilizer permits, pesticides, agricultural implements, and production loans. Though some of these items might be ill-suited to the locality or of no interest to most farmers, others were certain to be in great demand. The extension agent would therefore condition the sale or distribution of a high-demand article on the willingness of the recipient to take a low-demand item with it. As a result of such a quid pro quo, a farmer might count himself fortunate to have obtained a permit to buy fertilizer at a subsidized rate and an AEO would be relieved to have made progress toward fulfilling his target for the sale of green manure seeds nobody wanted. Neither would be particularly disturbed by the fact that the farmer would simply throw out the seeds.

The Vicious Cycle of Intense Supervision

Mechanisms of intense feedback control, then, produced reactions on behalf of extension agents that were counterproductive of real development goals. Deception and coercion replaced dedication and service as the dominant features of extension work.

The tendency of behavior patterns in a closely supervised bureaucracy to degenerate into a "vicious cycle" is well documented.[7] Close supervision fosters alienation that leads to a decline in work habits that

[7] See, for example, Alvin W. Gouldner, *Patterns of Industrial Bureaucracy* (Glencoe, Ill.: The Free Press, 1954), p. 160; Michel Crozier, *The Bureaucratic Phenomenon* (Chicago: Phoenix Books, The University of Chicago Press, 1964), pp. 187–94.

triggers a further intensification of supervision. An especially pernicious cycle developed in Indian development administration, however, when central planning and intense feedback control were imposed on a structure designed to accommodate planning from below and cadres of extension workers who had been preprogrammed to act as autonomous change agents. The cycle can best be understood by first considering the heavy workload imposed on the extension staff.

Two features of Tamil development administration reinforced and aggravated normal bureaucratic predilections to develop new programs without eliminating older and less productive ones. First, no structural mechanism existed to control and coordinate the number and mix of schemes and programs that were centrally planned and passed down through numerous hierarchies for implementation by Gram Sevaks. Even when a single agency such as the Department of Agriculture developed its programs, it did so without the capacity to plan and coordinate their interrelationship at the local level. Second, traditional compliance practices of colonial bureaucracy were to establish heavy demands on subordinates in order to maintain the pressure and threat that were felt to be essential to effective supervision.

The pressures for more programs and targets led to the placement of unmanageable levels of demands on Gram Sevaks and AEOs. Consequently, even allowing for the protective strategies employed by the extension agents, increasing numbers of failures to achieve targets were reported up through the hierarchies. The reaction of superiors in the chains of command to these reports was to intensify the application of feedback control procedures. Monthly reports on a series of targets were to be supplemented by weekly or bi-weekly reports on schemes of special interest. Reports of final achievements (such as acreage planted in a new variety) were to be preceded by preliminary progress reports containing detailed accountings of efforts undertaken.

The increasing amount of time extension agents spent in the preparation of ever-more-detailed, ever-more-frequent reports reinforced their tendency to ignore initial requests and early reminders of reports due. Thus clerical staffs spent increasingly more time in the preparation of depressingly voluminous and angry reminders of mounting urgency. The remedy, then, simply intensified the problem.

It had other effects as well. First, it led to a pervasive alienation and disillusionment among the field workers. As Gram Sevaks and AEOs discovered that they were not trusted to work under a system of preprogrammed compliance, their self-esteem and motivation to carry out agency goals declined. As targets exceeded capabilities and field agents increasingly relied on adaptive strategies that conflicted with real development goals, their alienation from their role and its symbolic rewards became more intense. This led to a progressive lessening of their psychic involvement in their jobs and a weakening of their sense of identification with the agency and its goals.

As the preprogrammed field agents found themselves increasingly deprived of psychic, status, or achievement rewards for performing well in their jobs, they were increasingly inclined to work at the lowest level of output and effectiveness that could be maintained without antagonizing their superiors. As a result, a self-fulfilling prophecy was created. Middle- and upper-level supervisors, imbued with dharmic and colonial assumptions about the laziness and deceitfulness of subordinates, found ample evidence to confirm their views that harsh and threatening techniques were the only effective means of extracting work from subordinates.

In addition, the extension agents' strategies of deception were producing misinformation in reports to higher levels of administration: levels of achievement were inflated and serious problems in implementation of programs were not reported. Middle level supervisors showed little interest in verifying the accuracy of most reports because the aggregation of inflated figures from their subordinates made their own reports look better in the eyes of their superiors. Even on personal inspection tours of village programs, supervisors ignored practical problems and concentrated on the specific and quantitative issues for which they were directly responsible. Operational problems brought to them either by extension agents or by specific villagers were treated as self-interested excuses or complaints, which were not representative of actual conditions. Thus, the quantitative indicators that showed up on consolidated reports encouraged the view that programs were operating reasonably well and could be brought up to the mark with a little more pressure on the subordinate staff. Inquiries into the need for modification of programs were thus discouraged, and the planners turned their attention to the creation of more new programs.

Conclusion

In brief, then, the attempt to reform a colonial bureaucracy by preprogramming a band of young workers with the ideologies of Gandhi and the community development movement was swamped by the pervasive domination of colonial and dharmic models of compliance systems. The result was not simply a routinization of procedure, but a severe and progressive deterioration of performance, integrity, and morale.

Notwithstanding this general pattern of deterioration, some individuals retained allegiance to the idealism of the Gandhian and community development traditions. Some Gram Sevaks continued to derive, as late as 1968, distinct satisfaction from their self-images as altruistic workers concerned with the well-being of the people. Their working patterns, however, departed so strikingly from the norms established in the community development ideology that they had had to undergo tortured changes in views to sustain their motivation. They argued that the need to develop the country quickly, combined with the low level of literacy and knowledge in the villages, had made classical extension efforts impractical. Instead, rational criteria had to be used to define village needs and then villagers had to be forced to try new ways of working. Thus, the focus on targets became a necessary part of the program. One of the few highly motivated Grams Sevaks in North Arcot sustained his own enthusiasm by reconciling the community development ideal with the realities of a closely supervised feedback control system in the following terms:

> There is no contradiction between extension methods and our actual work. The government gives us only very useful schemes but the people, because of their ignorance and illiteracy, often don't understand them. So it is our duty to make them understand the usefulness of these schemes. In the beginning they won't come forward, but if we compel them once or twice then they will realize the benefits and come forward themselves.

The DAO from Polur was perhaps the most enthusiastic advocate of using human relations techniques to motivate subordinates. In his efforts to create a sense of personal involvement and enthusiasm among his subordinates, however, he found that his attention to their needs and

practical difficulties had a very different effect. Just as the colonial mythology suggested, they worked less effectively because his lack of
harshness was interpreted as a "weak-kneed policy." In his brief tenure
at Polur he managed to dispel that notion, but he was not able to noticeably modify the enthusiasm or commitment of his subordinates.

The Ranipet DAO took a less doctrinaire but perhaps more successful approach to the problem of motivation. By beginning with the normal and expected criticism, he made it clear to his subordinates that he
had within him the harshness to command respect. This made it possible
for him to then listen to problems and involve his subordinates. Although he was personally concerned with bringing about change in agricultural production patterns, his rhetoric contained little that was designed to stimulate the same concern in his subordinates. He did,
however, often encourage them to help farmers with specific needs, even
at the expense of meeting their targets.

Perhaps the most important counterforce to the pervasive pressures
for close supervision, with all of its behavioral consequences, came from
a group of senior officers in the Department of Agriculture who had
received advanced training in the west, been actively involved in the
Ford Foundation's project in Tanjore District, or both. They were
largely responsible, for example, for a March 1967 meeting of DAOs in
which, for the first time, joint directors actively solicited the views of
their subordinates. A tone of openness was established and a great deal
of information about the actual operation of many programs, and the effect of many administrative decisions, was conveyed from district
officers to the planners in the Madras headquarters.

Three years later, in the course of a brief follow-up visit to North
Arcot, I found evidence that this new openness to information from the
field had begun to have significant consequences for the agricultural bureaucracy. Many of the most onerous features of the AEOs' work situations had been improved. Though the number of reports they were
responsible for had not noticeably declined, they had been given assistants to help in the handling of block agricultural depot accounts. And
though the number of schemes and programs on the books appeared to
be only slightly reduced, the AEOs were clear in their own minds that
the HYVP was a priority program and that work on many of the other

schemes could legitimately be slighted. As a result of these changes and the general success of agricultural programs, there was a noticeable improvement in the AEOs' sense of involvement and self-esteem.

The continually worsening plight of the Gram Sevaks was in striking contrast to the modest improvement in the position of the AEOs. The numbers and levels of their targets had, if anything, increased, but nothing had been done to augment the resources at their command. Most simply continued to try to carry out their duty in a proper way. For those who had, three years earlier, still retained an enthusiasm and a sense of hope, the enthusiasm had waned and hopes had, in most cases, turned to despair.

CHAPTER EIGHT

Between Bureaucrats and Farmers: The Transformation of Extension Work

Relationships between farmers and field agents of the Tamil Nadu development administration provided the critical link between the elaborate structures of government and the citizens whose behavior they were designed to influence. Just as culture, historical experience, and ideology infused the inner workings of the bureaucracy with a distinctive character, so also did they shape the link between bureaucracy and citizenry. The arrival of Gram Sevaks in the rural areas of Tamil Nadu was seen by villagers in the light of years of accumulated experience with government representatives. Village perceptions were filtered through a distinctive dharmic view of their own community's structure and its relationship to outsiders. The extension agents had been widely trained in appropriate community development approaches to farmers, but the realities of bureaucratic pressures under which they operated seemed to require strategies of village work that were radically different from those they had been trained to follow. These conflicting traditions, perceptions, ideals and pressures had all to be worked out in the context of a changing political climate. The state's representative institutions created effective channels for the expression of public discontent to executive leadership, and in the late 1950s, these institutions were supplemented by publicly elected panchayats and panchayat union councils with direct powers over block bureaucracies. The pattern of behavior that evolved out of these circumstances is the subject of this chapter.

175

Three Views of the Farmer-Bureaucrat Relationship

The firmness, harshness, and impersonality used by British authorities in handling their Indian subordinates were in turn employed by those subordinates in their dealing with villagers. This colonial approach, which became known disparagingly among community development workers as "the official way," was a product both of the paternalism of colonial bureaucracy and of the related sense that fear and awe were the emotions most likely to cause farmers to pay taxes and otherwise cooperate with the representative of an extractive bureaucracy.

"The official way" of dealing with citizens relied on the authority and prestige of office. Bureaucrats made no attempt to gain the friendship or trust of villagers. They emphasized instead their own superior status and their ability to cause uncooperative citizens endless difficulty and expense. Officials felt themselves accountable to superior officers and in the service of an administrative machine that was not ultimately responsible to the people. Their goals and those of the agency were to control citizens and to extract resources from them. The bureaucracy's strict rules became weapons in the hands of its officials. Elaborate regulations facilitated their postures of aloof and formal inflexibility, but were easily forgotten when they received offers of "gifts" to appease the harshness of their feelings.

Villagers thus had a well-established image of the exploitative, extractive, and disdainful government worker which they naturally applied to extension agents when they first began to appear in rural areas. Gram Sevaks and AEOs, however, behaved in ways that reflected a radically different tradition. Community development ideology was explicit in its insistence that extension workers not perpetuate "the official way" of dealing with villagers. They were instead to be friends and helpers of farmers, stimulating their sense of the possible and helping them find practical ways to formulate and achieve goals that had previously been beyond consideration. Gram Sevaks were to be accountable to their villagers, with whom they would work toward a common goal of village development. The government hierarchy was to be a source of financial, technical, and programmatic support that would help villagers achieve their newly defined goals. The influence of Gram Sevaks was to depend not on their official position and their ability to induce fear, but on their qualities of sincerity and technical competence, and on their power to mobilize government resources for the benefit of their villages.

Even where Gram Sevaks and AEOs managed to break down stereotypes of government servants, however, powerful barriers to effective extension relationships remained. Two of these barriers were products of distinctive village perceptions of the role that extension agents were performing and of the implications of taking advice.

Tamil farmers are deeply conscious of their duties as members of specific families, castes, and villages. They perform those duties in the knowledge that their activities help to sustain the order, balance, and stability of their community. Extension agents who entered their villages had no rights or duties in the community, but it was clear that they did have rights and duties relating to their membership in some remote government bureaucracy. Thus, village farmers saw extension agents as performing a set of duties designed to perpetuate and benefit institutions of government. There was no reason, either logically or historically, for them to believe that the activities of extension agents were also designed to benefit the villages. Indeed, in a world that had never known sustained secular economic growth, there was every reason to believe that activities which would benefit external institutions of government would impose equivalent costs on the village community.

Attitudes toward the roles of extension agents were further shaped by the assumption that any individual does his duty either because tradition imposes it on him or because it has been assigned to him by a recognized authority figure. Just as a Tamil farmer would not be concerned about the consequences of the performance of his duty, so also would he not expect an extension agent to be concerned with calculating the consequences of his work.

Thus, when urged by extension agents to plant a particular variety of rice or use a specific quantity of a special fertilizer, Tamil farmers were highly skeptical of protestations that such advice was for their own benefit. Rather, they were much more likely to believe that extension agents were simply repeating advice they had been told by superiors to give, that the extension agents didn't know—and were not concerned with knowing—what the consequences of following their advice would be, and that following their advice would be more likely to benefit the government than the farmer or his village. One extension official who had worked with rare diligence to influence agricultural practices expressed his frustrations in the following terms. "Often farmers will think that I give them advice only because it is my duty. They think I must do so in payment for my salary. Since they think my advice is not given because of real interest in them, they are reluctant to take it."

A second aspect of villagers' perceptions that complicated extension work involved connotations that were associated with giving and taking advice. Recognizing a broad range of highly technical specializations is a characteristic of modern society. The resident of a sophisticated and complex urban center is used to acting on a mechanic's advice about his carburetor, a dentist's advice about his teeth, a plumber's advice about his drainage pipes, or an electronic specialist's advice about his television set. The scope of each specialist's expertise is clearly defined, however, and neither a recognition of inferior social status nor a willingness to accept nonspecialized advice is implied by the resident when he does as the technical expert advises.

For the Tamil villager, on the other hand, the recognition of status and authority is not highly differentiated. Superior status within caste and family hierarchies implies superior knowledge and understanding of the complex interrelationship of activities that is the dharmic ordering of the village. In giving advice, one assumes a superior position in this general hierarchy; in accepting and acting on advice, one accepts and validates that assumption. Thus, in villages like Marusoor, farmers are extremely cautious about giving and receiving advice. Information does circulate within the village on such matters as agricultural production practices, but the giving and receiving of advice is carefully limited to established hierarchies within castes, families, and factions.

Extension agents who went out to these villages had acquired some measure of expertise in agriculture through their training programs. Gram Sevaks were taught general principles of scientific farming practice, whereas AEOs had gone through the much more rigorous and detailed training associated with the requirements of a B.S. degree in Agriculture. Their reception in villages was conditioned, however, much more by their age, caste status, and family reputation than by their technical competence. The homes of most extension agents were remote from the villages to which they were assigned. Even where their caste and family status could be meaningfully identified by villagers, it rarely afforded them sufficient standing to give advice to prominent farmers.

The role of extension agents prescribed in community development ideology, then, not only conflicted with notions of duty current in a bureaucracy dominated by dharmic and colonial traditions, but was also foreign to fundamental assumptions, perceptions, and practices of the villages to which the agents were assigned. It should perhaps not be surprising to discover that the pressures of the bureaucracy quickly led to modifications of extension agents' village behavior that brought their activities into line with the assumptions and expectations of villagers. An examination of the impact of closely supervised feedback control on the village work of extension agents helps to illuminate this process.

The Vicious Cycle and Extension Agent–Farmer Relations

The pattern of close supervision through feedback control over extension agents deeply influenced their relationships with their village clients. Initial efforts to determine felt needs of farmers and to assist in cooperative planning for village development were quickly displaced by efforts to fulfill specific targets, irrespective of the particular needs or demands of individual villages. This change in goals shaped the patterns of activity that Gram Sevaks and AEOs followed in their village work. Since approved extension methods of informing farmers about, and persuading them to undertake, so many schemes would be impossibly time-consuming and would probably be unsuccessful in generating responses to many programs, extension agents developed alternative strategies. As noted in chapter 7, they distorted and inflated reports about what they accomplished in their villages, they concentrated their energies on targets that seemed to be engaging the attention of their superiors, and they conditioned their help for farmers on the willingness of those farmers to facilitate their meeting of particularly burdensome targets.

As the number of schemes expanded, so also did the number and variety of goods and services that extension agents had under their control. They became responsible not only for the sale of fertilizer, seeds, and pesticides, but also for the rental of equipment, the approval of loan applications, and the granting of permits to buy special varieties of fertilizer. Thus, conducting sales, rentals, and executing documents came to take up an increasing share of extension agents' time. It was in the skillful and occasionally manipulative conduct of these tasks that progress on targets could most effectively be made. The roles of Gram Sevaks and AEOs shifted, in short, from agricultural extension to agricultural administration. They acted not as agents of social and economic change, but rather as brokers who provided certain farmers with an accessible link to a procedurally complex development-oriented government.

An analysis of samples of working days for both Gram Sevaks and AEOs in 1967 and 1968 confirms the impression that they played primarily administrative and brokerage roles. The working days of 75 Gram Sevaks and 36 AEOs serving in North Arcot District were sampled by means of a one-page mailed form on which respondents were to indicate their primary activity during each half-hour period of the day they received the form. Each Gram Sevak was sampled once and each AEO twice. Responses were received from 50 Gram Sevaks (a 67 percent return rate). Forty-two of the 72 forms (58 percent) sent to AEOs were returned.

Gram Sevaks were found to spend 38 percent of their time in bureaucratic maintenance tasks, travel, and miscellaneous activities, and 10 percent in nonagricultural program work (see Table 8-1). Of the remaining 52 percent of their time that was available for work with farmers, 34 percent was devoted to agricultural administration and only 18 percent to agricultural extension. Among AEOs, 57 percent of the working time was spent in bureaucratic maintenance, travel, and miscellaneous activities, and 4 percent in nonagricultural program work. Of the 39 percent of their time spent with farmers, 25 percent was devoted to agricultural administration and only 14 percent to agricultural extension.

The relationships most extension agents developed with village farmers were, as these data suggest, built around exchanges of goods and services that were to the mutual advantage of both parties. Though they did not become integrated into intravillage exchange relationships, extension agents established themselves as useful centers of commercial exchange. Farmers dealt with them not out of friendship or the commitment of a social relationship, but rather out of commercial calculation. The resources of Gram Sevaks and AEOs were sufficiently rich and

Table 8-1. Time Use of Gram Sevaks and AEOs (in percent)

ACTIVITY	GRAM SEVAKS		AEOs	
Agricultural Administration	34		25	
Processing loans and permits		(25)		(9)
Sales, distribution of supplies		(3)		(7)
Inspecting loan-supported projects		(2)		(3)
Seed Procurement		(–)		(–)
Other work for farmers		(4)		(6)
Agricultural Extension	18		14	
General		(14)		(7)
Inspections, demonstrations		(4)		(7)
Bureaucratic Maintenance	14		33	
Mail, reports		(6)		(14)
Staff meetings		(4)		(2)
Verifying stocks and accounts		(2)		(9)
Discussions with superiors		(2)		(5)
Discussions with subordinates		(–)		(3)
Travel	18		20	
Nonagricultural Program Work	10		4	
Miscellaneous	6		4	
TOTALS	100		100	

varied to make it worthwhile to help them in carrying out their bureau-cratic duties.

Thus, as administration and commerce replaced extension as the primary concerns of Gram Sevaks and AEOs, their roles became increasingly comprehensible to villagers. As representatives of a closely supervised bureaucracy implementing centrally planned programs, they *were* doing their duties as explicated by their superiors, and they could not afford to be concerned about the consequences of following the advice they gave. It also became clear, however, that whatever the government's interest in defining the duties of the extension agents, the carrying out of those duties could be beneficial to farmers who knew how to take advantage of them.

Many villages maintained, then, what turned out to be a reasonably accurate view of extension worker roles. They understood and accepted the institutional imperatives of the Gram Sevaks' lives. Sunderambal was willing to help Marusoor's Gram Sevak with his targets because he, in return, provided her with useful services. The relationship was much more congenial than were most dealings with government servants because the Gram Sevak lacked the coercive power and the extractive duties that typified most government incursions into the village.

The differences in style and tone between "the official way" and the commercial approach to farmers were well articulated by a BDO who had himself worked as an extension agent.

The key to being a successful BDO is adjustment. For example, if a farmer comes for some seed and there is none in stock, we can't just say, "There's no stock. Go away," as we would be able to do by the rules. Rather we must treat the person politely and explain to him that there is no stock and if he will return the following month, stock should be available. This kind of treatment is necessary because the following day I may have to go to that fellow and ask him to grow ADT–27 and if I acted like an official he would pay no attention to me.

Or, for another example, if a farmer comes for seed at 5:30 in the evening and our closing time is 5:00, we cannot just say that our working hours are over; we have to oblige him. Otherwise when we go to him the next day with a request to grow ADT–27, he will say, "What sir? When I came to you yesterday you said your working hours were over. Well, my working hours are over for today," and he will walk away!

In approaching farmers we must first cultivate their affection. We can't just go to them and say: "Apply such and such a fertilizer." Instead we must first sit down with them and inquire about their family and talk with them. Then, after we have associated ourselves with them for some time, we can ask them to use this fertilizer. Otherwise they will say, "I have already heard that advice. You can go." We can't use the official way.

When a new extension officer comes, he may start to behave in an official manner with the people, but within two months and often much sooner he comes to realize his position through experience. He will then begin to work in a better way. If he just stops working with the people, I will go to him and tell him that it is his duty to do this work, and that the Collector is pressing me for these results. Usually they will understand my position and will work in order to help me.

In performing the brokerage and administrative functions, extension agents play an important role in agricultural development. These activities are especially important in countries such as India, where programs depend so heavily on government agencies to control, and frequently to carry out, the distribution of such critical commodities as fertilizer, pesticides, and seeds. Even most production loans are administered by government agencies. In the case of the HYVP, the administrative and commercial activities required to assure timely distribution of production inputs were absolutely necessary—if not sufficient—conditions for the success of the program. The relative efficiency and effectiveness with which these activities were carried on reflects very favorably on the diligence of the extension staffs and the administration of the feedback control system. The experience in North Arcot in 1967 confirmed the positive reputation in India of Tamil Nadu bureaucracy.

Nevertheless, the administrative-commercial roles of extension agents left much to be desired. Distributive functions had been placed in the hands of public bureaucracies because of a pervasive Indian distrust of the profit-oriented middleman. This suspicion is probably not entirely misplaced, for in a nongrowth economy, greatest distributive profit opportunities lie not in expanding one's market but rather in creating large profit margins by the shrewd manipulation of inventories and prices in fluxuating markets. Public bureaucracies, however, generate their own distributive pathologies. In this case, supplies were established by planners calculating what farmers ought to want, and sales were calculated by extension agents to maximize the fulfillment of targets. As a result, short supplies of high-demand items were used to induce the movement of items for which there was no demand. Thus, farmers still ended up paying premium prices for the commodities, but the premiums were in unwanted purchases which helped extension workers meet their targets rather than in cash which swelled the excess profits of the private retailer.

Perhaps the most serious effect of the administrative-commercial role the extension agents adopted was that it further complicated their already difficult task of providing authentic extension support to farmers. Seen as representatives of a governmental interest that was external to the village, extension agents were treated properly, but with caution. They, in turn, were polite and respectful, but confined by their commercial role. Pursuit of targets was both time-consuming and frequently in conflict with the best interests of farmers.

Thus the slow and painful process of developing legitimacy as "servants of the villages" rarely advanced beyond preliminary stages. Gram Sevaks were supposed to live in the villages they served, but only rarely were they and their families integrated into tightly knit village social structures. Rather than endure the intense isolation of living in a foreign village, they frequently found housing for their families in the less restrictive social atmospheres of nearby towns.

One of the great ironies of extension work was that Gram Sevaks, though greatly overprogrammed, were often underworked. Their targets frequently went unmet, but at the same time they felt unable to keep busy in the villages. During one informal discussion I had with several Gram Sevaks, they wanted to know if it was true that American extension agents felt they did not have enough time to do their village work. As one of them explained, "When we are in the village the time is heavy on our hands and we are concerned about what to do with ourselves." This reflects the very limited character of village relationships which most Gram Sevaks were able to develop as commercial agents. The challenges of extension work were enormous, but the roles appropriate to such work could not easily be reconciled with the demands of meeting externally imposed targets.

Agricultural Bureaucracy and Agricultural Change

The rapid spread of ADT–27 throughout North Arcot District in 1967 and 1968 was not, then, the result of the extension work of Gram Sevaks and AEOs. Their efforts at education, demonstration, and persuasion were minimal and generally ineffectual. Rather, a three-step pattern of dissemination produced this remarkable pattern of innovation.

First, each DAO had developed and maintained relationships with a number of "progressive" farmers living in his jurisdiction. These farmers were generally wealthy, educated, and powerful men whose contacts and influence extended beyond their own villages. Among the farmers the Ranipet DAO knew personally, for example, were the district's public prosecutor from Dusi village and Govindaraj, the Panchayat President of Nesal. Frequently such men would be familiar with new agricultural developments and would search out their DAO to learn more about them. Indeed, I found that many progressive farmers in North Arcot had been in regular contact with district agricultural offices since before the community development program began.

When ADT–27 was first introduced, this small group of farmers, who had some notions of scientific agriculture and ample wealth to absorb the cost of experiments that failed, were the first to use it. In almost all cases initial experiments with it were strikingly successful. In almost any soil condition and with almost any application of fertilizer, ADT–27 seemed to yield better results than conventional varieties.

The second step in the diffusion of ADT–27 in North Arcot was through a complex pattern of marriage relationships that span the district's villages. In south India, marriages are generally arranged between families of the same caste living in different villages. The new wife forsakes her childhood home for that of her husband, but visits are frequently exchanged between households during festivals and important family events. These intervillage patterns of communication were repeatedly cited to me as the means by which ADT–27 was first introduced into villages throughout the district. It was through such visits, for example, that the new variety reached Marusoor from Nesal. A similar network of family marriage relationships brought K. M. Krishnaswamy Naicker—known in Marusoor as Arni Krishnan—into contact with Shanmugam, the young AEO who convinced him to try ADT–27.

Unlike the commercial-administrative relationships maintained by most extension agents with their village farmers, these family relationships were characterized by shared interests and mutual trust. Sunderambal's son-in-law, Sunderamurthy, was a much more persuasive agent of change than was Marusoor's Gram Sevak, though the latter was presumably more competent technically.

The third step in the diffusion of ADT–27 was the result of observation and informal discussion within villages of North Arcot. In Dusi, farmers observed the fields of the public prosecutor, talked with the men who supervised his agricultural work, and decided to try the variety in a part of their fields. In Marusoor, farmers saw the successes of first Arni Krishnan, then Sunderambal, and then Nadesa Udaiyar. They talked with these village leaders, listened to radio programs about the variety, and then decided to experiment with it on their own fields.

Thus, extension work went on with great effect while Gram Sevaks and AEOs were busy attending to agricultural administration and the fulfilling of their targets. There were serious drawbacks to this pattern of diffusion, however, for at each step in the process the accuracy and detail of the information transmitted deteriorated badly. Progressive farmers who had dealt directly with DAOs were generally well informed about the best "package of practices" to use in growing ADT–27. Most farmers in Marusoor, however, had learned about the variety at third or fourth hand. Their methods of preparing seedbeds, transplanting, and applying fertilizer produced yields that were well below what they might have obtained.

Inadequate use of fertilizer was to become a particularly serious problem. New varieties such as ADT–27 produced spectacular yields in large part because they make extensive and efficient use of soil nutrients. It is essential that these nutrients be replaced by fertilizers if high levels of productivity are to be sustained. Thus, farmers who used conventional fertilizer in their initial experiments with ADT–27 found that their yields dropped off in subsequent seasons unless they invested in greater amounts of fertilizer.

Varieties that offered still greater yield increases were introduced into North Arcot after I left in 1968. These proved to be less adaptable than ADT–27, and farmers who planted them were faced by severe problems involving scheduling, pest control, and irrigation practices that they did not understand. A few were able to get advice and help from the DAOs, but most lacked access to professional advice that they felt would be reliable.

When I returned to North Arcot in 1971, many farmers seemed to be undergoing a crisis of confidence in their attitudes toward agricultural modernization. What had begun as a low-risk venture with ADT–27 had proven to be a much greater gamble with other varieties. Gram Sevaks, limited in technical skills and hemmed in by an ever-growing set of targets, could make only marginal contributions to their needs. AEOs, with greater technical abilities and an administrative hierarchy that had begun to respond to the realities of the field situation, offered somewhat greater hope.

In Marusoor, I found that disillusionment had become widespread. In the wake of numerous problems with new varieties, many farmers had gone back to planting the seeds that they had been using before ADT–27 made its spectacular appearance. They had become involved in a pattern of ecological change that they did not understand or know how to manage. Unable to get trustworthy technical advice, it was perhaps inevitable that they would turn back to agricultural patterns that were more familiar and reliable.

CHAPTER NINE

Cognitive Models and the Rationalization of Ritualistic Behavior

The basic behavior patterns of Gram Sevaks, AEOs, and other members of block extension teams were largely shaped by the demands, pressures, incentives, and controls under which they operated. These factors were the products of two processes of interaction between institutional and cognitive forces. First, the organizational structure of community development bureaucracy, shaped generally by the requirements of rural reconstruction, was given specific form by the imperatives of community development ideology. Second, the vicious cycle of ritual behavior evolved out of bureaucratic response patterns to the conflicting approaches to motivation and control of the British colonial, dharmic, community development, and Gandhian cognitive models of organization.

A third aspect of institutional and cognitive interaction, the process of cognitive adjustment to empirical pressures and realities, further shaped and defined behavioral patterns in Tamil community development bureaucracy. Individuals strive to maintain balance and order between their cognitive and behavioral worlds.[1] Bureaucrats thus seek to develop and sustain a world view that is consistent with their perceptions of their working roles. Where dissonance or imbalance develop between beliefs and attitudes on the one hand and perceptions of reality on the other, numerous cognitive mechanisms exist for restoring balance or reducing dissonance. Beliefs and attitudes can be changed, reality can be misperceived, or the salience of either beliefs and attitudes or the incongrous aspects of reality can be reduced.

Preprogrammed control develops, through its training programs, a

---

[1] For an introduction to balance and dissonance approaches to attitude change, see Roger Brown, "Three Models of Attitude Change" in *New Directions in Psychology*, no. 1 (1965).

cognitive framework that gives meaning and direction to bureaucratic activities. The individual is encouraged, in such symbolic incentive systems, to identify strongly with his organization, its goals, and the significance and value of his own work. Individuals who are motivated by
material incentives—as in most systems of feedback control—may identify positively with their organization, but are likely to attribute little
cognitive saliency to their own working role.

The problems of cognitive adjustment are especially important for
the individual who is trapped in the activities of a system that has developed a vicious cycle of close supervision and ritualistic response. One's
activities in such situations frequently become so distorted by intensive
supervisory pressures that they come into direct and obvious conflict
with the stated goals of the organization. Three cognitive mechanisms
can be useful—either separately or in combination—in maintaining balance in this type of situation. First is that of psychic withdrawal from
one's working role. One works automatically, without considering the effect of what one is doing. Second, one can derive satisfaction not from
the work itself, but from the material and social opportunities it gener-
ates. Third, one can misperceive the nature of one's work so that it does
seem valuable and meaingful. The classic means of doing this is, in the
words of Robert Merton,

> transference of the sentiments from the aims of the organization onto the
> particular details of behavior required by the rules. Adherence to the rules,
> originally conceived as a means, become transformed into an end-in-itself;
> there occurs the familiar process of displacement of goals whereby "an in-
> strumental value becomes a terminal value." [2]

Cognitive adjustments to reality are strengthened and made more vi-
able when they become part of a comprehensive world view. For
members of Tamil extension bureaucracy, who were faced with the pervasive dissonance between the ideology of community development and
the reality of their own work behavior, dharmic ideology provided a familiar world view that not only condoned, but extolled as positive values, psychic withdrawal from one's work and the displacement of goals
from organizational aims to "the particular details of behavior required
by the rules."

[2] Robert Merton, "Bureaucratic Structure and Personality," in Merton, *Social Theory and Social Structure* (Glencoe, Ill.: Free Press, 1949), p. 155.

Many of the ritualistic behavioral patterns among Tamil community development bureaucrats were defended in terms that were fully consistent with the dharmic code. Expressed values focused on the performance of specifically defined actions, for example, and duty was generally defined as the fulfillment of specific targets. Consequences of specific actions were not calculated on the grounds that higher authorities had thought through the implications of patterns of duty assignments and that all of these, when taken together, would produce positive results. Duties were widely seen as being of equal importance and not subject to ranking in terms of relative priorities.

It is a difficult task, however, to move from the proposition that perceptions of bureaucrats are consonant with dharmic views to the proposition that dharmic views give specific shape, strength, and persistence to the cognitive framework that sustains ritualistic bureaucratic behavior. One means of providing evidence of such a relationship is by eliciting statements from bureaucrats that show elements of the cognitive frameworks they use to support and explain their own behavioral patterns. The specific means of eliciting such statements will vary with the thought processes and styles of communication in individual cultures.

In India, as in many traditional societies, one of the most important styles used in the transmission of cultural norms is the story. Both folk tales and stories out of the great tradition provide standards and reflect implicit assumptions. Indeed, it is the process of drawing analogs from stories—as well as other sources—that forms a dominant means of reasoning in Indian society. It is useful, then, to explore stories as a potential source for information about the cognitive structuring of attitudes and values relating to the performance of bureaucratic duty. Clearly, however, these should be stories chosen and told by bureaucrats themselves. As part of a questionnaire that was administered to 351 extension and clerical personnel in block headquarters throughout North Arcot District, each respondent was asked the following open-ended question: "What story would you tell to your younger brother in order to give him a good example of proper performance of duty? Tell the story briefly in the space below." [3]

[3] The questionnaire was in Tamil and most of the stories written in response to this question were also in Tamil. Versions of stories which appear in this chapter were jointly translated by K. Sivakumar and the author.

Such a question was especially appropriate in the cultural context of Tamil Nadu for three reasons. First, it is widely held among Tamils that giving advice is the most effective method for changing attitudes. Second, giving advice is the appropriate role of a family status superior, and the elder-brother–younger-brother relationship is familiar to most respondents. Indeed, the most effective Tamil political leader of the 1960s, C. N. Annadurai, head of the Dravida Munnetra Kazhagam (DMK) and Chief Minister of the state from 1967 until his death in 1969, used with great effect the fact that the shortened form of his name, "Anna," is the Tamil word for elder brother. A major channel for the development of party morale and information was "Anna's" regular letters, published in the party's magazines, to his "tambigul"—younger brothers—containing advice and exhortations to further service and accomplishments. Third, as we have suggested, the story provides a dominant cultural vehicle for the persuasive proffering of advice in Tamil Nadu and throughout India.

The appropriateness of this item as a means of eliciting information from respondents is perhaps best attested to by the fact that, of 351 respondents, 247 provided coherent stories in response.

A much more complex question, however, is: what do these stories really tell us about the attitudes, values, and cognitive frameworks of the respondents? It is well to be clear, first of all, about what the stories do not do.

First, they cannot be taken as *sources* of attitudes. Though stories *can* influence the formulation of attitudes, they can just as well serve as ex post facto means of legitimizing and refining already-held attitudes. Thus, as an individual acquires points of view and patterns of behavior, he is attracted by and inclined to remember stories that support those views. The stories may be retrieved from his childhood recollections or they may be more recent products of adult experience.

Second, it is risky to assume that each story accurately reflects the attitudes of the individual who told it. A respondent may have told the only appropriate story he could remember at the time—a story that had stayed with him not because its moral particularly appealed to him, but simply because it was an arresting or memorable story or because he had heard it recently. Alternatively, he could have chosen a story, knowing it would be read by a foreigner, which would reflect well on his nation or his linguistic and cultural community.

More subtly, the story may reflect certain attitudes of the person telling it but conflict with some of his other attitudes. The analyst, then, is in danger of focusing on the "wrong" moral or theme in the story if his goal is to draw conclusions about the attitudinal ramifications of the story for the person who told it.

Finally, since stories are presumably of greater importance in the transmission of traditional Hindu culture than they are in western culture or in more modern forms of Indian thought, there is some danger that they will reflect a disproportionate share of traditional attitudes. What is striking, however, is the degree to which nontraditional sources have been tapped for stories about duty. Even when the content and media of cultural transmission change, the style of transmission shows remarkable continuity. Gandhi, in trying to modify attitudes toward duty, wrote stories of his own "experiments with truth." The DMK, in its attempts to change Tamil social and political attitudes, turns primarily to film stories. Even the Department of Agriculture, in its propaganda efforts, has been strikingly successful in its use of stories dramatized as radio plays.

With all of these cautions, however, the stories are highly revealing if they are used with appropriate care.

First, they provide evidence as to the cultural traditions that have reached and stayed with these respondents.

Second, they provide evidence of the form and content of the traditions as they are received at this level, and of the meanings that have been attributed to them. Fortunately, in the summaries of the stories given by the respondents, morals are frequently made explicit.

Third, they provide, when compared to the original versions, indications of how stories have been shaped to fit the requirements of local attitudinal patterns. This is of special interest in the case of stories from western sources which have, for some reason, become known in India.

Fourth, they provide us with a sense of what kinds of situations were seen as important and problematical. Certain themes recur in many of the stories, suggesting that they represent key issues in the proper performance of duty.

Fifth, the stories also give us a sense of what issues were generally ignored in considerations of duty. Clearly this is a culturally relative kind of insight, but for the western observer it is of great interest to discover what is *not* in these stories.

Finally, the stories taken together can legitimately be used as indicators of attitudinal patterns toward duty among the respondents. Responses of 247 government servants provide a wide range of stories, and patterns within this range are reasonably clear. Though there are undoubtedly examples to the contrary, dissonance theory suggests that an individual is not likely to recall and retell a story which he perceives as advocating views that are incompatible with his own.

The stories related by respondents to this questionnaire are of great intrinsic interest and value simply because of their richness in variety and detail. Their usefulness as data is further enhanced when they are analyzed quantitatively along several dimensions. The 247 responses that formed coherent stories with a set of related events leading to a conclusion were all coded with respect to each of the following issues:

1. On what grounds does the main character in the story determine (or ought he to determine) what his duty is in the given situation?

2. What is the nature of the dilemma or conflict posed in the story?

3. How does proper action relate to the consequences of that action? Each of these three dimensions will be discussed separately in the remainder of this chapter, drawing liberally on respondents' stories for illustrative purposes.

In addition, the main focus of each response, whether it constituted a coherent story or not, was coded by source: the cultural tradition from which it was drawn. The results (see Table 9–1) give an indication of the diversity of traditions that served as sources for the stories. Nearly one-half were drawn from traditional Indian sources. In addition, many of the stories from modern Indian sources reflect traditional dilemmas and attitudes.

Table 9–2 summarizes the categories into which stories were divided with respect to the basis on which duty was appropriately determined. In 24 percent of the stories this dimension was ambiguous or did not fit any of the five major categories. Of the remaining stories, 47 percent (36 percent of the total) showed duty being defined by the *role* of the person involved, and an additional 20 percent (15 percent of the total)

Table 9-1. Cultural Traditions from Which Stories Were Drawn

SOURCE OF PRIMARY RESPONSE	NUMBER	PERCENTAGE
Traditional Indian sources	165	47
Non-Tamil epics	(75)	(21)
Tamil stories of the great tradition	(35)	(10)
Indian folktales	(55)	(16)
Modern Indian sources	98	28
Gandhi	(41)	(12)
Other modern historical figures	(12)	(3)
Films, true stories, and stories made up by respondents	(45)	(13)
Western sources	31	9
Bible	(17)	(5)
Other	(14)	(4)
Other: unidentified or none	57	16
TOTALS	351	100

had it defined by obedience to a status superior; a specific form of role-determined norm-setting. Examples from each category will help to clarify the specific issues involved.

1. *Duty defined by known role requirements.* The traditional means of identifying occupational duty is through knowledge of caste role expectations. This pattern was most frequently reflected in stories relating to the duties of Kshatriyas, who are warriors by occupation. Indeed, more respondents chose to recount an episode from the *Bhagavad Gita* than any other single story. As one version relates,

A fight was going on between the Pandavas and the Gowravas. Arjuna refused to kill the Gowravas because they were his relatives, and also because Bhismer and Thronar were his teachers. At that time

Table 9-2. The Means by Which Duty is Defined

	NUMBER	PERCENTAGE
1. Defined by known role requirements	89	36
2. Defined by a status superior	38	15
3. Defined in terms of general social norms: thrift, politeness, cooperation, etc.	25	10
4. Defined by inner-directed moral principle such as honesty or justice	31	13
5. Defined by results of analysis of specific situation	4	2
6. Other, ambiguous	60	24
TOTAL	247	100

Krishna told him that on the battlefield he should think of them not as his relatives but only as his enemies. He said, "It is the duty of Kshatriyas to fight. So you should fight without thinking about the consequences."

So, everyone should do his duty without fail.

Other stories drew analogies about duty from the role expectations of animals. Two versions of the following story emphasize different points, both of which are central to the *dharmic* concept of duty: first, that one failure in the performance of duty leads to other failures; second that the order of the system is destroyed when one person does a duty appropriate to the role of another.

I

A dhobi [washerman] was living with a donkey and a dog. The dog did his duty by watching the dhobi's house. One day the dhobi did not give food to the dog. That night some thieves came to his house and took away all the clothes. The dog, though he saw the thieves, did nothing to stop them; but the donkey, instead of the dog, cried out. This made the dhobi angry and he beat the donkey soundly. Only the next morning did he realize that he had beaten the donkey for its good work and that his own failure to give food to the dog was the reason for its failure to catch the thieves.

2

There was a dhobi in a village. He kept a donkey to carry the clothes and a dog to watch his house. The donkey felt that the dog didn't do any work; he only barked during the night. One day a thief came to rob the house and the dog was sleeping. The donkey cried out when he saw the thief, but the dhobi thought that the donkey was just disturbing his sleep. So, he went out and beat the donkey.

What we understand from this is that everyone must only do his own duty. We should not do other people's duty.

Two stories from the Tamil classics that were told by a number of respondents emphasize justice as being a paramount duty of kingship. The first is from the most popular of Tamil epics, the *Silappadigaram:*

Pandiyan Neduzhiyan was ruling Madurai. One day a soldier came to him and told him that they had arrested Kovalan, who was trying to sell the queen's jewels after stealing them. The king without thinking whether that was true or not ordered them to cut off Kovalan's head. When Kannagi, Kovalan's wife, heard this she came to the king and told him the jewels were hers and she proved it by showing the remaining jewels. The king immediately died, after accusing himself of having failed in his duty. So, we should not fail in our duty.

What is striking about the second of these Tamil stories—and of many others in the genre—is not the king's interpretation of what is just (the appropriateness of the punishment is immediately self-evident to the Tamil reader), but rather that the king is selfless enough to implement the punishment:

Porkai Pandiyan was ruling Madurai. He used to go out in disguise during the night to see to the people's welfare. One night when he was doing this, he heard a newly-married couple talking. The wife was saying, "You are going out. How can I stay alone?" The husband replied, "There is no need to worry in Pandiyan's kingdom," and went away. So, the king watched that house regularly at night from that day on. The husband returned from his trip. He and his wife were talking very happily. When the king heard a male voice he was shocked and knocked at the door. The husband opened the door and asked, "Who is there?" The king recognized the husband and discovered his mistake. Therefore he knocked on all the doors in that street. The next day the people reported the matter to him at court. The king asked them what punishment he should give to that person. They told him that a hand should be cut off. Immediately the king cut off his own hand with his sword. The people understood his action and praised him for doing his duty.

Other stories emphasize duties associated with family role expectations. The following story illustrates a use of Gandhi's life story to support traditional values. The clerk who wrote it departed from Gandhi's version in a number of respects, most strikingly in recalling that it was Gandhi's mother, rather than his father, who died on this occasion.

Gandhi never failed to do his duty to his parents nor did he disobey them. He got married. Even after his marriage he was doing his duty to his parents. One night he was talking with his wife when his mother was on her death bed. The next day when Gandhi came to see her, his mother was dead. Then he felt very badly about that because when he failed to do his duty (to be with his mother) his mother died. I will tell my brother that, like Gandhi, he should do his duty. If he fails in his duty then he will suffer because of that in the future.

2. *Duty defined by a status superior.* In many of the stories featuring parent-child relationships, the duty of the child is part of a general role expectation. In others, however, a specific duty is defined explicitly by a

parent. An episode of the *Ramayana* that was recounted by many respondents illustrates this means of identifying one's duty.

King Dasarathan had four sons. Raman was eldest and the others were Bharathan, Laxmannan, and Chatrukuna. Dasarathan decided to make Raman king since he had himself gotten old. Bharathan, though younger than Raman, was Karkayi's first-born son. She asked Dasarathan to grant her two wishes. The first one was that Raman should go to the forest for fourteen years and the second was that Bharathan should be made the king. But when Bharathan returned from a trip, he was very angry with his mother. He went to the forest and asked Raman to come back . . . But Raman refused to return since he wanted to keep his father's promises.

Stories drawn from Gandhi's autobiography were also used to emphasize obedience to a superior as a central aspect of duty.

Gandhi went to England; his mother gave him a necklace and told him he should not remove it from his neck. He did as his mother asked him. In England, others criticized him because of that necklace, but he wore it throughout his stay in order to obey his mother's word. Like that we should also obey our parents. That is our duty.

3. *Duty defined in terms of social norms.* Of the stories that emphasize general social norms, over 80 percent focus on cooperation and the importance of unity. The two most frequently told stories were the following:

I

Four bulls were living in a forest. A lion came to kill and eat them. The bulls joined together and drove the lion from that place. The bulls had some misunderstanding and started to go out separately. The lion killed them one by one and ate them. From this we understand that we should cooperate with one another.

2

An old man was living with his seven sons. When he was on his death bed his sons asked him to divide the property equally among all of them. Then he asked his sons to break a bundle of sticks together. They were not able to do so. But when they were asked to break the sticks separately they were able to break them. The old man advised them that union is strength, and asked them to live together.

In the balanced and ordered life of the traditional village, one's caste, family, and occupational duties do not presumably come into conflict. The following story suggests the use of a general social norm to resolve a modern conflict between family and occupational duties.

Vallabhbhai Patel, who took part in the Independence movement, was a lawyer. He received a telegram when he was arguing a case. He did not lose heart when he read the telegram. He continued his argument and won the case. At the end, the judge asked him what was in the telegram. He said, "My wife has died," and shed tears. Hearing this, the judge was surprised and asked him, "Is the client more important than your wife?" Patel said, "Yes, my first duty is to complete the work I have started." I will tell this and ask my brother to do his duty well.

4. *Duty defined by inner-directed moral principle.* Besides using Gandhian stories to illustrate unquestioning obedience to a superior, many respondents used themes from Gandhi's life to illustrate adherence to principle in defiance of authority (usually a teacher).

One day Gandhi went to school. That day there was a spelling test. The teacher asked the boys to write the spelling of some words on the blackboard. Gandhi was not able to spell "kettle" correctly. The teacher made signs to Gandhi, asking him to copy from the next boy, but Gandhi didn't do that. We should also be truthful like Gandhi in our work.

Though most of the stories in this category were either about or were popularized by Gandhi, some others were from western sources, most frequently from the Bible.

"Love others as you love yourself." I will tell an example told by Christ. One day a person came to Christ and told him that he was acting according to the Bible and asked him what else he should do. Christ replied, "Love others as you love yourself." The man asked Christ, "Who is the other person?" Christ replied, "One person was travelling. On his way he fell down and suffered some injuries. Parichyan and Sathuchyan were also traveling that way. They did not do anything for the injured person and went on their way. But Samariyon, who came that way, went to him, applied medicine to his wounds, gave him food, took him on his donkey, and left him in a nearby chowltry [building for ceremonies]." In the same way you too should love others.

5. *Duty defined by results of analysis.* Since in the west stories do not constitute an important medium for the transmission of attitudes toward duty, it is difficult to imagine what a sample of stories told by American respondents would look like. Impressionistically, however, one would ex-

pect to find a significant number of stories in which the main character analyzes a situation and acts in a way that is calculated to produce a certain result. Indeed, many of Æsop's Fables, stories by Uncle Remus, and other favorite childhood tales emphasize this quality. Among the stories told by these Tamil respondents, however, only 2 percent suggest that duty should be determined in this way, and these stories seem to be drawn heavily from western sources. One of these, told by a number of respondents, is about the Dutch boy and the dike:

The people in Holland have built a wall around their city so that sea water will not come inside their city. One day a small boy was walking along the wall and he saw a small hole in that wall. He thought that through the hole water would come inside the city. He covered that hole with his hand throughout the night. The next morning, people found him and they appreciated his sense of duty to the country. His name and action became part of history from that day on. Only his adherence to his duty made it possible for the government to repair that wall and save all of them.

Another is a folk tale:

A crow felt very thirsty. It was not able to get any water. It went around the city. There was no water anywhere. Behind a house there was some water in a pot. The crow thought for some time. Then it took small stones and put them in the pot. The water level came up. The crow drank the water. That we also should live wisely is the main point of the story.

Another, more traditional, rendering of this story failed to take note of the creativity in finding a solution, but rather simply pointed out that, when faced with difficulties, one must "try again and again."

Patterns of Dilemmas and Conflicts

A second dimension along which the 246 stories were categorized is the type of dilemma or conflict emphasized in the story. Clearly, not all stories have definable conflicts. Many simply emphasize the importance or benefits of doing one's duty well, without explicitly suggesting why one might be inclined to do otherwise:

A rich landlord was living in a village. He employed a man to assist him and that man was doing his duties well. All of a sudden he died.

The landlord did everything for him and helped his family. He got all of that help because he did his duty well.

Though about one-third of the stories cannot be reliably categorized along this dimension, the remaining 163 stories are of sufficient interest to more than compensate for the lack of complete coverage. Table 9-3 summarizes the basic categories and the results of coding the stories along this dimension.

Table 9-3. Major Dilemma or Conflict in Story

	NUMBER	PERCENTAGE
1. Duty conflicts with well-being of family, caste members, or close friends.	54	22
2. Duty conflicts with personal well-being.	50	20
3. Duty conflicts with laziness, inattention, or neglect.	36	15
4. Duty conflicts with fear, timidity, or cowardice.	3	1
5. Duty conflicts with one's perceived prestige, honor, respect, or status.	6	2
6. Duty is not clear; dilemma is to decide on proper action through analysis or creative thought.	3	1
7. Other dilemma or conflict.	16	7
8. Nature of dilemma or conflict is not clear, or there are more than one important dilemmas.	78	32
TOTAL	246	100

1. *Duty conflicts with well-being of family.* In 22 percent of the stories, duty conflicts with the well-being of the family, caste members, or close friends of the main character. Three of the most popular stories taken from the epics were generally used to point out this conflict. For many of the respondents, this was the major point of the *Bhagavad Gita* story:

The Pandavas and the Gowravas had started their fight. There were more soldiers on the Gowravas' side than on the Pandavas'. Lord Krishna was driving Arjuna's chariot. Arjuna was a great person in all respects. Arjuna's grandfather and his former teachers were fighting on the Gowravas' side. Seeing them, Arjuna told Krishna, who was driving the chariot, "Krishna! I do not want to kill and fight when I see the opposing army of the Gowravas. The reason is that it is not good to kill my teachers, grandfathers, and relatives." Krishna replied, "The war is not between Pandavas and Gowravas. It is a war between *Dharma* and *Adharma*. It is your duty to uphold *Dharma* by crushing *Adharma*. Only by doing your duty can you be relieved of your *karma*." After receiving this advice Arjuna fought with them and killed the Gowravas. The Pandavas won the war. *Dharma* won over *Adharma*.

Another well-known story, from the *Mahabharata,* focuses on the conflict between duty and love for brothers that was faced by Karnan:

Karnan did not know that the Pandavas were his own brothers. He was with the Gowravas and was working for them. At the time of the war he came to know, through his mother, Kunthi Devi, that the Pandavas were his brothers. But still, with the feeling that he should do his duty, he helped the Gowravas and fought against his brothers. I will make my brother understand that duty is more important than love for brothers.

The most popular of the Tamil stories of kings who not only have an unerring sense of what is just, but also the duty-consciousness to implement justice unhesitatingly, is the story of Manuneethi Cholan:

Manuneethi Cholan was ruling Chola kingdom. One day his son went along the street in a chariot. On his way, he did not notice a cow and her calf and, as a result, he killed the calf by driving the chariot over it. The cow came to the palace and rang the bell. The king came out and learned that his son has killed the calf. Then he ordered that his son be killed in the same way in order that justice be done for the cow.

In this way, when we are doing our duty we should not think about our relations or anything else. Duty is more important.

The Tamil film industry has capitalized heavily on the strong appeal of this type of dilemma. The modern reincarnation of the epic theme usually involves the conflict between the duty of the policeman and his family loyalty. The two stories that follow are representative of this genre:

I

A rich man named Gopal Mudaliar was living in a certain place. He had two sons. The younger son tried several times to learn from his father how he was getting his money, but he did not get a satisfactory reply. He did not like to keep quiet. One day he went to the police and told them about his father and about his own suffering. Then he was given an appointment as a police officer. After ten years he became a member of the CID [Criminal Investigation Division]. One day he caught a person who had a smuggled watch. He questioned him and from him he learned where he bought that watch. He went to search that place. He found that the watch belonged to his father. He arrested his own father. So, duty is important for everyone.

2

A poor farmer was living in a village. Because of his poverty he sold his second son to the rich man of the village. The boy who was in the rich man's house never studied and became very bad. He started to drink and spend all of his money in bad ways. Later he became poor. But then he became the head of a gang of thieves and the whole village was afraid of him. The first son of that farmer suffered from poverty, got a government scholarship and studied well. He became a big CID officer. He came to his native place and inquired about the well-being of the people. He did not tell the people that he was a big CID officer. He came to know, when his father was about to die, that the great thief in the village was his brother. Nevertheless, he captured him and put him in jail. He did not fail in his duty.

2. *Duty conflicts with personal well-being.* In 20 percent of the stories the hero is faced with the dilemma of doing his duty or doing what is in his short-term personal interest. Many of the epics extoll selfless performance of duty. Raman deprives himself of the throne and the comforts of urban living for fourteen years, and Porkai Pandiyan unhesitatingly cuts off his own arm. Even Gandhi's adherence to his pledges of avoiding meat, wine, and prostitutes was frequently seen as a form of self-deprivation. The statement that he renounced these things in England "though it was very cold," reflects a commonly held view that meat and liquor are necessary for survival in a cold climate.

The military tradition provides further examples of this conflict. A subtle but significant feature of most of these stories is that the emphasis is not on bravery and courage but rather on a strong sense of duty. In the following story, the dream is assumed to be a reliable guide to what will happen if Velaiyadevan is firm in his sense of duty:

Velaiyadevan was a General under Veerapandiya Kattabhoman. He was ordered to fight against the British. He went to his house to take leave of his wife. She asked him not to go until the following day because she had had a bad dream [which foretold of his death on that very day]. But Velaiyadevan refused to stay and went out to fight against the British that same day. He obeyed the King's order and did his duty. He died in the battle.

Many of the stories emphasizing cooperation point out the necessity of self-sacrifice in the interests of unity. One respondent concluded his story about the bundle of sticks with this speech by the father: "You were able to break the sticks easily one by one, but when they were together you were not able to break them. In like manner, you should also live together and sacrifice something so that you can accommodate others."

3. *Duty conflicts with laziness or neglect.* The third common conflict in the stories was that between proper action and laziness, inattention, non-persistence, or unexplained neglect. A story of a vendor illustrates the point.

In a village, an old lady was selling sweets in the street. She felt thirst and, after putting her basket near a tree, she went to get a drink of water from a well nearby. A crow came and took one sweet. A dog took another and rolled the basket in the street so that all the sweets came out of the basket. When she found this, the old lady felt very sad. Her duty was to sell correctly. Apart from that, she might have placed her basket in the house nearby or might have taken it to the well with her. She lost all the money because of her failure to do her duty well and correctly. So, our duty is to do one thing correctly and well.

Several respondents held up ants as models of active, hard-working creatures:

1

We should be active in our lives like the ants. Ants never waste their time. To be successful in our lives it is essential that we be active.

2

Look at the ants. How small they are! They get their own food briskly. They store their food for the rainy season. So you also should be smart and brisk, and should do your duty as do the ants.

4. *Duty conflicts with fear or cowardice.* Courage and bravery figured in only three of the stories. One of these reflects perceptions of the ever-presence of violence in America:

Swamy Vivekananda's sense of duty is the best example. Swamy Vivekananda was to talk in Chicago. At that time, one city man got permission to test Vivekananda's courage and his sense of duty. While he was speaking in the meeting, a bullet went very close to his ear. But still, Vivekananda did not fail in his duty and did not stop the speech.

5. *Duty conflicts with a sense of honor or prestige.* Six of the stories present conflicts between duty and the maintenance of prestige, honor,

status, or respect. Gandhi emphasized the honorable nature of all work and this principle is reflected in many of the extension training programs. One Gram Sevak wrote:

We should do any work without looking down on that work. Example: A man was ashamed to sweep his own house when he was alone. So the house became dirty and there was a lot of dust in it. But if he had tried to sweep his own house, the house would have been clear and free of dust. So I will advise [my brother] to do any work and ask him to do it well. That is his duty.

6. *Duty requires creativity or analysis.* Only three of the stories presented situations in which the hero was to use creativity or analysis to solve a problem or achieve a desirable result. The story of the crow that put pebbles in a pot to raise the water level is perhaps the best example of this theme.

The Role of Consequences

In many respects, the most interesting theme in these stories concerns the consequences of doing one's duty properly. In more than a third of the stories, the hero does his duty in the face of evidence that the short-term material consequences of his actions will be negative (Table 9-4, categories 1, 2, and 3). In an additional 31 percent of the stories, duty is specified but the consequences of action are not mentioned—again suggesting the irrelevance of results for what must be done. Fewer than one-fourth of the stories show material consequences as important and logically linked to behavior.

1. *Negative consequences of proper action should not be considered.* The traditional view is simply that one should do one's duty without thought of consequences. The cosmic ordering of dharma is such that ultimate good will result from adherence to duty no matter what the temporal and immediate consequences may appear to be. It is a great virtue to do one's duty in a proper way even when all of the temporal consequences promise to be negative. The 19 percent of the stories that are in the first category reflect this tradition. Again, the paramount example is from the *Bhagavad Gita:*

Arjuna refused to fight in the battle when he discovered that among the important persons who were fighting against him in the war were his relatives, brothers, and teachers.

Table 9-4. The Role of Consequences

	NUMBER	PERCENTAGE
1. Negative consequences of proper action should not be considered	48	19
2. Negative material consequences of proper action are compensated for by religious or moral reward	19	8
3. Unanticipated forces overcome negative expectations of proper action	27	11
4. Consequences not related to proper action	77	31
5. Correct action is logically linked to favorable material consequences	59	24
6. The role or significance of consequences is ambiguous	17	7
TOTALS	247	100

At that time Krishna told him many things from the *Bhagavad Gita*. He said "I am responsible for all things. I am doing everything. You need not worry about this. Everyone has to do his duty when the time comes for it." Immediately, Arjuna realized his duty and started to fight. Krishna made clear to Arjuna that if you want to benefit everyone by removing bad and evil things, then without hesitating each person should do his duty. He made Arjuna fight by explaining the *Bhagavad Gita*.

This theme is also prominent in many versions of other traditional Hindu stories: Raman abandons his realm without hesitation or thought on the grounds that it was his duty to do so; Velaiyadevan and others of the martial tradition go to war, not out of bravery and courage or a determination to defeat the enemy, but because their duty so dictates. Karnan, in the following story, fights against his relatives and on the side of evil because it is his duty to do so:

When Kunthi heard from Krishna that Karnan was her son, she went to Karnan and told him that she was his mother. For some time they exchanged affection and then Kunthi asked him to come and join with the Pandavas and fight against Duriyothanan. Karnan answered, "Mother, though Duriyothanan is doing the wrong things, he helped me to become a great man. So I will not do any harm to him by joining with you. My duty requires me to help Duriyothanan." He refused to join with her and the Pandavas.

One of the most frequently told western stories highlights the virtue both of obedience and of performance of duty without regard to consequences:

A sailor brought up his son with love and affection. He never took him in the ship because he was very young. The boy lived with his mother in the house. The sailor was ready to go on tour. He took his son and sailed to other countries. The ship was sailing on the sea. The sailor kept his son in a room and asked him to stay there until he called for him. The ship caught fire. The room in which the sailor's son was staying also caught fire. He called for his father several times. But he did not move from that room. So, he died in the fire. He did his duty as it was told to him by his father. As a result of that he had to give his very life. You also do your duty even if you are faced by difficulties.

2. *Negative material consequences of proper action are compensated for by religious or moral reward.* The great heroes—the Arjunas, Ramans, and Karnans—manage to do their duty without thought of consequences, simply because it is their duty. Many of the stories seem to recognize, however, that the general run of fallible humans require greater incentive to keep them on the path of dharma. The traditional incentive is tied to the doctrine of karma, which suggests that one's position in future lives will be determined by one's behavior in the current life. As the version of the Arjuna-Krishna encounter quoted earlier notes, "Only by doing your duty can you be relieved of your *karma*." The 3 percent of the stories in category 2 reflect this tradition.

3. *Unanticipated forces overcome negative expectations of proper action.* Far more common in the stories is the lesson that if one does one's duty without thought of consequences the results will somehow turn out well.

Two brothers, Raman and Krishnan, were living in a village and they were unemployed. One day a saint came to that village. They asked the saint to help them get a job. He told them to go daily and sit on the steps of the government office. So, both went every morning and returned every evening, as the saint asked them to do. Krishnan did not like to do this and one day he did not go. But Raman sat on the steps daily. The officer asked why he was doing so. Raman told him that he was sitting there to get a job. Then the officer asked him about his brother. Raman told him that his brother did not like to sit there. The officer appreciated Raman's endurance and gave him a job. "Do not expect results. Do your duty well and the results will be good."

4. *Consequences are not related to proper action.* Nearly a third of the stories do not refer to the consequences of proper action. In many of these, the impact of the story comes from the demonstration of continuing allegiance to duty in even the most trying of circumstances.

She is a mother. She wanted her son to be a great person, so she avoided all harshness in raising him. As a result, the son began doing whatever he wanted. He wanted to marry a dancer in his town, but the dancer thought he was too young for her. To get rid of him, she asked him to bring her the eyes of his mother if he wanted to marry her. The son plucked out the eyes of his mother and was running with them to the dancer's house when he tripped on a rock and fell. Seeing this happen, his mother's eyes filled with tears and said, "Be careful, son. Don't fall down. You might hurt yourself."

The mother was always thinking of her son's well-being, as was her duty.

5. *Action logically linked to consequences*. Twenty-four percent of the stories show a direct concern for consequences and establish direct links between proper action and good results, or between improper action and bad results. Again, most of these stories do not come from traditional Indian sources. The major exception to this generalization is the stories emphasizing cooperation and demonstrating the bad results of disunity. Several respondents related the story of the Good Samaritan and a number drew from the parable of the Prodigal Son the moral that straying from the path of obedience to elders will produce bad consequences:

One man was living with his two sons. The eldest was a good man, but the youngest son used to be friendly with bad people. He became bad himself and asked his father to give him his share in the property. He spent all his money in bad ways in a short time. He took a job as a swine keeper and he was given only the worst food. Only then did he recognize his bad ways and return to his father.
I will ask my brother to obey the words of his elders in his life.

A number of stories of more recent Indian origin also emphasize the importance of results. Stories of bureaucrats doing their duties properly, for example, frequently stress the promotions that follow. A final story illustrates the impact of modern ideas on traditional themes. Obedience to parents, an unquestioned duty in traditional stories, is here supported by reference to the positive results that come from taking the advice of a modern technical specialist.

There lived a *ryot* [farmer] named Murugan in a village. He always believed that he knew everything and he never paid any attention to the advice of others. A Gram Sevak went to that village. He advised the ryots about the benefits of modern techniques of agriculture. The ryots followed his advice and as a result they were able to get more benefits. But Murugan laughed at the Gram Sevak and did not follow his advice. So he was not able to get better results.

Like the other people who benefited from the Gram Sevak's advice, you will also be successful in your life if you obey and follow your father's words in your youth.

So always act in accordance with the words of your parents.

 CHAPTER TEN

Planning, Implementation, and the Management of Change

Cognitive models of organization were not only influential in shaping the behavior of Tamil extension agents and their supervisors, but program planners and agency executives were also subjected to conflicting models of authority roles, planning imperatives, and management strategies. In order to explore these issues it is necessary to go somewhat beyond the four primary models of organization presented in chapter 2. At this level, the conflicts are between dharmic notions and a set of ideas that are inherent in much western development thought and administrative practice. Although these western ideas are implicit in the community development literature, they must be made explicit if the contrasts with dharmic views are to emerge clearly.

Two Approaches to Planning, Implementation, and Change

The dharmic tradition recognizes two distinct but complementary faces of temporal authority. Dharma itself is the proper ordering of relationships into patterns approximating the cosmic order. Danda is the coercive power that enforces the dharmic order.

Dharmic authority is concerned primarily with providing order and coherence to a system through defining relationships in terms of duties and rights *as they ought to be*. For a government officer responsible for evolving developmental policy and programs, this becomes a matter of defining what his government department ought to provide and to whom. In creating a model of appropriate relationships, he must be concerned with defining duties and rights of specific groups of citizens as well as those of functionaries in the bureaucracy.

208

The criteria by which one determines appropriate patterns of duties and rights are implicitly clear in the dharmic framework. One strives for a comprehensive formulation of programs within one's frame of reference because all segments of a community must be integrated into the whole. One strives for a form of distributive justice that will sustain the existing balance between components of the society. And, one develops program and policy goals on the basis of what justice, balance, and order require, not on the basis of resources and capabilities. All of these considerations are inherent in the goal of providing a normative model for one aspect of human interaction. One's success is judged not in terms of the reality-orientation, practicality, or cost-effectiveness of the proposals, but rather in terms of their internal coherence, comprehensiveness, and distributive justice.

Implicit within the dharmic cognitive model of organizations is the goal of maintaining a steady-state system. Stability, balance, and order are traditionally achieved through the preservation of the existing structure of relationships and the maintenance of a roughly constant flow of goods and services. Variations in population levels and agricultural production create strains, but the system has built-in mechanisms designed to cope with such fluctuations.

Also part of the dharmic model is a distrust of competition and incentives. In a steady-state economy, striving for one's own economic self-interest seriously threatens the social order, for increased wealth is seen as being achieved only at the expense of others. As George M. Foster has pointed out very persuasively, the "image of limited good" that is associated with steady-state economies emphasizes the importance of self-restraint.[1] Dharmic tradition, as a highly developed Indian rationale for sustaining a steady-state society, sees individual duty and individual economic self-interest as opposing values. The one sustains social order; the other threatens to tear it apart.

Dharmic ordering of society cannot, therefore, be based on a structuring of personal incentives. Individuals and groups must receive rights and compensations commensurate with their duties, but they must be restrained from trying to achieve excess benefits. If an individual tries to perform duties in excess of those assigned to him, he deprives someone

---

[1] "The Image of Limited Good," *American Anthropologist* 67 (1965) pp. 293–314.

else of the opportunity to do his duty and claim compensation rightly due him. To encourage individuals to work in their self-interest beyond the proper definition of their duties flies in the face of reason, for to do so is to stimulate imbalance, conflict, and disorder.

Dharmic ordering must, however, be complemented by danda. Authority must maintain the mechanisms for enforcing proper performance of duty. Danda is the coercive face of authority, necessary because of man's natural reluctance to fulfill his duties and accept only those rights due him. Since appropriate behavior is defined in the dharmic ordering, the role of danda is a narrow one of enforcement. Within an organization, each official must be constantly vigilant in the supervision of his subordinates. In managing large-scale programs affecting the lives of citizens, elaborate control mechanisms must be maintained to assure that relationships are properly conducted. When the social order is threatened by the nonperformance of duty (whether in the form of deviations, negligence, or excesses) then the mechanisms of control must be strengthened.

Though they are two complementary faces of authority, dharma and danda operate independently. The dharmic ordering is normative, determined by an assessment of fairness to all parties. Danda enforces that ordering, without adding to or changing it; without providing information relevant to the redefining of that order.

British colonial bureaucratic practice reinforced many aspects of dharmic approaches to authority. Early imperial goals were largely directed toward reestablishing the social order of a subcontinent that had been convulsed by the shifting fortunes and ambitions of warring rulers. The massive field operations of the British raj were devoted to the maintenance of social order and a consistent and fair collection of land revenue.

As western goals and administrative practice evolved, however, significant conflicts between Indian and western models of organization began to develop. One of the more important changes in administrative practice involved the introduction of a distinction between line and staff roles in administration. Clear and unitary lines of command were seen to be essential to orderly administrative processes. Particularly at senior levels, however, officials in these lines of authority would require various forms of assistance and support. Thus staff roles were conceived as those which provided line officials with the capabilities necessary to exercise their authority efficiently and wisely. Much attention was devoted to the proper structuring of line authority, supporting staffs, and relationships between the two in formal organizations.

In these formulations, line authorities had responsibility for the development of policies and for the implementation of programs. Staff services would provide the technical knowledge and information necessary for intelligent policy-making. General policy directives would be issued by top-level line authorities, and at each level in the line hierarchy they would be refined and made more explicit. Information on field conditions and program implementation would flow up the chain of command and would provide the basis for changes in program design and implementation.

The goals of western public administration moved increasingly away from stability and toward the creation and maintenance of secular economic growth. As economic and social theory evolved, the notion of development as a process of self-sustaining change took shape. This change was seen as involving not only continuing expansion, but also continuing modification in the structure of the economy as new technologies demanded new patterns of relationships between productive sectors.

Growth was produced, in this western model, by the strivings of individuals to create new wealth through more efficient use of capital and labor. The rationale for growth, spelled out in Adam Smith's *The Wealth of Nations*, argued that the pursuit of economic self-interest by the individual was not only consistent with, but essential to, the best interests of society. Increasingly it was argued by latter-day theorists that government had to play a constraining role in order to maintain a competitive marketplace and compensate for excessive distributive injustices, but the proposition that individual interests and societal interests are complementary has continued to dominate much western economic thought. Deriving from this proposition is the notion that a primary role of public bureaucracies is to design incentives that motivate individuals to act in the public interest.

Western concepts of line and staff roles have been integrated into the administrative structure of Indian community development bureaucracy, and western notions of growth underlie much of community development ideology. Moreover, much criticism leveled at Indian development efforts by western—and especially American—critics derives directly from the vast differences in Indian and western views of the role of public authority and the nature, promise, and threat of developmental change. Investigation of these differences, and their consequences for the planning and policy-making process in Tamil Nadu agricultural development, suggests hypotheses about the general nature of policy planning and implementation in India.

The Dharmic Approach to Line and Staff Roles

The twin concepts of dharma and danda provided a natural model for Indians who, having been raised in the dharmic tradition, entered western bureaucratic structures that differentiated between line and staff roles. On the surface, the parallels seem very close. The dharmic function is that of ordering, planning, and the development of organizational forms and relationships—functions generally associated with a staff in an administrative agency. Danda is implementation; the line activity of carrying out action programs. Under closer examination, however, it is clear that the western approach to staff and line functioning on the one hand, and an approach based on the analogy with dharma and danda on the other, are radically different.

In the western approach, action, excitement, and challenge are centered in the line. Staff personnel value their positions, for the most part, when they are close to and have influence on line authority. For it is in line positions that one must make realistic and practical decisions based on complex and incomplete information; and it is in line positions that one is most likely to face the challenge of training, motivating, and leading subordinates.

In the dharmic model, action, initiative, and intellectual challenge are in staff positions. Here one is involved in the Brahmanic task of discovering the orderly patterns that sustain a society. Here one creates models of fair and just relationships that will restore balance and order to a social and economic system. And here one establishes the proper pattern of relationships between one's subordinates. In the line role, on the other hand, the dharmic analogy suggests that opportunities are limited to the narrow, coercive role of danda. Assigned specific duties, a line official has the limited responsibility of overseeing subordinates to make sure that they carry out their duties.

Evidence from the study of Tamil Nadu agricultural development bureaucracy indicates that these dharmic notions of authority have been very influential in shaping the behavior patterns of Tamil bureaucrats. At the district level and below, line officials generally conceive of their roles in very narrow terms. Duty is limited to the extraction of work from subordinates and that work consists of fulfilling narrowly defined targets. Even the Collector, a man with very extensive powers, saw his development role as one largely limited to the implementation of programs and policies established elsewhere.

The line of authority in the Department of Agriculture ran from the director to a second level of deputy directors, each responsible for all extension operations in a region of the state. The deputy directors, in turn, each supervised a group of about eight DAOs. The role performed by the deputy directors, however, was very limited. Their primary functions were to superintend the collection of statistics from the DAOs and pass them on to the state headquarters, to distribute regional targets among the DAOs, and to conduct occasional inspection tours to make sure that the DAOs were carrying out their duties in a proper way.

The great efforts of the AEOs and DAOs to meet their targets received almost no attention in the departmental headquarters. Their reports were generally reviewed only by senior clerical personnel. DAOs knew that letters they received criticizing them for inadequate performance on their targets were initiated by this clerical staff rather than by their superiors in the department.

It was in the staff roles of the Department of Agriculture that agricultural policy was formulated, and in the office of the Secretary to Government for Agriculture that it was ratified. Working under a generalist IAS director, the joint directors of agriculture developed programs and established the basic directions of agricultural policy. These staff jobs, with no direct authority over field personnel, were the positions of prestige and influence to which ambitious agricultural specialists in the department aspired.

Dharmic imperatives seemed to shape patterns of staff operations in the department. The need for comprehensiveness, for example, was a continuing concern of planners. The joint director in charge of commercial crops felt that he had to develop and maintain programs for all types of commercial crops that might be grown in the state. Tamil staff planners were similarly concerned with the need to develop programs for all groups of farmers. Several senior administrators expressed the feeling that such diversity of programming was necessary, not simply because of political demands for equity, but because it was the responsibility of the Department of Agriculture to cater to the needs of all farmers.

Staff planning also showed a lack of concern for the relationship between programs and resources. The budgeting process brought together a great diversity of programs from the several joint directors, and limited departmental and central funds were spread thinly to cover the wide array of efforts. Cost-effectiveness of various programs was not seen to be an important consideration in determining how funds were to be distributed. A rhetorical concern for priorities was occasionally expressed, but this generally reflected the idea that one should simply rank order programs, not that new programs of secondary importance should go unfunded. Rather, the primary concerns expressed were for balance and comprehensiveness. If adequate funds were not available, I was frequently told, the resources available would somehow have to be stretched to cover the necessary programs. This attitude was splendidly illustrated by the cartoon showing the then Chairman of the Planning Commission of India, D. R. Gadgil, when the Fifth Five Year Plan was being developed. Gadgil, depicted as a milk merchant unable to get sufficient resources out of his cow, is seen diluting the milk with water in order to fill the jug, which represents the plan.[2]

Perhaps most striking, though, was the lack of staff consideration for the practical realities of extension work in program development. Joint directors toured widely in rural areas of the state, but their inquiries were generally directed to the specifics of target implementation. When they were confronted with serious problems during efforts to implement some programs, their usual response was to urge that more intensive supervision be exerted. Thus, occasional suggestions that farmers were simply not interested in the green manure seed program

[2] The cartoon, drawn by "Kutty," appeared in *The Indian Express*, Sept. 21, 1967.

evoked the view that the program was a good one and that the farmers had to be advised more vigorously to take it up.

It is this disjunction between staff planning and line implementation that is so striking to many western observers of Indian bureaucracy. The conventional view that there is an enormous gap between the elaborate and sophisticated Indian plans and inept and half-hearted efforts at implementation reflects several aspects of the dharmic approach to staff and line roles. Planning is indeed the valued activity, and great pride is taken in the preparation of elaborate plans. Implementation, much less valued, is viewed as routine and of little interest. The gap between the two is of concern to Indians as well as westerners, but the processes remain clearly separated and the problems of implementation are not seen as being appropriately reflected in planning for what ought to be done.

An approach to staff work that draws on the dharmic analogy bears clear resemblance to patterns of staff work in ritualized western bureaucracies. Wildavsky, for example, has described the incremental nature of change in the American federal budget-making process, and cost-effectiveness criteria for program evaluation are frequently rejected in favor of concerns for distributive equity.[3] It would be dangerous to infer, therefore, that the dharmic analogy is the *cause* of staff and line patterns of action. The expressed norms of many officials certainly suggest, however, that their implicit application of the dharmic analogy to staff and line roles both reinforces ritualist predispositions and imparts a distinctive quality to line-staff relations in Indian bureaucracies.

The Nature and Management of Change

Differences in dharmic and western perceptions of economic growth processes also shape patterns of behavior within Indian bureaucracy. The nature of development and the role of incentive and control mechanisms as public management tools are two areas that have been continuing sources of conflict within India and of confusion to westerners.

The concept of development is in three respects alien to the dharmic view. First, it implies that the quantity of goods and services produced by a society is constantly expanding. Second, it suggests that structural rela-

---

[3] Aaron Wildavsky, *The Politics of the Budgetary Process* (Boston: Little, Brown, 1964).

tionships within an economy will change as new technologies are introduced and new goods produced. Finally, development implies an acceptance of the ever-presence of change.

The first aspect of development is clearly the least disruptive of traditional dharmic patterns and perceptions. The thought of a society that produces growing quantities of goods while maintaining existing relations essentially intact is manageable within the context of a dharmic world view. Development as involving the substantial modification of structural relationships is much more difficult to accept. Dharma is so important because of the fear that without a well-defined pattern of duties and rights, society would become a chaotic human jungle, with each individual working in his own self-interest and with no thought for the community as a whole. Thus, development as social and structural change is an unattractive and, indeed, threatening prospect for the individual who views it from the perspective of a dharmic world view. Development as the acceptance of the ever-presence of rapid social change strikes at the very heart of the dharmic world view. When patterns of relationships are in constant flux, it becomes impossible to retain a sense that order in the system is being maintained by the imposition of a complex set of rights and duties.

As the contemporary generation of Indians attempts to grasp the meaning of development as it is applied to a society's economic system, the strong tendency is to think of it in familiar terms. Thus, many Indian administrators operate from an implicit model of development as the expansion of the supply of goods within the context of a relatively stable structural balance. There is, as a result, a substantial bias toward balanced rather than imbalanced growth. It is extremely hard for many administrators to conceive of a model of planned imbalanced growth that would involve a few selected programs creating a set of dynamic discontinuities that would, in turn, stimulate new areas of activity and produce new kinds of growth, new discontinuities, and still further growth. Most Indian administrators are much more at home with a model of development that sets out the entire range of major programs at the beginning and then carries them forward together. This pattern of balanced incremental growth is consistent with the maintenance of controls over the social and economic organism.

A second basic perspective that derives from a dharmic view relates to the usefulness of competition and incentives. The essential function of the dharmic order is to preserve the coherence and stability of society by limiting and restraining competitive self-seeking. The replacement of the dharmic order by competition would lead not to a dynamic process of growth and expansion through striving to improve one's own well being, but rather, in the context of a view of limited goods, to social disintegration. Herein lies the root of widespread Indian fear and distrust of any system of social or economic organization that depends on competition, structured incentives, or an appeal to the "invisible hand."

Conversely, these perceptions contribute to the great Indian concern for cooperation. A social unit is seen as being strong only so long as its members work cooperatively and limit their individual desires. The theme is so important in Indian culture not because Indians are more cooperative by nature than the rest of us, but because they feel so threatened by the failures of cooperation, which are everywhere so apparent.

Finally, the dharmic world view clearly suggests what one does when programs are not working. The role of government is to provide order for society. When problems arise or disorders erupt, the Indian administrator instinctively moves to refine and tighten the definitions of duties and to intensify the controls at his command.

One important technique of the western administrator is to manipulate incentives so that the self-interests of component groups come into accord with the general good of the society as a whole. The manipulation of incentives, however, is not within the dharmic administrator's vocabulary of operations. He maintains the strong presupposition that the self-interest of the individual and the good of the society at large are inherently contradictory.

The problem with the view of administration as the process of defining rights and duties and then enforcing their observance is that under conditions of change it becomes an extremely burdensome task. As the need for rules and controls increases, a bureaucratic body of individuals charged with the enforcement of those rules and controls is created. These individuals are routinely tempted by self-seeking people in the society whose self-interests require that they try to circumvent existing rules. The resulting corruption stimulates within the bureaucracy the creation of more refined rules and punishments. The complex mesh of controls thus tends to expand inexorably, stimulating new bureaucratic growth and new temptations for the self-seeking.

Conclusion

Approaches to planning, implementation, and the management of change illustrate the interrelationship between the processes of modernization and westernization. The acceptance and expectation of self-sustaining change is a *sine qua non* of modernization, and the steady-state assumption of dharmic thought represents a fundamentally traditional feature of that world view. The displacement of that assumption by first the expectation of secular growth and subsequently the anticipation of structural transformation and continuous change represents the progressive modernization of this tradition.

Many alternative world views are consistent with steady-state economic processes. Foster has suggested belief patterns that are likely to be integral features of such world views,[4] but other anthropologists have documented the great variety of social, religious, and cultural institutions that have sustained traditional societies. The dharmic ordering is certainly one of the most fully articulated cultural models for social organization in a steady-state environment. Modernization involves the adaptation of that specific model to the conditions of growth; westernization involves the adoption of institutions and assumptions that are associated with conditions of growth in the west but alien to an indigenous tradition.

Thus the development of some form of social organization capable of coordinating large numbers of individuals in complex and interrelated tasks is a necessary aspect of modernization. Indian adoption of the line-staff pattern of role differentiation to meet this need incorporates, however, an implicit commitment to western notions of authority that conflict with traditional Indian authority notions associated with dharma and danda. Any of three patterns might evolve out of this conflict. First, line and staff roles could be consciously redefined to correspond to the characteristics of danda and dharma, and bureaucratic structures redesigned

---

[4] *Ibid.* See also his "The Anatomy of Envy: A Study in Symbolic Behavior," *Current Anthropology* 13, no. 2 (April 1972): 165–86.

to meet the needs and capabilities of those roles. Alternatively, the implicit western role assumptions associated with line and staff positions could be made explicit, and bureaucrats educated to accept and fulfill those role assumptions. Or third, the conflict could go unrecognized. It would continue to generate inefficiencies and bureaucratic failures, which would be attributed to unknown malevolent forces or some basic flaw in Indian character. Unfortunately, this third option has so far prevailed on this issue. As recognition of the conflict becomes more widespread, however, its resolution through the modernization of dharmic authority roles or the westernization of attitudes toward authority roles becomes possible.

Attitudes toward incentives and self-interest pose more serious problems for Indian development. Self-restraint is not only a key element in the rationalization of a steady-state society, but also a deeply held and deeply prized value in Indian culture. The doctrine that short-term economic self-interest is consonant with societal interests not only conflicts with the experiences of India as a steady-state society, but also argues for open and aggressive competitiveness that is ethically and religiously repugnant to much of the society. A central unresolved issue in the evolution of Indian social thought concerns the nature and range of motivations that should be encouraged to generate dynamic patterns of growth and change. To date, normative thought and economic policy have eschewed individual self-interest as an engine of growth, though tacit acceptance is given to the entrepreneurship of traditionally marginal commercial groups such as Marwaris and Parsis.

Closely associated with the issue of incentives is that of strategies for public management of change. In a dynamic economy opportunities for entrepreneurship flourish. If public authority attempts to rigorously control the exploitation of those opportunities, its control problems accelerate rapidly. In attempting to channel patterns of growth into balanced, orderly expansion, Indian authority has created enormous incentives for self-interested individuals to subvert the elaborate system of regulations and controls of government. Somehow, motivations, values, and institutional capabilities must be better reconciled, whether through acceptance of western notions of management by incentives, or through the evolution of new and more meaningful appeals to duty-consciousness in a changing social and economic order.

CHAPTER ELEVEN

Conclusion

Tamil community development administration in the late 1960s was the product both of patterns of bureaucratic behavior that transcend cultures and of goals, norms, and attitudes that were unique to that time and place. The construct of cognitive models of organizations facilitates the analysis and understanding of the complex processes that have produced this—or any—bureaucratic system. The value of the construct is two-fold. First it encourages differentiation among the several distinctive traditions that may have shaped any single system, and second, it encourages a conscious searching for sources of conditions that are frequently the independent variables of research on organizations.

Tamil bureaucrats appear faithful to the general behavioral patterns established in western organization theory. The pathologies associated with close supervision in the United States or France were also clearly present in Tamil community development bureaucracy. To document the validity of organization theory predictions, however, is to provide only a partial explanation of the bureaucratic system. It leaves unexplained the choice of the structure within which bureaucrats worked, the reasons for the application of close supervision, the response of authorities to indications of institutional failure, the choice of public management strategies, and the definition of bureaucratic goals.

It is these characteristics of bureaucracy which cognitive models of organization help to explain. The identification and description of specific models deriving from distinctive traditions—whether cultural, historical, or ideological—is an important part of this analytic process. In the case of south Indian development administration, the identification of a Tamil political culture rooted in dharmic thought was an insufficient basis for understanding the character of the system. At least four distinctive models of organization had influenced the structure and processes of

220

that bureaucracy. Implicit in the analysis are hints that further models might have been elaborated. A change- and development-oriented variant of British colonial bureaucracy developed in the twentieth century, for example, and the model of organization implicit in that sub-tradition might have been spelled out. Also, American agricultural specialists in the Ford Foundation and several American universities had imparted a variant of the community development ideology to a small but influential group within the Department of Agriculture, and the distinctive features of that tradition might have been described.

Finally, a longer-term historical approach to this subject would certainly have singled out the Moghul tradition of administration for analysis, since the British Indian bureaucracy was in fact the product of a mixing of Anglo-Saxon and Moghul models of colonial administration.

This analysis, in short, required the exercise of judgment both as to what constituted a separate tradition and as to which traditions were of sufficient importance to merit treatment as sources of distinctive cognitive models of organization. That another analyst might have made different judgments in studying the same system should be neither surprising nor distressing. This study is both preliminary and partial. It attempts to identify major traditions and salient patterns of behavior on the basis of an empirical sample that was limited in time, geography, and type of program.

It focuses on selected aspects of structure and behavior that seemed at that time consequential but not readily explainable. It must be judged on whether or not the application of separate cognitive models of organization to the analysis of Tamil bureaucracy contributes to an understanding of that system of institutions and behavior. If it does, then subsequent work can elaborate, refine, and more accurately measure the variables and patterns of association that come out of the analysis.

Cognitive model analysis will hopefully do more than just contribute to the understanding of a bureaucratic system at a given time. For it is the introduction of new cognitive models into a bureaucratic system, and the creation and resolution of conflicts between the new and established models, that defines much of bureaucratic change. The evolution of Tamil development bureaucracy during the 1950s and 1960s can be seen in large part as a product of the introduction of Gandhian and community development models of organization into structures and processes that were rooted in radically different models. The elaboration of the individual models within comparable categories reveals the specific conflicts created by this change. One sees that reliance on the symbolic rewards of preprogrammed control was opposed by the established use of material rewards of feedback control; that ego-satisfaction of program achievement and team identity were opposed by a ritual devotion to duty; that planning from below was opposed by central determination of targets; and that flexible and responsive line authority was opposed by the application of danda as an analogical model for the behavior of line authority.

The failure of many community development ideas to survive as some of these conflicts have been settled is better understood when the coalitions in opposition to them are made explicit. Assumptions of needs for harsh and rigorous supervision in the dharmic and British colonial traditions, for example, generated opposition to the preprogrammed control orientations of community development ideology that could not be effectively resisted. Dharmic and Gandhian values of nonattachment and selflessness overwhelmed community development emphasis on ego-centered symbolic rewards.

Specification of cognitive models also contributes to our understanding of—and hopefully our ability to predict—the consequences of institutional change. Thus, in retrospect, it is clear that training programs and structural designs of community development origin had many complex and unintended consequences for development administration in Tamil Nadu. Explicit formulation of assumptions in cognitive models that inspire future reforms should suggest the lines of conflict such reforms would be likely to generate, and strategies likely to produce rapid and congruent solutions to those conflicts.

At a higher level of abstraction, a cognitive model analysis of change can provide suggestive insights about the nature of modernization and westernization. Both processes, this analysis suggests, should be seen as involving continuing series of discrete choices that must be made in order to resolve conflicting demands of alternative cognitive models. The Gandhian reformulation of duty as the Truth that must be defined by the individual in each situation, for example, represents an effort to modernize the concept of dharma so as to make it adaptive to change. The introduction of line and staff roles into Indian administration is a form of modernization because it permits greater task differentiation and institutional capacity to develop. However, it also involves westernization in that it assumes adherence to western notions of authority roles. To accept the western form of structural differentiation but retain inconsistent notions of authority roles is to generate institutional conflict and inefficiency. The conflicting demands of western structure and Indian authority roles can be reconciled either by extending dharmic concepts of authority to differentiated bureaucratic roles (even if they are still called line and staff), or by westernizing Indian authority behavior to meet the assumptions of line and staff roles.

The effort to integrate community development and Gandhian models of organization into an existing Indian bureaucratic system illustrates the complexity and dangers inherent in efforts to modernize through westernization. Integral to the western extension ideology that shaped new structures and training programs was an extensive set of assumptions—some explicit, others not—about goals, goal setting, motivation, control, the meaning of duty, and the function of line authority. The failure to establish planning from below and preprogrammed control, combined with the lack of awareness of other assumptions, produced a set of institutional conflicts, many of which continue to bedevil development administrations not only in Tamil Nadu but throughout India. Proposals for the resolution of Indian development administration problems are offered by Indians and westerners alike. With each proposal, however, there is always the danger that it contains hidden assumptions and implications that will generate more conflicts and incongruities than it will resolve.

The adoption of modern elements of structure and process in any bureaucracy creates the potential for increases in institutional capacity that result from greater differentiation, better communication, or more effective control. At the same time, such innovations are likely to generate new conflicts and incongruities that reduce institutional capacity. The challenge of administrative development is to modernize in such a way that the first dynamic achieves greater force than the second.

Tamil administration undertook an ambitious program of modernization when it created the structure and programs of community development. The progress of its administrative development, however, has been much more difficult and uncertain. Its future success will depend on the insight and creativity of those who develop new models of organizations and the skills of those who struggle to resolve the dilemmas and conflicts created by demands of new models impinging upon the old.

Bibliography

This Bibliography is divided into five parts:
(1) Political and Administrative Culture Studies; (2) Organization
Theory and Public Administration Studies; (3) Sources on the Four Cog-
nitive Models of Organization; (4) Sources on Tamil Nadu (Madras
State) and North Arcot District; (5) Sources on Contemporary Indian
Public Administration.

1. Political and Administrative Culture Studies

Abegglen, James C. *The Japanese Factory: Aspects of Its Social Organization*. Glen-
coe, Ill.: Free Press, 1958.
Abueva, Jose Veloso. "Administrative Culture and Behavior and Middle Civil
Servants in the Philippines." In *Development Administration in Asia*, edited by
Edward W. Weidner. Durham, N. C.: Duke University Press, 1970.
Almond, Gabriel A., and Sidney Verba. *The Civic Culture: Political Attitudes and
Democracy in Five Nations*. Princeton, N. J.: Princeton University Press,
1963.
Bradburn, Norman M. "Interpersonal Relations Within Formal Organizations in
Turkey." *Journal of Social Issues* 19, no. 1, pp. 61–67.
Crozier, Michel. *The Bureaucratic Phenomenon*. Chicago: University of Chicago
Press, Phoenix Books, 1964.
Grossholtz, Jean. *Politics in the Philippines: A Country Study*. Boston: Little,
Brown, 1964.
Hardgrave, Robert L., Jr. *The Nadars of Tamilnad: The Political Culture of a Com-
munity in Change*. Berkeley: University of California Press, 1969.
Kakar, Sudhir. "Authority Patterns and Subordinate Behavior in Indian Organi-
zations." *Administrative Science Quarterly* 16, no. 3 (1971): 298–307.
La Palombara, Joseph. "Values and Ideologies in the Administrative Evolution of
Western Constitutional Systems." In *Political and Administrative Development*,
edited by Ralph Braibanti. Durham, N. C.: Duke University Press, 1969,
pp. 166–219.

Pye, Lucian W. *Politics, Personality and Nation Building: Burma's Search for Identity.* New Haven: Yale University Press, 1962.

Riggs, Fred W. *Administration in Developing Countries: The Theory of Prismatic Society.* Boston: Houghton Mifflin, 1964.

Scott, James C. *Political Ideology in Malaysia: Reality and the Beliefs of an Elite.* New Haven: Yale University Press, 1968.

Solomon, Richard. *Mao's Revolution and the Chinese Political Culture.* Berkeley: University of California Press, 1971.

Thompson, James D., et al., editors. *Comparative Studies in Administration.* Pittsburgh: University of Pittsburgh Press, 1959.

2. Organization Theory and Public Administration Studies

Clark, Peter B., and James Q. Wilson. "Incentive Systems: A Theory of Organizations." *Administrative Science Quarterly* 6, no. 2 (1961): 129–66.

Etzioni, Amitai. *A Comparative Analysis of Complex Organizations: On Power, Involvement and Their Correlates.* New York: Free Press, 1961.

—— *Modern Organizations.* Englewood Cliffs, N. J.: Prentice-Hall, 1964.

Fainsod, Merle. "The Structure of Development Administration." In *Development Administration: Concepts and Problems,* edited by Irving Swerdlow. Syracuse: Syracuse University Press, 1963.

Fesler, James W. "Approaches to the Understanding of Decentralization." *Journal of Politics* 27, no. 3 (1965): 536–66.

Frey, Frederick W. *Concepts of Development Administration and Strategy Implications for Behavioral Change.* Cambridge, Mass.: Massachusetts Institute of Technology, Center for International Studies, mimeo, n. d.

Golembiewski, Robert T. *Organizing Men and Power: Patterns of Behavior and Line-Staff Models.* Chicago: Rand McNally, 1967.

Gouldner, Alvin W. *Patterns of Industrial Bureaucracy.* Glencoe, Ill.: Free Press, 1954.

Merton, Robert K. "Bureaucratic Structure and Personality." In Merton, *Social Theory and Social Structure.* Glencoe, Ill.: Free Press, 1949.

Selznick, Philip. *TVA and the Grass Roots.* Berkeley: University of California Press, 1949.

Skinner, G. William, and Edwin A. Winckler. "Compliance Succession in Rural Communist China: A Cyclical Theory." In *A Sociological Reader on Complex Organizations,* 2nd. ed., edited by Amitai Etzioni. New York: Holt, Rinehart and Winston, 1969, pp. 410–38.

Smith, Brian C. *Field Administration: An Aspect of Decentralisation.* London: Routledge and Kegan Paul, 1967.

Wildavsky, Aaron. *The Politics of the Budgetary Process.* Boston: Little, Brown, 1964.

3. Sources on the Four Cognitive Models of Organizations

Beidelman, Thomas O. *A Comparative Analysis of the Jajmani System.* Locust Valley, N. Y.: J. J. Augustin, 1959.

Bendix, Reinhard. *Work and Authority in Industry: Ideologies of Management in the Course of Industrialization.* New York: John Wiley and Sons, 1956.

Brown, W. Norman. "The Content of Cultural Continuity in India." *Journal of Asian Studies* 20, no. 4 (1961): 427–34.

Cary, Lee J. *Community Development as a Process.* Columbia, Mo.: University of Missouri Press, 1970.

Cohn, Bernard S. "Anthropological Notes on Disputes and Law in India." *American Anthropologist* 67, no. 6, part 2 (1965): 82–122.

—— "Some Notes on Law and Change in North India." *Economic Development and Cultural Change* 8, no. 1 (1959): 79–93.

Dikshitar, V. R. Ramachandra. *Hindu Administrative Institutions.* Madras: University of Madras, 1929.

Drekmeier, Charles. *Kingship and Community in Early India.* Stanford: Stanford University Press, 1962.

Dumont, Louis. *Homo Hierarchicus: An Essay on the Caste System.* Chicago: University of Chicago Press, 1970.

Foster, George M. "The Anatomy of Envy: A Study in Symbolic Behavior." *Current Anthropology* 13, no. 2 (1972): 165–86.

—— "The Image of Limited Good." *American Anthropologist* 67 (1965): 293–314.

Frankel, Francine R. "Ideology and Politics in Economic Planning: The Problem of Indian Agricultural Development Strategy." *World Politics* 19, no. 4 (1967): 612–45.

Frykenburg, Robert. *Guntur District, 1788–1844: A History of Local Influence and Central Authority in Southern India.* Oxford: Clarendon Press, 1965.

Gandhi, Mohandas K. *An Autobiography or the Story of my Experiments with Truth,* translated by Mahadev Desai. Ahmedabad: Navajivan Publishing House, 1940.

—— *My Varnashrama Dharma.* Edited by Anand T. Hingorani. Bombay: Bharatiya Vidya Bhavan, Pocket Gandhi Series, 1965.

Gould, Harold A. "A Jajmani System of North India: Its Structure, Magnitude and Meaning." *Ethnology* 3, no. 1 (1964): 12–41.

Greenberger, Allen J. *The British Image of India: A Study in the Literature of Imperialism, 1880–1960.* London: Oxford University Press, 1969.

Harper, Edward B. "Two Systems of Economic Exchange in Village India." *American Anthropologist* 61, no. 5, part 1 (1959).

India. *Reports on the Reorganization of the Central Government* [the Tottenham Reports]. Reprinted by the National Institute of Public Administration, Karachi, 1963.

India. Secretariat Procedure Committee. *Report* [the Llwellyn Smith Report].

Delhi: Supt. of Govt. Print., 1920, reprinted by the National Institute of
Public Administration, Karachi, 1963.

India (Republic). Committee on Plan Projects. Team for the Study of Community Projects and National Extension Service. *Report* [the Balvantray Mehta
Committee Report]. New Delhi, 1957.

Ishwaran, K. "Customary Law in Village India." *International Journal of Comparative Sociology* 5, no. 2 (1964): 228–43.

—— *Tradition and Economy in Village India*. London: Routledge and Kegan Paul,
1966.

Iyer, Ramaswamy R. "Understanding Our Bureaucracy." *Indian Journal of Public
Administration* 12, no. 4 (1966): 697–716.

Lingat, Robert. *Les sources du droit dans le système traditionnel de l'Inde*. The Hague:
Mouton, 1967.

Madras (Presidency). *Gazetteer of North Arcot*. Madras: Government Press, 1903.

Madras (Presidency). *A Manual of the North Arcot District in the Presidency of Madras*. Compiled by Arthur F. Cox. Madras: Government Press, 1895.

Mathur, K. S. *Caste and Ritual in a Malwa Village*. Bombay: Asia Publishing
House, 1964.

Mayer, Albert. *Pilot Project: India*. Berkeley: University of California Press,
1959.

Mencher, Joan. "Growing Up in South Malabar." *Human Organization* 22, no. 1
(1963): 54–65.

Misra, B. B. *The Administrative History of India, 1834–1947: General Administration*. London: Oxford University Press, 1970.

Neale, Walter C. "Reciprocity and Redistribution in the Indian Village: Sequel
to Some Notable Discussions." In *Trade and Markets in the Early Empires*,
edited by Karl Polanyi, et al. Glencoe, Ill.: Free Press, 1957.

Radhakrishnan, S. *Eastern Religions and Western Thought*. London: Oxford University Press, 1959.

Rudolph, Susanne H. "Consensus and Conflict in Indian Politics." *World Politics*
13, no. 3 (1961): 385–99.

Ruthnaswamy, Mariadas. *Some Influences That Made the British Administrative System in India*. Madras: University of Madras, privately printed, 1939.

Singh, Baij Nath. "The Etawah Pilot Project." In *History of Rural Development in
Modern India*, vol. 1, edited by Sugata Dasgupta. New Delhi: Impex India,
1967.

Spengler, Joseph J. "*Arthaśāstra* Economics." In *Administration and Economic Development in India*, edited by Ralph Braibanti and Joseph J. Spengler. Durham, N. C.: Duke University Press, 1963, pp. 224–59.

Symonds, Richard. *The British and Their Successors: A Study in the Development of the
Government Services in the New States*. London: Faber and Faber, 1966.

United Nations. Economic and Social Council. *Report of the Mission on Community
Organization and Development in South and South-east Asia*. Prepared by Horace
Belshaw and John B. Grant. New York: 1953.

Wiser, William H. *The Hindu Jajmani System*. Lucknow: Lucknow Publishing House, 1936.

Wren, Percival Christopher. *The Dark Woman*. Philadelphia: Macrae Smith, 1943.

4. Sources on Tamil Nadu (*Madras State*) and North Arcot District

Dupuis, Jacques. *Madras et le nord du Coromandel*. Paris: Librarie d'Amerique et d'Orient, 1960.

Krishnaswami, S. Y. *Rural Problems in Madras*. Madras: Government Press, 1947.

Madras (State). *Handbook on Administration of Madras State*. Madras: Director of Stationery and Printing, 1966.

Madras (State). "Descriptive Memoir of Dusi Village." In *Census Handbook, North Arcot District, 1951*. Madras: Director of Stationery and Printing, 1953.

Madras (State). *District Census Handbook: North Arcot, 1961*. Madras: Director of Stationery and Printing, 1966.

Madras (State). Law Department. *The Madras Panchayats Act, 1958*. Madras: Director of Stationery and Printing, 1966.

Slater, Gilbert. *Some South Indian Villages*. London: Oxford University Press, 1918.

Thomas, P. J. and K. D. Ramakrishnan. *Some South Indian Villages: A Resurvey*. Madras: University of Madras, 1940.

5. Sources on Contemporary Indian Public Administration

Dube, S. C. *India's Changing Villages: Human Factors in Community Development*. London: Routledge and Kegan Paul, 1958.

Fritz, Dan. "Evolution of Official and Non-official Roles in Mysore State's Panchayati Raj." *Indian Journal of Public Administration* 19, no. 2 (1973): 163–76.

Hanson, A. H. *The Process of Planning: A Study of India's Five-Year Plans, 1950–1964*. London: Oxford University Press, 1966.

Hart, Henry C. "The Village and Development Administration." In *Spatial Dimensions of Development*, edited by James S. Heaphey. Durham, N. C.: Duke University Press, 1970.

Khera, S. S. *District Administration in India*. Bombay: Asia Publishing House, 1964.

Maddick, Henry. *Democracy, Decentralisation and Development*. Bombay: Asia Publishing House, 1963.

Neurath, Paul M. "Radio Farm Forum as a Tool of Change in Indian Villages." *Economic Development and Cultural Change* 10, no. 3 (1962): 275–83.

Panikkau, K. Kesava. *Community Development Administration in Kerala*. Ph.D. thesis, Department of Politics, University of Kerala (1966).

Potter, David C. *Government in Rural India: Introduction to Contemporary District Administration.* London: London School of Economic and Political Science, 1964.

Reddy, G. Ram. "Some Aspects of Decision-Making in Panchayati Raj." *Economic and Political Weekly* 5, no. 41 (1970): 1699–1704.

Taub, Richard P. *Bureaucrats Under Stress: Administrators and Administration in an Indian State.* Berkeley: University of California Press, 1968.

Tinker, Hugh. "The Village in the Framework of Development." In *Administration and Economic Development in India,* edited by Ralph Braibanti and Joseph J. Spengler. Durham, N. C.: Duke University Press, 1963, pp. 94–133.

Index